Wiccan Roots
Gerald Gardner and the Modern Witchcraft Revival

Philip Heselton

Wiccan Roots

©2000 Philip Heselton

ISBN 186163 110 3

ALL RIGHTS RESERVED

No part of this publication may be reproduced, stored in a retrieval system or transmitted in any form or by any means, electronic, mechanical, photocopying, scanning, recording or otherwise without the prior written permission of the author and the publisher.

Cover design by Paul Mason
Cover painting by Arnold Crowther, by kind permission of Patricia Crowther

Published by:

Capall Bann Publishing
Freshfields
Chieveley
Berks
RG20 8TF

Dedication

To two great pioneers of the
modern witchcraft revival

Gerald Brosseau Gardner
(13th June 1884 - 12th February 1964)

Doreen Valiente
(4th January 1922 - 1st September 1999)

Picture Credits

Ann Cook: 26. Patricia Crowther: Cover picture. Newscom plc: 10, 11, 12, 14, 17, 52, 53. Ian Stevenson: 30, 31, 32, 34, 38, 41. Bill Wakefield: 20, 23. The author: 5-9, 13, 21, 22, 24, 27, 28, 33, 35, 37, 42-44, 43-51, 54. All other illustrations in the collection of the author. The author has made every effort to identify copyright holders and to obtain their permission but would be glad to hear of any inadvertent errors or omissions.

Extracts from the *Christchurch Times* are quoted with the permission of Newscom plc.

Contents

Illustrations	iii
Foreword	1
Introduction	3
Chapter 1 Gerald Brosseau Gardner	11
Chapter 2 Naturism and the New Forest	24
Chapter 3 "A Goddess Arrives"	41
Chapter 4 The Rosicrucians and the Crotona Fellowship	52
Chapter 5 Activities At The Ashrama	63
Chapter 6 "The First Rosicrucian Theatre in England"	78
Chapter 7 Mabs and the Co-Masons	91
Chapter 8 "The Most Interesting Element ..."	97
Chapter 9 Dafo	116
Chapter 10 Dorothy St. Quintin Clutterbuck	126
Chapter 11 Dorothy's Diaries	156
Chapter 12 Initiation	177
Chapter 13 Old Dorothy - High Priestess or Red Herring?	188
Chapter 14 The New Forest Coven?	205
Chapter 15 The Threat of Invasion	217
Chapter 16 "Operation Cone of Power"	226
Chapter 17 Their Finest Hour	242
Chapter 18 Learning the Ways of the Witches	261
Chapter 19 Witch Beliefs and Practices	275
Chapter 20 "In Another Part of the Forest ..."	295
Chapter 21 A New Myth?	304
Appendix A Acknowledgements	309
Appendix B References	314
Appendix C Further Reading	327
Index	328

by the same author

Skyways and Landmarks Revisited
(with Jimmy Goddard and Paul Baines) (1985)

Earth Mysteries - An Exploratory Introduction
(with Brian Larkman) (1985)

Tony Wedd - New Age Pioneer (1986)

The Elements of Earth Mysteries (1991)

Secret Places of the Goddess (1995)

Earth Mysteries (1995)

Newland School - 1896-1996
Our Past Prsent and Future (1996)

Mirrors of Magic (1997)

Magical Guardians - Exploring the Spirit & Nature of Trees (1998)

Leylines - A Beginners's Guide (1999)

Illustrations

1. Gerald Gardner's birthplace - The Glen, Blundellsands   13
2. Gardner with his wife, Donna, aboard his Customs launch on the Johore River, Malaya   20
3. Rushford Warren, Mudeford   28
5. The New Forest and Surrounding Area   31
6. The Rufus Stone   33
7. The Christchurch Area   36
8. Highcliffe   37
9. Southridge, Highland Avenue, Gardner's home in Highcliffe   38
10. George Alexander Sullivan (1890-1942)   55
11 & 12. The Academia Rosae Crucis 1937 Annual Conclave in the grounds of the Ashrama. Christchurch   64
13. The Vicinity of the Ashrama and Garden Theatre, Somerford   65
14. The Academia Rosae Crucis Annual Conclave pictured in their academic robes outside the Ashrama, Christchurch   67
15. Mabel Besant Scott's Bungalow - Iocris   73
16. Letterheading for Christchurch Garden Theatre   78
17. George Alexander Sullivan laying the Foundation Stone of the Garden Theatre on 13 March 1938   80
18. The Garden Theatre, Somerford, Front View   83
19. The Garden Theatre, Somerford, Auditorium   84
20. Rosicrucian Plaque inside the Ashrama, Somerford   87
21. The Mason Family Tree   101
22. Beechwood, Beechwood Hall and the Observatory 1 Osborne Road, Portswood, Southampton   103
23. Ernie Mason in Rosicrucian robe - June 1953   109
24. Mill Cottages, Malton Edith Rose Wray's Birthplace   118
25. Mill Cottages and Lady Well, Malton   121
26. Edith Rose Wray February 1917   122
27. 67 Osborne Road, Portswood, Southampton Edith Woodford Grimes' home from 1920 to 1937   123
28. The Clutterbuck Family Tree   127
29. Chewton Mill House and the Walkford Brook   134
30. Chewton Mill as a working mill   135

31. Chewton Mill House following alterations about 1910
with a figure who may be Thomas Clutterbuck   136
32. Chewton Mill House about 1910 with a figure who may be
Dorothy Clutterbuck   137
33. Orpheus, on the exterior of the Music Room Mill House   138
34. The Mill House Players in a performance of "The Yeomen
of the Guard" in 1929. 140
35. The Fordham Family Tree   142
36. Letterheading from Fordham's Ashwell Brewery   143
37. Broom Hall, Bedfordshire Rupert Fordham's home from
1989 to 1932   144
38. Latimers, Highcliffe . Dorothy Fordham's home from
about 1935 until her death in 1951   145
39. Plan of Latimers accompanying 1933 sale document   147
40. An extract from Dorothy's Diary for 1942   150
41. Dorothy St Quintin-Fordham in about 1950   151
42. An extract from Dorothy's Diary for 1942   157
43. Mill House and the stream   170
44. Mill House in 1998   181
45. The Porch Mill House   182
46. Mill House. The room where Gardner may have been
initiated   183
47. Rupert Fordham's Gravestone Churchyard, St Mark's
Church, Highcliffe   194
48. Thomas and Ellen Clutterbuck's Gravestones.
Churchyard, St. Mark's Church, Highcliffe   195
49. Ram's Head Chimneypiece, Mill House   201
50. The Naked Man   214
51. Possible site of the 1940 Rituals near the Rufus Stone.   231
52. Review of "A Goddess Arrives" by Walter Forder   245
53 . Report of the wedding of Rosanne Woodford-Grimes and
Cecil Thompson in The Christchurch Times 24 August
1940   265
54. Avenue Cottage, Avenue Road, Walkford, Edith
Woodford-Grimes' home from 1940 until her death in
1975   267

Foreword

by Ronald Hutton, Professor of History at the University of Bristol

'Modern Pagan Witchcraft, in all its various branches, is now a worldwide religion, found all over the continents of Europe and North America and across Australia and New Zealand. As such, it is an important and remarkable component of contemporary human spirituality and has a global significance. It also, however, has a peculiar place in English history, for it is the only religion which England has ever given the world. The English have certainly produced throughout history their own distinctive varieties of faiths which have originated elsewhere, and exported some of these across the globe. Pagan witchcraft, in its primary form of Wicca, is still the only self-contained religion which has its roots in the land and culture of the English, even though its adherents are now more numerous in the New World. It is therefore all the more important, intriguing, and frustrating, that its origins remain mysterious and controversial.

Philip Heselton's book represents a major landmark in the recovery of those origins. It is a work of considerable primary research which solves several long-standing problems and questions and furnishes a quantity of solid information upon the subject greater than that provided by any previous publications. This data derives from both local and national archives and is presented with meticulous care and in a charming and engaging style. It gives a quantum leap to knowledge, and represents the indispensable starting-point for any future research.

Mr Heselton also sets out a theory of his own to interpret that evidence and to explain the appearance of Wicca. While this is certainly inconclusive, and the case which it makes remains unproven, it has two considerable merits. The first is that it is based upon this new body of excellent information, and sustained by it. The second is that throughout the supporting data is laid out so clearly and carefully that readers have the opportunity of making the best possible judgement as to the strengths and weaknesses of the author's ideas. If it is possible to suggest alternative hypotheses from the same material, then this is only because he has provided the latter so well.

I can therefore praise this book for having fulfilled the two greatest requirements of scholarship; it is a considerable achievement.'

Introduction

Some of those reading this book will be familiar with the principles underlying the religion of witchcraft, the 'Craft of the Wise' or 'Wicca' as it is often known. But it may be as well before going any further to try to answer the question: "What sort of thing is it?"

Whilst many would call it a religion, I think it is probably more accurate to say that witchcraft is, as the name implies, a craft which works with the unseen world, the subtle realms, which all witches, from their own experience, know to be real. They use the psychic sense, if not as easily as the other five senses, then certainly with the realisation that this can potentially be achieved. And yet it is a religion also - and firmly rooted in paganism - the religion of the earth and of the god and the goddess - archetypes of the energies of which the universe is made up. This usually leads, for example, to a firm acceptance that the present is just one of many lifetimes.

There are claims of continuity with the religion of the prehistoric people and, whilst these are unrealistic in practical terms, they do demonstrate some underlying truths. One is that paganism is a religion that you don't have to teach. Unlike Christianity, Judaism or Islam, which would cease to exist if all knowledge of them disappeared from the world, paganism would regenerate spontaneously because its roots lie in the depths of each individual and their relationship to the earth and not in any outward teaching. And it is a common theme amongst witches that they have been reborn into the Craft, that they were members in a previous lifetime and have come back to where they belong.

Thus, the hereditary family still remains an important way in which the knowledge and power is passed on. But witches also recognise that this does not always occur and that those who were 'of the Craft' in a previous lifetime will be drawn back into it. This has been called 'witch blood', which can be both physical and/or spiritual.

So witches have both practical skills, such as in the use of herbs for healing the deeper part of the individual, and techniques for raising power for the working of magic on the subtle levels.

Their religious observance tends to be focused on Nature, on the cycles of the day, the moon and seasons, through harmony with the earth.

Many have claimed that writers such as Charles Godfrey Leland and Margaret Murray introduced the idea that witches formed themselves into groups, although much has recently been written about traditions of witchcraft, very frequently with a strong hereditary component, which claim to go back much further. These have, for the most part, yet to be properly investigated, but it seems a possibility that the tradition with which I will be dealing was just one of many.

This book explores the origins of the current revival of interest in and practice of the religion of witchcraft. This revival took place initially almost entirely as a result of the writings of one man - Gerald Brosseau Gardner. This is not, however, primarily a book about Gardner, fascinating though his story undoubtedly is. It is about how he, in the latter part of his life, discovered a surviving witchcraft tradition, and what he learned of their beliefs and practices.

Gardner is the central thread and we follow him through the crucial nine years from his retirement to the end of the Second World War in 1945. There will be diversions along the way and I have probably written far more about the Crotona Fellowship and Dorothy Clutterbuck than can be justified. But they are fascinating in their own right, so I make no apology.

Why have I written this book?

Since the late 1950s I have had a strange affinity with witchcraft which seems to have its origins in a previous lifetime. I wanted to know more about its recent history, but what I could find was more myth than reality, frequently contradictory, vague and uncertain. I began to realise that far more was known about the events surrounding the origins of Christianity 2000 years ago than about the witchcraft revival a mere 60 years ago.

There are some who acknowledge the need for mystery in life and therefore consider that the origins of the modern revival should remain shrouded in mist. I appreciate the mystery in those hidden aspects of nature which, for me, are at the heart of paganism. But there is equally, in my view, the need for a knowledge of the source from whence we sprung, whether it be our own family history, the evolution of the place where we live, or the religious and philosophical movements to which we belong.

This book attempts to clear away some of the myth and misconceptions which surround the recent history of witchcraft, but there is still a vast amount which remains hidden and probably always will remain a mystery.

I wanted to know more, but what I was presented with was almost an article of faith:

"Retired civil servant, Gerald Gardner, moved to the New Forest in 1939 and was initiated into one of the last surviving witch covens by its High Priestess, Dorothy Clutterbuck."

It was not that I wanted to throw doubt on this, but I was keen to find out more - to clothe such a bald statement with details, by talking to those who knew Gardner and the area where these events were reputed to have taken place, as well as accumulating evidence from a variety of sources.

One of the things which I emphasise throughout the book is that it is important to look at what people (particularly Gardner) have said, rather than what we think they said. If we read something carefully, with an open mind, we can often be surprised.

I was inspired by the Appendix entitled "The Quest for Old Dorothy" which Doreen Valiente wrote for the Farrars' book *The Witches' Way*. In it she demonstrated that Dorothy Clutterbuck, as a key person in the modern witchcraft revival, both existed and corresponded to what Gardner had said about her.

5

I was also inspired by the first broadcast performance of Elgar's *Third Symphony* in February 1998. Elgar died in 1934, leaving notes for a third symphony and little more. And yet the composer Anthony Payne has deciphered these notes, realised the significance of some of them for the first time, and, inspired by the spirit of Elgar, has been able to elaborate on these notes to produce the complete symphony, perhaps not as Elgar would have done it, but a valuable contribution to the repertoire nonetheless. I would like to think that, at least in part, I have done the same.

At a ritual at Samhain 1997, we did some scrying in some water in an antique wooden bowl which I possess. I remember seeing clearly the face of Gerald Gardner in the bowl and feeling his presence and desire to help very strongly. This gave me confidence to continue with this enterprise (for surely Gerald is very busy at that time of year!). The following Samhain I was aware of him again, giving me a fairly specific message which has proved fruitful in connection with this work. There have been remarkable coincidences, as I shall mention in the pages of this book, which have convinced me that I am doing the right thing. And the circle was completed when I presented the finished book, in thanks, at a ritual at Samhain 1999.

When I set out on this work, I wasn't quite sure what I wanted to achieve. In the course of my researches, I identified the main areas that I hoped to cover. I wanted to draw together what had already been published about the modern witchcraft revival, including vital books such as *Gerald Gardner: Witch* and obscure articles in defunct magazines, which could nevertheless reveal some unusual aspects of the subject.

I also wanted to delve into all sorts of unpublished records. Let alone anything else, this has been a valuable educational exercise in the sources of historical information. I have shared space with those researching their family histories whilst searching through records of Births, Marriages and Deaths. The *Christchurch Times* has been amazing in its store of information. And people's wills have often provided a revealing and personal link with those individuals.

I have spoken with many people, and they were, overwhelmingly, supportive of what I was trying to achieve. Some have provided a wealth of material, and others perhaps only the odd snippet. But that seemingly insignificant snippet could be, when seen in the context of others, the vital piece in an important corner of the jig-saw. For my research has been very much like doing a jig-saw puzzle. The problem is that one doesn't know how big the puzzle is; those pieces that are not lost for ever are scattered in a variety of unusual and unexpected locations; and one can't always decipher the picture on each piece anyway!

When starting this research, I knew perfectly well that I would not find out everything that I wanted to know. I am only too conscious that this book is incomplete and far from being the last word on the subject. This is hardly surprising. We are dealing with something that was still illegal in 1939 and things that were written down were carefully protected from falling into the wrong hands. None of the original participants is, after over 60 years, still with us. However tempting it is to delay publication awaiting the key pieces to the puzzle, I have gone ahead in the hope that, at the very least, I have shed some light into some very dusty corners which might make it easier for other researchers to follow. I hope very much that it will inspire others to take the work further. There should be sufficient pointers to further research and I will do what I can to set those interested in the right direction (though I somehow feel this subject has not finished with me yet!).

But I have found out many things, certainly enough to engage in what I call "intelligent speculation" - in other words, to think sensibly about what might have happened. I hope that I have been careful not to present them as facts, but such conclusions are the results of thinking about the known facts of the case, or facts that became known as the result of my research.

So there is plenty of mystery left! To take just one example, Old Dorothy still remains an enigmatic figure. This book contains three chapters devoted to her - far more than has ever previously been written - but I still feel that I do not have the independent evidence of Dorothy's role in the Craft which would back up Gardner's own statements. Indeed, I have, I hope in a good-natured way, refused to bow to pressure from those who, on the one side, want to "clear her name from accusations of witchcraft" and on the other to confirm clearly her role as Gardner's initiator. I have resisted such pressure, but I hope that I have dealt with Dorothy honestly, have given a fair picture of her and have provided material so that those who want to continue the debate will at least conduct it on a higher level of knowledge.

It is of course real live people who have helped me most. I mean it when I say I could not have written the book without them. To show my appreciation, the Acknowledgements is not just a page or two listing names: I felt that the contribution of others to a book of this sort was worthy of something longer. I have put this as an Appendix so that those who have read right through the book will better appreciate the contributions which have been made.

The basic text I have followed is *Gerald Gardner: Witch* by J.L. Bracelin, originally published by Octagon Press in 1960[1]. Much key information comes from this book and I quote it throughout. Patricia Crowther has told me that, when her late husband, Arnold, put it to Gardner that he had written the book himself, Gardner agreed. It is a little more complicated than that because there are places in the book where the author specifically quotes Gardner and puts his words within quotation marks. The implication is that, in the rest of the book, the author is not using Gardner's own words - he is re-writing material, paraphrasing, editing, rearranging and generally performing the function of any writer.

In some cases the author specifically states that he is using Gardner's own words, for example in a passage relating to the ritual carried out in 1940 to stop the threatened invasion of Britain. This is quite a long passage to quote verbatim, and I think what probably happened is that Gardner told his story directly onto tape and that this was the "raw material" from which the book was written.

There is now convincing evidence, from Fred Lamond and others, that the book was actually written by Idries Shah (1924-1996), the prolific writer on Sufism and other topics. He was introduced to

Gardner, probably in the mid-1950s, and got to know him well. I understand that a biography of Gardner was suggested because he felt that he hadn't got many years left in this lifetime and that it was important to get something published quickly which would answer various verbal attacks which were being levelled at him. When the book was completed, Shah felt unhappy about using his own name, possibly because it was such a different book from those which he normally wrote, and Jack Bracelin, another friend of Gardner's, agreed to put his name to it. So, as the book is formally attributed to Bracelin, I use that name in referring to it.

It has been assumed that the book is effectively autobiographical, in other words that Gardner would have had the opportunity to read through the text carefully and make amendments where necessary, i.e. where Shah had got it wrong or misinterpreted what Gardner had told him. Theoretically this is true, but knowing Gardner's personality, he may not have been that careful in checking it and even left things in that he knew were misinterpretations even though they may have thrown people "off the scent", because he had that sort of mind! The book cannot be read uncritically, but I am pleased that a new edition by I-H-O Books has now been published.

The story which is central to my investigations is, appropriately, Chapter 13 - Into the Witch Cult. I have used this as a framework for my investigations. I have found the broad outline of the story to be as Gardner gives it, but there is much inaccuracy of detail and, I suspect, some deliberate "putting off the scent". The chapter traces Gardner's move to Highcliffe before the war and his contact with the Rosicrucian Crotona Fellowship, where he claimed to have met certain people who finally initiated him into a surviving witchcraft tradition. My investigation of the story as told in that chapter constitutes the heart of this book.

I have, of course, also used Gardner's own writings: his works of fiction - *A Goddess Arrives* (1939)[2] and *High Magic's Aid* (1949)[3]; his non-fiction books *Keris and Other Malay Weapons* (1936)[4]; *Witchcraft Today* (1954)[5] and *The Meaning of Witchcraft* (1959)[6].

Gardner was not very good at spelling. Whether this was anything to do with the fact that he was self-taught and never had any formal lessons in the rules of spelling, I don't know, but he had a tendency to spell things phonetically - working it out each time from how you say a word. It has been said that it was just his typing that was bad, but it is clear from examining his typed letters that it was, in fact, his spelling. Where I am quoting from original manuscripts and letters, I have kept to his way of spelling as I think in some ways it enables one to get closer to him. I have heard it said that Gardner was marginally dyslexic. I am no expert on the characteristics of dyslexia, so I make no comment on that.

Details of other books, articles and documents which I have referred to in the course of writing this book are to be found in the References and Further Reading sections.

I will end by saying that I have tried to write the sort of book which I would want to read and find interesting myself. I hope that I have succeeded and that others will find it interesting as well.

Chapter 1
Gerald Brosseau Gardner

Witchcraft, or Wicca, as it has become known to many of its adherents, is one of the most rapidly growing religious movements in the world today. Its revival is the subject of the current book and in particular the role of one man in helping to bring about that revival.

It is difficult to say how many witches there are, because of the way the Craft (as it is frequently known) is organised. There is no central body to which members subscribe and which accepts individuals into membership. It is rather organised at the level of the individual group, or coven, and there is a growing number of solitary witches who are accountable to no one but themselves. A seemingly realistic estimate by Professor Ronald Hutton puts the number of initiated witches in Britain alone at about 10,000.[1]

Whenever the modern witchcraft revival is mentioned, Gerald Gardner's name is not usually far behind, often (mistakenly) quoted in the context of having invented the whole thing. He it was who first said, in *Witchcraft Today*[2], published in 1954, that witches had not died out in the 17th Century: they still existed. Not only had he talked to them about what they did and believed, but he had actually been initiated as a witch himself.

Gardner was the director of the only museum in the world devoted to magic and witchcraft and, as a result, obtained much publicity for his views, being interviewed for newspapers, magazines, radio and television. A revival of interest was the result, initiation being passed, in succession, to many thousands of people, in Britain and America and around the world.

Just as Columbus did not 'discover' America (the native people of that continent were well aware of its existence for thousands of years before he made his voyage) so Gardner did not discover that witchcraft had survived - the witches were well aware of the fact a long time before Gardner came on the scene. In fact, Gardner was not the only one to be saying that witchcraft still survived, only the most well-known. Others were sometimes disparaging about what he was promulgating, giving it the epithet 'Gardnerian'. But like many such names it has now been adopted by the very group it was intended to denigrate, and Gardnerian Witchcraft is now a major current in the stream of the modern witchcraft revival. But it was Gardner who publicised their survival and if we are to find the truth about what actually happened it is by following his story that we stand the best chance of success.

So, it is reasonable that any investigation into the origins of that revival should follow the path which Gardner trod in uncovering what he claimed was a surviving tradition of witchcraft, and to do this we first need to look at the person and life of Gerald Gardner himself. There is much more to be discovered about the Gardner family and the influences on his life, and I am sure there is fascinating material waiting to be found by anyone willing to undertake the amount of work required to research and write a full biography of Gardner - it would be a fascinating document. My present purpose is more limited - to set out the main course of his life up to the moment when he took the first steps which would lead him to meet the people who would change that life - the witches. I have concentrated on his character, on the influences upon him, the ideas he became attracted to, organisations which he joined and, above all, the people that he met.

Childhood

Gerald Brosseau Gardner (1884-1964) was born on 13th June 1884 at The Glen, The Serpentine, Blundellsands, an exclusive planned estate of low density Victorian villas on the coast a few miles north of Liverpool.[3] His father was William Robert Gardner, a partner in the firm of Joseph Gardner and Sons, founded in 1748, and the largest hardwood importers in the world.[4] The firm had yards in Bootle, on the northern fringes of Liverpool and many of the family lived in Blundellsands. The family were very rich and Gerald shared in this affluence, particularly following the inheritance he received following the death of his father in 1935.

A major theme in Gardner's life was asthma, from which he suffered badly. This has long been known as 'the occultist's disease', which afflicted such well-known characters as Aleister Crowley. It resulted in the Gardner family doctor's advice that he might be better if taken abroad to avoid the English winter. Fortunately, the family was in a position to afford such a treatment, so, at the tender age of four, he was entrusted to a companion (or nurse-maid), Josephine McCombie (known as 'Com') and taken on voyages to the Mediterranean and Canary Isles.

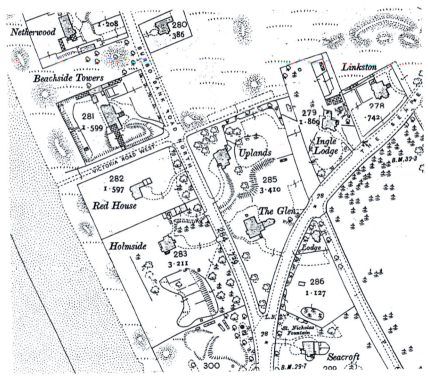

1. *Gerald Gardner's birthplace - The Glen, Blundellsands (Extract from 1891 25-inch Ordnance Survey map - reduced in scale)*

One of the consequences of this was that Gardner missed out on any formal schooling, which is not to say that he didn't receive any education. He certainly did, but it was of a very unorthodox sort and was largely of his own making. Bracelin recounts how Gardner learnt to read:

This he accomplished by intelligent use of the old Strand Magazine. He would look at the pictures in it, then plague people to explain the letters above and below them. Later, when he had the letters firmly in his mind, he would practise on the fairy tale published at the back of each issue. At last he realised that he was reading, and rushed triumphantly in to Com, shouting "I can read! I can read!". It must have been a moment as blinding as that which led to Archimedes' "Eureka".[5]

Gardner later attributed such scholarship as he had to this early learning of the importance of the written word and the avid reading of everything he could lay his hands on which resulted.

Weapons

Gardner also had a lifelong interest in weapons, particularly knives. At the age of seven, when they were in the Canary Islands, he noticed the knives which seemed to be worn by all the men. With his pocket money he bought one for himself, but it was confiscated by Com. She soon relented, however, and he quickly amassed a sizeable collection. As Bracelin says:

He would get away and try to add to his accumulation of weapons. One could find Napoleonic cutlasses and bayonets, from those whose grandfathers had fought in those wars. One could find, perhaps, local daggers, or knives imported from Africa.[6]

Spiritualism and Philosophy

Another major theme in Gardner's life started while he was in Madeira with Com, as Bracelin reports:

Whatever books other guests left behind when they returned to England, he would find on the shelves and read. It was in this way that he came across a book which was to be the first real step in his life's destined journey. It was There Is No Death by Florence Marryat, and purported to explain and prove the truth of spiritualism.[7]

He found more of Florence Marryat's works in the local library when he was visiting Ryde, on the Isle of Wight. He read them avidly and Bracelin says that Gardner "dates his firm belief in the survival of the spirit from this time".[8] He found it difficult to accept the conventional Christian idea of God, and warmed to the idea of 'local gods and spirits'.[9]

On Madeira, he developed a taste for discussing philosophical and religious matters with one Billy Dewey, an 80-year old Nonconformist with a long white beard. As Bracelin says, it "first opened up to him the possibility of trying to find his own answers to perennial metaphysical questions".[10]

Ceylon

In 1898, Com married David, a tea-planter in Ceylon. In 1900, at the age of 16, Gerald joined her, as his parents thought that it might be a good idea for him to work on the plantation and learn about tea. Gardner found the work unsatisfying, but he kept his mind active and thought a lot about the doctrine of reincarnation that the local Buddhists accepted. After two years, he had had enough of the life and got a paid job on another plantation. This meant that he: "... could spend more time in the jungle, in walks and in talking to the people, studying their beliefs and taking a part in their lives".[11]

It was in Ceylon that he first made a relationship with the land in which he was living. Bracelin recounts it thus:

One day, Gardner was hunting deer in the jungle, when he lost his way. Caught by the sudden sundown, he decided to lie down and sleep. He had always thought of the darkness as being in some way friendly, and was quite used to the jungle and its noises. The coolies who were sent to look for him went a hundred yards or so among the trees and squatted, not even bothering to look for him. They knew that he was at peace in the wildness and among the animals: he would come home in due course. The jungle gave him shelter, as it did all who were its friends. Next morning, Gardner found his way back, exhilarated by the experience, unable to understand the uneasiness which the unknown had created in the minds of his well-meaning friends.[12]

In fact, Gardner was developing an intuition which would guide him throughout the rest of his life. As Bracelin says:

In his heart remained the streak of mysticism which was to guide and shape him, whatever others might think about the reasons for his actions. The intuition, the feeling in the solar plexus which piloted his decisions, was something that he kept very much to himself. It gave him the guidance, he felt, to choose the experiences he wanted.[13]

He had heard something about the Freemasons, who had a lodge (The Sphinx, 113, I.C.) in Colombo. He felt that he might learn something connected with his inner feelings there and he frequently took weekend leave to attend their meetings.

Visits Home

Whilst Gardner, on his retirement, had never lived in England since he had been a small child, he was not totally out of touch with life in his native land. As well as frequent correspondence and newspapers, he also came back for extended visits. Between going to Ceylon with Com in 1900 and his retirement in 1936, Gardner paid four visits to his native land, in 1905, 1916, 1927 and 1932, each for several months. Each visit made a particular contribution to his life and his way of thinking. It is interesting to speculate on whom he might have met on his visits home, but I have no evidence that he met any of the individuals who would later be important in influencing the course of his life.

In 1905, he visited England, and met his elder brother, Harold, who had been living in America, for the first time for many years. He also made the acquaintance of the Surgenson family - Ted and Nellie and her sister Gertrude. The family had, as he put it, "a faint and inconclusive interest in the occult", with Edith, another sister of Nellie, being a palmist and crystal gazer.

[Ted] *believed that he could see the Little People, and there were some in his garden. He kept a part of it wild for them, feeling that they were there; sometimes he could see them. This matter was more or less taken for granted by most people. The comment was: "Old Ted, he sees things, you know."*[14]

Gardner also learned something very interesting about his grandfather. Joseph Gardner (1791-1865) did not, by all accounts, have a happy marriage with his wife, Maria, and, indeed, it was rumoured that he "kept a second and happier home" with a woman by the name of Ann "somewhere up north". Gerald had learned about this because, through the Surgensons, he had met a doctor and his sister with the surname Gardner who turned out to be the children of Joseph and Ann. He was informed that Ann was a witch and "had witchpower" and that she used to take Joseph "up into the hills for secret meetings and horrible rites". Strange things were supposed to have gone on.

Where were the hills? Possibly the Lancashire Pennines, around the Forest of Bowland or even Pendle, with its witchcraft associations. We know nothing more, except for the fact that "everyone said that Gerald was very much like his Grandfather".[15]

Borneo

In 1908, Gardner answered an advertisement for rubber planters in Borneo. He got the job and travelled to Jesselton via Singapore.

In his spare time away from his work, Gardner learned about the local native people - the Dyaks. He was particularly interested in their weapons and their beliefs and customs. Gardner felt in sympathy with their worship of local deities. They knew that magic worked and that the spirit survived physical death. These spirits could be contacted at what might be called 'seances', which Gardner frequently attended.[16] The seance would start with the *pawang* (usually translated as 'witch doctor') chanting for about an hour. Then he would put the subject into a trance, and the spirit would speak through her. Anyone who wanted to ask questions could do so. When things had come to an end, the subject awoke.

Most precious of all, perhaps, he had learned to adopt their belief in the naturalness of the occult, had come to take for granted as they had some contact with those who had died, the possibility of developing faculties of concentration, mind and energy which in the West had fallen into general disuse. This was a development in his thinking which was to bear fruit many years later.[17]

A bout of malaria caused Gardner to give up his job, and he intended to move back to the more congenial climate of Ceylon. In between, in 1910, he visited Sarawak, talking to Charles Brooke, the White Rajah, about his researches into the beliefs and customs of the Dyaks. Brooke had done some research himself, but commented that few Europeans were prepared to take such things seriously.

Malaya

Gardner left Borneo in 1911 and was intending to travel to Ceylon via Singapore. While there, however, he was offered a job as assistant on a rubber plantation in central Malaya. In 1916, Gardner paid another visit to England. It was in the middle of the war. He wanted to sign up, but his health prevented it. He spent a month in Tenby with Bob and the Surgensons. Finally, he was taken on as a hospital orderly in Liverpool. Towards the end of the year, his malaria returned badly and, because he could be no use in Europe, was sent back to Malaya.

In 1923, Gardner applied for, and got, a Government post as an inspector of rubber plantations at Muar, in Johore. He enjoyed this work, being alone for much of the time, travelling around and seeing the country.

Gardner's growing close friendship with the Malays and his long-standing interest in weapons led him to investigate the *kris* - a wavy dagger which was considered to contain a spirit and to have magical properties. He discovered that there were ritual dances involving the kris. Gardner studied the *kris* for some 20 years, finally producing a book in 1936, the year he returned to England, entitled *Keris and Other Malay Weapons*, upon which he had become the world's foremost authority.

Typical of Gardner's approach is the way he got to know the Sakis. These were a Stone Age people living in the jungles of Malaya, so isolated that many had denied their very existence. But Gardner managed to contact them and realised that they used magic as a normal part of life. He found that when one was surrounded by a community which accepted that magic worked, then one's whole thinking could change, necessitating, as Bracelin puts it, "a new attitude towards the whole question of the supernatural".[18]

In 1926, the Commissioner of Customs put Gardner in charge of inspecting the chandu shops - registered Government premises where opium could be sold. Gardner's view of opium was that it promoted deep relaxation and hard work, and that only one in ten thousand became addicted to it. He felt that it was much less dangerous than hashish or alcohol. In 1927, he visited England again. This coincided with the total eclipse of the sun on 29th June, the only one to be seen in England during Gardner's lifetime, the path of totality of which passed directly over Blundellsands. It would seem characteristic of Gardner to have arranged the trip, at least in part, to experience it. But he was lonely - his mother, Ted and Gertrude had all died, and Nellie was grief-stricken.

When ... someone mentioned a spiritualist church near Liverpool, he felt a twinge of curiosity. He remembered the books on survival after death he had read as a boy, and the demonstrations he had watched in Borneo. Was it possible that as close to home as this he would discover the truth about spiritualism as it existed among Europeans? He decided to investigate.[19]

He felt that the performance was fraudulent, but was told that the good mediums were all in London, and one Hewart Mackenzie was particularly recommended. He visited three mediums at the London Spiritualist Alliance. They each mentioned an "Uncle John" and a "Cousin Anne", both of whom Gardner denied having. His brother later told him that he did indeed have an Uncle John, whom Gardner didn't know, and Cousin Anne was identified as Gertrude, who also predicted his marriage. In addition, automatic writing from one medium was recognised as being identical to his mother's.

This had a profound effect on Gardner. As Bracelin puts it:

In a sense this seance was a watershed in his life. He had almost always believed in spiritualism, and in the existence of a spirit

2. *Gardner with his wife, Donna, aboard his Customs launch on the Johore River, Malaya*

world. In Borneo, he had seen impressive confirmation of this certainty. But never before had this touched him directly, nor had he ever been able to prove, to his own satisfaction, the truths of his beliefs. Now he had done so; from now on he had a personal, as opposed to a merely intellectual, conviction that life survives what is called death.[20]

He also applied for a reader's ticket at the British Museum in July 1927 to study Basque and Welsh folklore, which shows that Gardner's interest in people's beliefs and practices was, even at that time, not limited to the Far East.[21]

Gardner did indeed meet a young woman, Donna Rosedale, a nursing sister at a London hospital, who was actually his brother's sister-in-law's step daughter. He knew from the moment he saw her that he would marry her. Donna accepted his proposal, and a special licence was obtained. She sailed back with him to Singapore, arriving on Christmas Eve 1927.

Archaeology

Gardner's new job took him throughout Johore, up rivers and into the jungle, and in the process he got to know the country in that area really very well. He began to take an interest in its history and to look at the sites of ancient cities that had now disappeared.[22] There was one called Johore Lama which he studied in great detail. Everyone said there was very little left, but he found a lot, including gold coins and stone beads - evidence of trade at an early period. He found it difficult to convince the authorities at the Singapore museum, but he gradually got more help and support, though it was not until 1953 that he was finally vindicated.

Gardner was due more leave in 1932. Instead of going straight back to England, he went to the Middle East. He spent a week in Egypt and then to Gaza. His friend, McAlpine Woods, had given him a letter of introduction for Sir Flinders Petrie, the archaeologist, who was doing a dig at an ancient city there. Petrie was encouraging about Gardner's activities in Johore:

"Archaeologists are the most jealous people in the world", he said. *"But you must butt on. You've found the beginnings: you've proved that there really was a Malayan civilisation. Now others can follow the trail."* And Gardner reflected that, although he would have loved to remain in the Middle East, the work he was doing in Johore was his own; no one else was working in the field there, nor had anyone before him dug anywhere in Malaya or found anything.[23]

Gardner then went to England, via the prehistoric caves in France. With Donna he worked on digs in Devon and other parts of the country, and he met Keiller, who was carrying out excavations at Avebury and Windmill Hill.

In 1936, Gardner was again due for leave, but as he would have only 18 months to serve if he came back, it was decided he could retire with full pension rights as he went on leave. He was 52. He came back to England slowly. To start with, he joined the excavations of the ancient city of Lachish in Palestine, under the directorship of J.L. Starkey. Travelling back via Turkey, Greece and Germany, he arrived back in London in about May 1936. The rest of his life, and probably the most significant part, was about to begin.

There are certain themes which run like threads through Gardner's early life which would remain with him and which would form the backdrop for his involvement in witchcraft, for which he is now largely remembered.

He was self-educated and had the ability to find information in unusual ways - to study unconventional subjects in unconventional ways. He had a life-long interest in weapons, on which he was a recognised authority. This knowledge was valuable to him in his study of witch tools, ancient and modern, and their significance. He was conscious of the dimension of time, and that we live in history as much as we live in places. He was always wanting to increase our perspective on things by looking at the historical dimension, and prominent in this would be archaeological techniques.

Gardner was always interested in the local people of an area, and in their beliefs and practices - and he found out what he could by making friends with them and talking to them - not a universal way of doing things at the time. And he was impressed by the way the native peoples that he came across accepted magic as a normal part of life - as something which worked. Through his own experiences, he found himself, quite naturally, adopting a similar attitude, for there was in Gardner an inbuilt awareness of the reality of the 'otherworlds' which was intensified and strengthened by his experiences 'out East'.

The way in which Gardner applied the knowledge and insight gained during his working life to the new challenges of his retirement will be revealed in the course of this book.

Chapter 2
Naturism and the New Forest

Donna had gone straight back to England and had found a flat on Charing Cross Road, some time before Gardner returned in about May 1936. The English climate did not suit him, as he tells in his book *A Goddess Arrives*, where, referring to the hero, Denvers (recently retired from work in Malaya and clearly based on Gardner), he says: "Long years in Malaya had thinned his blood and made of these English winters a torment"[1] Gardner, as usual, caught a cold, which, as Bracelin records, "hung about him"[2]. On visiting his doctor, Gardner received the following advice:

"I could suggest something that would cure you, but I expect you will refuse to do it". It was a visit to a nudist club. "I'll die there", said Gardner, but the doctor was adamant that it would help him.[3]

Despite this sceptical response, Gardner had actually had a previous demonstration of the benefits of sunshine and naturism. It was while he was living in Malaya and he developed synovitis in his knee. He was admitted to hospital and had undergone a variety of treatments without success: in fact his leg had bent and refused to straighten. While lying in his hospital bed, he began to long for fresh air and sunshine and asked for his bed to be wheeled out. Reluctantly this was agreed. As Bracelin recounts:

For a long time Gardner lay thus in the sunshine, feeling its rays penetrate the skin, feeling health and vitality creep back into his body. Later in the day, the sister came out to him. "I've come to rub your leg again", she said, briskly. Gardner lay back and submitted to this daily therapeutic ritual. And, to their amazement, on this day, suddenly and without warning, the recalcitrant leg straightened under her ministrations.

This near-miracle had far-reaching effects on Gardner's opinions. ... It led him, much later, to accept medical advice and take up nudism seriously.[4]

On his visit to England in 1932, he asked about nudist clubs, but was told (wrongly) that they did not exist: it was, in fact, several years before Gardner discovered otherwise, in 1936, when he took the advice of his doctor, as Bracelin recounts:

He was thus introduced to a club in Finchley. This was a huge house, with a ballroom and gymnasium, club room and all. He made many friends there, and got rid of his cold.[5]

The club was known as the Lotus League. Michael Farrar, Archivist for the Central Council for British Naturism writes that it:

... operated from early 1934 to 1939 at Cardrew House, 92 Friern Park, Finchley, London N12. The proprietor was Mrs. Denise Bedingfield. It seems to have been under the wing of the Sun Bathing Society, ... the organisation founded by Notley Frank Barford, who published Sun Bathing Review. It had been called the League of Light before moving to its Finchley premises. By Spring 1938 it was under "revised management". At the end of 1938 it was about to move to "de luxe premises, much nearer town", but vanishes in Autumn 1939 on the outbreak of war.

... there was a garden, entirely screened from public view, open to members from 9am to sundown every day except Wednesday. This included a lawn, 50ft by 100ft for sunbathing and a hard court for games such as badminton, deck-quoits etc. All meals were served outside when weather permitted. Inside the house, which had 20 rooms, there were three large public rooms for the use of members including a beautiful dance room with parquet floor, a pleasant lounge with coal fire in cold weather and a games room with ping-pong table. There was a dormitory for men and several guest rooms. There were social evenings on Tuesdays, Thursdays, Saturdays and Sundays from 4.30 to 11.30. There were physical culture classes in the dance room, and an ultra-violet lamp. Nudity was obligatory for men from the first visit, but ladies could retain their clothing for

their initial visit. Shoes could be worn if desired. Subscriptions were £4.4s a year for men, £1.10s for ladies.[6]

From then on, naturism became a major theme in Gardner's life. As well as benefits to his health, there were other attractions, as Bracelin confirms:

...he felt that he met people in this way whom he did not know existed in England; interesting people, prepared to talk, argue and discuss. Many had a faint occult interest: fortune telling, palmistry, astrology, vague spiritualism. He felt healthier, too, and liked the lack of class-consciousness which naturism brought.[7]

Indeed, Arnold Crowther, who had met Gardner in 1939 at a lecture on folklore given by Christina Hole, told his wife-to-be, Patricia, of some meetings which seemed to be of this nature:

... Gerald once took him to the home of a lady called Vanda. She frequently held soirees where various artistes, intellectuals and writers, were able to commune with their equals and let down their hair by 'peeling off', as Gerald put it, and sitting around sky-clad.[8]

It is possible that Gardner was introduced to these meetings by some of the naturists whom he had met at Cardrew House.

Witchcraft

Gardner was already thinking about witchcraft about the time he joined the Folk-Lore Society, which he did in March 1939, having been sponsored by a Dr. Hildburgh.[9] Gardner's first written contribution to the Society's Quarterly Transactions, *Folk-Lore*, appeared in the June 1939 issue. It was an account of a box of witchcraft relics. Gardner does not indicate how he acquired it, merely stating that: "Within recent years a box containing what appear to be witchcraft relics has come into my possession."

The only other clues to the origin of these items are [i] a label on the back of the box, written, according to Gardner, about 1890 to 1900, stating that it was "given to me by my father Joseph Carter, of Home Farm, Hill Top, near Marlborough, and contains the finger, etc. of Mary Holt, a notorious Wiltshire Witch. Signed S. Carter."; [ii] a label, on old paper, in old writing, which read: "Witches Moon-dial, used by them at Moonlight. It is made of human bone, with only seven sections, the Seven Hours of Dread. Found near Weyland [sic] Smith's Cave, on the borders of Berkshire and Wiltshire."[10] I think we can assume that they probably came into Gardner's possession following his return to England in 1936, although the possibility cannot be ruled out that he acquired them in 1932 when he came back on a visit and spent some time helping in excavations throughout the country.

The big question, of course, is how Gardner came to acquire these items, three years before he claimed to have been initiated into a surviving witchcraft tradition. It might have been through naturism, as Gardner admits that many of the naturists had a 'faint occult interest' and there is a suggestion, which I shall explore in greater detail later, that he may have met a witch before moving to Hampshire. The article referred to above also stated that: "The relics have been examined by Dr. Margaret Murray, and Fr. Ward of the Abbey Folk Museum, who believe them to be genuine..." Both Murray and Ward were to be important figures in Gardner's future life, so it is interesting that he probably met them and discussed with them both the artifacts and, almost certainly, witchcraft in general, probably in late 1938 or early 1939 in preparation for the article.

The New Forest Club

By early 1938, Gardner and his wife, Donna, were living at 23a Buckingham Palace Mansions, right opposite Victoria Station. This was much larger and could accommodate all their various possessions, including Gardner's large collection of weapons.[11] However, as Bracelin points out:

Civil defence plans were that in the event of war, every house within half a mile of each large London railway station was to be evacuated. The flat which he shared with his wife was just across the road from Victoria terminus: and he was determined that his collection should not be destroyed.[12]

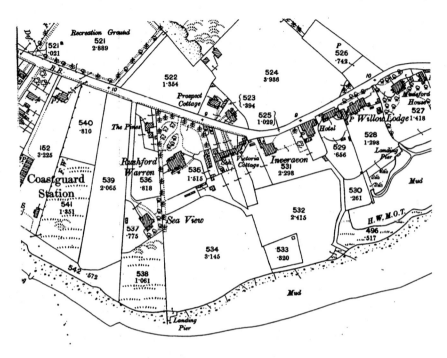

*3. Rushford Warren, Mudeford
(Extract from 1896 25-inch Ordnance Survey map - reduced in scale)*

So, Gardner was looking to move out into the country. Bracelin states that "The only place in England where he had friends was the region of the New Forest, and he managed to get a house there, where wife and collection were duly installed."[13] It seems clear that Gardner could make friends fairly readily and he had been back in England for some two years, so we don't really know who these friends were. However, Gareth Medway considers it likely that the friends referred to were naturists.[14]

In the mid to late 1930s, naturism was still very much a minority interest, and there weren't so many clubs around. It is therefore highly likely that Gardner would have been aware of the existence of the New Forest Club. This was initially opened on 1st May 1934 in the woods and grounds of "Forest View", West Moors, Dorset, on the fringes (or at least within sight) of the New Forest.

In the early 1930s, it was usual for a naturist club to rent a clearing in a wood and for members to do any construction work themselves. Spartan conditions were to be expected. In contrast to this, the New Forest Club was run as a business. The two proprietors were Leonard Lloyd and J.W. Joseph, who had provided the necessary capital (about £300) and had works carried out so that, when the club opened, services had been laid on, a pavilion had been erected, and meals were provided.

The club was very successful and, seeking to expand and provide a greater range of facilities, it closed at the end of March 1936 and re-opened on 9th April that year on a new four acre site at Rushford Warren, Mudeford, on the shores of Christchurch Harbour. This spot, characterised as it was with abundant large houses in their own grounds, seemed to attract such enterprises, for in the immediate vicinity was the Inveravon Guest Home, Centre for Spiritual Healing.[15]

The brochure advertising the club gives a vivid impression of what Gardner would have experienced:

The new home of the Club is a large country house with 24 rooms ... lying well back from the road. ... The place having been used as an hotel, the public rooms are necessarily spacious and eminently suitable for club use. As re-arranged for its present purpose, the building contains, on the ground floor, a large general club room, 30ft. by 25ft., suitably furnished and equipped, with wireless, pianola piano, library, etc., large dining room, games room, long sun lounge facing south and entirely glassed in, changing rooms for ladies and gentlemen respectively, reception room, private apartments for the resident proprietor and family, two bathrooms, and the usual kitchen quarters. Upstairs there are fourteen bedrooms, of which the greater number are available for resident members for whom a third bathroom on this floor is reserved. Many of these rooms have magnificent views overlooking the grounds and the sea. ...

The grounds are partly cultivated and partly natural woodland. The former part includes the big lawns where there are full size Badminton and ring tennis courts. ... The wooded portion of the

29

4. The Club House, The New Forest Club, Rushford Warren

grounds extends from the lawns to the sea front, and are gradually being cleared of undergrowth. ... The necessary clearings have been made for the chalet-huts which were a feature of the old location.

The principal feature of the Club at its new location is the water frontage of 400 feet, overlooking Christchurch estuary, Hengistbury Head and the Isle of Wight.[16]

The Club had its own distinctive and detailed "Dress Customs" as the brochure makes clear:

The organisers of the Club have not adopted the usual policy of making complete nudism compulsory on the part of its members when on the Club premises. THE NEW FOREST CLUB IS NOT A NUDIST CLUB in the usual sense of the words. We invite members to join us for the purpose of sun and air bathing, and the manner in which they do this is left to the individual taste of the members. COMPLETE OR PARTIAL NUDISM IS ENTIRELY OPTIONAL at all times and in all parts of the Club premises ...

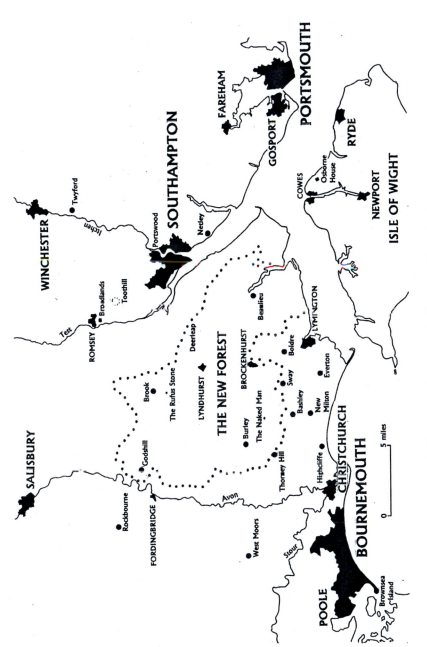

5. *The New Forest and Surrounding Area*

It had been publicised in the local *Christchurch Times* as being "Britain's First Seaside Nudist Colony"[17] In the late 1930s it was the only naturist club anywhere in the vicinity of the New Forest. Gareth Medway states[18] that Gardner and Donna joined the New Forest Club while they were still living in London and implies that this was where he formed the friendships which decided them to move to Highcliffe in 1938. This would make sense as we know that Gardner found the company of naturists congenial. Moreover, "the region of the New Forest" is just the sort of phrase one might use about the New Forest Club, named after the forest but really only in its vicinity.

As we have seen, the Club had accommodation for members to stay and it is quite likely that Gardner came down in June or July 1938, staying at the Club, contacting local estate agents and cycling round looking for property that might be suitable. The Club was bombed in September 1940, and thereafter closed permanently.[19]

The New Forest

The area of the New Forest lies on the south coast of England and is shown in Illustration 5. To the east lie the cities of Portsmouth, home of the Royal Navy, and Southampton, seaport and ocean liner terminal. It was from Southampton that the ill-fated *Titanic* started her maiden voyage in 1912. To the south lies the Isle of Wight, popular as a tourist destination since Victorian times, when Queen Victoria's favourite residence was Osborne House, on that island. And to the west lies Bournemouth, a large seaside holiday town, but also very much of a retirement spot, as is much of the south coast.

Between these lies the New Forest, which is itself relatively unpopulated. This is mainly due to the sandy soil, which is not good for agriculture. This was probably the reason why William the Conqueror declared it a royal preserve for hunting, where the penalties under the game laws for killing a deer were most severe. Whilst the New Forest does contain considerable areas of woodland, these have mostly been planted, and the more usual landscape is that of open heathland.

6. *The Rufus Stone*

One of the most significant spots historically for those interested in witchcraft and paganism is the Rufus Stone, at Canterton, near the village of Brook. It is a metal three-sided pillar and it tells its own story:

Here stood the Oak Tree on which an arrow shot by Sir Walter Tyrrell at a Stag glanced and struck King William the second, surnamed Rufus, on the breast, of which he instantly died, on the second day of August anno 1100.

King William the Second, surnamed Rufus, being slain, as before related, was laid in a cart, belonging to one Purkis, and drawn from hence to Winchester and buried in the Cathedral Church of that City.

Margaret Murray[20], Hugh Ross Williamson[21] and others have speculated that this was in fact a ritual killing of the Divine King and that Rufus, as well as being openly Pagan, was actually a willing victim. There are many pagan themes in the story and the works quoted are well worth studying.

Christchurch

The town of Christchurch has an important role in our story, although in fact the main events took place in the neighbouring villages of Highcliffe and Mudeford, and in Somerford, which is really a suburb of Christchurch.

The earliest settlers lived on St. Catherine's Hill, which is prominent to the north of the town, and Hengistbury Head, which encloses Christchurch Harbour to the south.

Christchurch Priory is the subject of two legends. One is a classic 'church moved by night' tale. De Crespigny and Hutchinson tell it as follows:

The old abbey lay low, and the monks caught rheumatism. They proposed, therefore to remove it to higher ground, namely, to the top of St. Catherine's Hill. Every night, however, the stones which had been taken to the top of the hill during the day were brought down to the bottom of it again by unseen hands.[22]

In the end they resigned themselves and built the new abbey at the foot of the hill. Such a story emphasises the pagan associations with St Catherine's Hill. The other legend is that Christ was one of the workers on the new abbey, who never came to claim his wages.

The site of the modern town lies between the rivers Stour and Avon near the point where they flow into Christchurch Harbour. The old name for the town, Twynham, emphasises this fact. Christchurch was described as a small market town in the Domesday Book and was particularly prosperous in the early mediaeval period. Smuggling became a major 'industry' in the 17th and 18th Centuries. Christchurch has remained a prosperous town in the 20th Century, being affected by the growth of neighbouring Bournemouth.

Highcliffe

Highcliffe takes its name from the high cliffs which characterise the coast at this point but it is actually a relatively recent name.[23] Until the beginning of the 19th Century it was largely open farmland, with the nearest settlements being at Chewton and Walkford. There was also a group of cottages at Slop Pond on the main Christchurch to Lymington road. Further houses were built here in the 1830s and the residents decided on a change of name to Newtown. It gained its own church, St. Mark's, in 1843. Development continued and at the turn of the 20th Century the name was changed to Highcliff. (The 'e' at the end seems to have gained in popularity as the century progressed.)

Highcliffe Castle, the local 'stately home', is really a series of gradual accretions to an older building, but is mostly 19th Century, although incorporating ancient stonework from France.

Highcliffe expanded greatly during the 1920s and 30s as part of the growth of Bournemouth and other seaside locations, being particularly popular with retired people. It is on the fringe of the New Forest and on the coast with magnificent views to the Isle of Wight, so was, and still is, considered a desirable place to live. Ronald Hutton puts it succinctly and well when he writes:

... its true socio-cultural context is as a part of that genteel conurbation which stretches along the coast between Poole and Lymington, with a healthy climate and picturesque hinterland which has made it especially attractive to people in retirement ...[24]

Gardner obviously must have considered that Highcliffe was a suitable and safer place to live than central London, even though it was close to the coast and possible invasion risk. I think that in mid-1938 the threat of invasion was thought much less likely than bomb and gas attacks on major cities, for Sheila Herringshaw confirms that children from Southampton and Portsmouth were evacuated to Highcliffe[25].

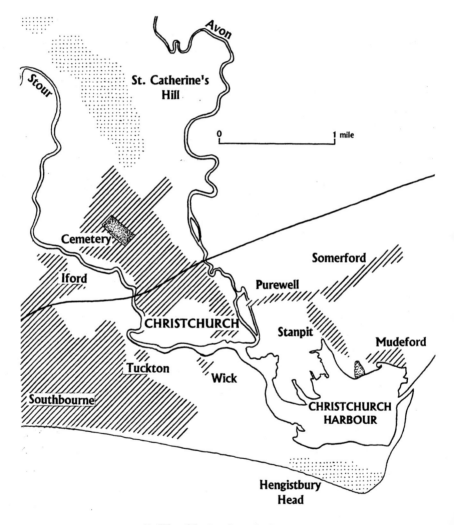

7. *The Christchurch Area*

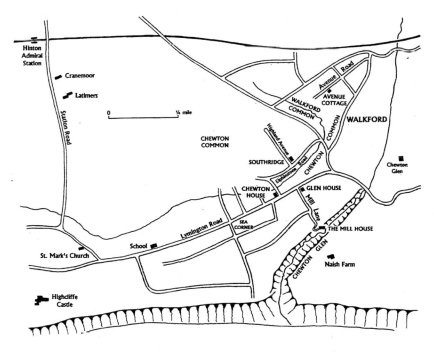

8. Highcliffe

Southridge

Gardner found the house he was looking for. It was called 'Southridge' and was situated on the corner of Highland Avenue and Elphinstone Road, Highcliffe. Also known as no. 3 or no. 5 Highland Avenue, it was built for the Misses Caroline and Ethel Estcourt in 1923, on a substantial plot of land measuring about 125 feet x 150 feet. The plot had several mature trees and was quite secluded, particularly in summer.

The house was in red brick, with a tiled roof and tall chimneys. The ground floor consisted of a porch leading into what is described as a "Lounge Hall" (21ft x 14ft), from which the stairs led to the upper floor. Adjoining this was a large (16ft square) Dining Room, really a projection to the house, with windows looking out onto the garden from three sides, along two of which was a verandah which provided an upstairs balcony for one of the four bedrooms.[26] I had always imagined Gardner's house as having a verandah. Perhaps I was picking up something from the

9. Southridge, Highland Avenue, Gardner's home in Highcliffe

ether when I thought about it: I certainly wasn't consciously trying to divine its character.

In about March or early April 1938, the Misses Estcourt moved out and put Southridge up for sale. This must have been around the time when Gardner was looking for property, and it seemed to suit him, for he moved in, probably in July or August 1938.

By November 1938, Gardner already had plans for the addition of a Sun Lounge to the house, presumably to pursue his naturist activities. Plans were submitted on his behalf by the local builder, A.V. Ridout, who happened to live next door to Gardner on Highland Avenue. The Sun Lounge and a Garage were constructed between March and August 1939. In fact, quite a lot of works were carried out to the house, including substantial repairs and renovations at a total cost of over £300.

Whilst Southridge was fairly secluded, Gardner's nudist activities in the recently-completed sun lounge had attracted some attention, as this humorous item in the *Christchurch Times* for 24th June 1939 makes clear:

The instant success (with the neighbours) of the Elphinstone Road Nudist Colony has been marked. Rooms with an uninterrupted view of the Island - and other items of interest, are, they tell me, at a premium. One old gentleman who has rented a second floor back says his outlook on life generally has entirely changed in the last few weeks. He has now no use for his car or fishing tackle, and wishes to exchange them for anything useful, such as telescopes, binoculars, or camera. Nearby householders have taken furiously to gardening and hedge trimming, putting in hours with their heads and shoulders buried in the macracarpa.[27]

It would seem that this was just Gardner and his friends, presumably those he had met at the New Forest Club.

Gardner was someone who seemed to change markedly in physical appearance, and also to quite a large extent in character, between his retirement in 1936 and the early 1960s when his books and museum had become world famous. We have the photograph of him on the river-boat in Johore, clean-shaven, bronzed, fitting in very well with his setting. But what seemed unexceptional in Malaya might be somewhat unusual on the streets of suburban Highcliffe. Ian Stevenson, in his youth, remembers Gardner as being a rather odd figure with a tanned skin who habitually wore shorts and sandals in all weathers! He says that the boys in the village considered Gardner a rather fearsome figure, with tattoos on his arms, and they always used to cross over to the other side of the road when they saw Gardner coming.[28]

Shortly after he moved to Highcliffe, Gardner started to attend meetings of the Rosicrucian Order Crotona Fellowship at their Ashrama Hall at Somerford, near Christchurch. Gardner says that he came upon them by chance, but, as we have seen, there has been a suggestion that certain members of the Fellowship might also have been members of the New Forest Club and that Gardner might actually have been introduced in this way. Whatever the truth of the matter, it was through the Rosicrucians that Gardner claimed to have met the group of people who brought him into the Craft. But before taking a close look at who these particular Rosicrucians were and what they believed and did, we must follow an 'interlude' in Gardner's story, one which took him back to a previous lifetime on the island of Cyprus.

Chapter 3
"A Goddess Arrives"

For many years Gardner had had, not a recurring dream exactly, but a succession of dreams, events and experiences which gradually built up into what seemed to him a very real life. It was set in ancient times, in a hot country, and Gardner was in charge of having a wall built, to repel invaders. As well as being the designer of the wall and supervising its construction, he was also responsible for organising the melting down of bronze cooking utensils for making weapons.

Gardner probably strongly suspected that these were memories of a previous lifetime, though not as coherent or detailed as those brought through by Joan Grant, whose memories of a life in ancient Egypt were to be published by Arthur Barker as *Winged Pharaoh* in October 1937.[1] These dreams did not engage Gardner's attention unduly. He felt that they might be a real place, and that it might be somewhere in the Middle East, as for some years he had had the strange feeling of "belonging" to that area.

A series of circumstances, however, led Gardner to a position where he could no longer ignore his experiences as being "merely dreams". In the winter of 1936/1937, Gardner had intended to return to Palestine to continue the dig, but Starkey had been murdered and everything had been cancelled as a result. Gardner wondered what to do. On an impulse, he booked a trip to Cyprus on a slow orange-boat, which took a month to get there.

On the eve of his departure he had another extraordinary dream. Bracelin described it as being "about a man who found that he was not wanted at home: so he dived into the past, seemingly with ease - where he was wanted."[2]

On the boat, the other passengers seemed intent on drinking and playing bridge, which didn't interest Gardner at all, so he made a decision to write a novel based on his dreams. I think he probably guessed that he would find the landscape of those dreams when he reached Cyprus, and so it proved to be.

As was to be expected, on his arrival in Cyprus Gardner went straight to the Museum in Nicosia. The Curator must have already heard of Gardner and his interest in weapons, for he posed him a problem. They did not have any idea how the ancient Cypriots hafted their swords. At first, Gardner tried to approach the problem analytically, but then allowed his mind to meditate freely on it. He says: "Then, suddenly and extraordinarily, my hands felt as if they knew" and he started, almost instinctively, to make a hilt which fitted perfectly. Gardner felt that this was all added confirmation that he had been a sword-maker in a previous lifetime in Cyprus.

The following winter, 1937/38, Gardner visited Cyprus again, recognising more places he had seen in his dreams, including a small round hill called Stronglos, at the mouth of a river. Bracelin recounts the experience thus:

This was the country of his dream; a place to be defended, a tongue of land with a knobbly rock upon it, beyond which lay the river, then a swamp, now hard ground, and a ravine. Part of his work in that past life, he thought, had been to build a wall from the ravine to the swamp. He remembers it all - foundations, earthworks, stones in position, towers. He even knew instinctively the points of the compass - the river flowed from north to south.[3]

Gardner went back to Cyprus, probably in the spring or summer of 1939, and managed to buy a piece of land in the area that corresponded to his dream landscape. He intended to build a house on it, or possibly even, according to Cecil Williamson, a temple of Aphrodite, but the war intervened.

All this time, Gardner had been writing his novel, which was to be entitled *A Goddess Arrives*[4]. It is a very competent first work of fiction, in many ways better written than his next book, *High*

Magic's Aid, which was published ten years later. It is certainly a long book and I think it likely that Gardner paid the costs of publication, or at least contributed to them, as it seems doubtful that a publisher would otherwise have been interested in a first novel running to over 380 pages.

A Goddess Arrives is important because its writing spans the three years from Gardner's retirement to his claimed initiation into the Craft. It may therefore reveal something of his thinking during that period. Certain themes, for example, may have been added in later revisions of the text as new ideas occurred to Gardner. As an author myself, I appreciate how this is a natural and expected part of the process.

In his other books, Gardner had help with spelling and other stylistic techniques. It is clear that someone must have helped him but, as no-one is acknowledged, it was obviously someone who didn't want their name to appear. My strong guess is Edith Woodford-Grimes, someone who will play an important part in the story. She knew Gardner well, certainly had the skills to act as editor, and would not have wanted any publicity for what she did.

In outline, the book tells of the Egyptian Invasion of Cyprus in 1450 BCE and of the legend of Venus emerging from the sea. As Gardner says in his introduction:

In Cyprus, Venus (Aphrodite) is a very real person. She was a Goddess, yes; but she commanded armies, and won great victories over hordes of black troops. She rose from the sea at Paphos, where her great Temple is, but she built castles and palaces, many of which still remain. She made laws, she buried treasure; the place where she was stoned to death and the site of her tomb are still shown, and of nights she is still sometimes seen at the head of her ghostly armies.

She evidently was a real person, who made a great impression on popular fancy, and on whom legends were fastened, as with King Arthur.

How it would be possible for a woman to be received as a Goddess, rising from the sea, I have endeavoured to show.[5]

The book starts in the London of the 1930s. Robert Denvers, the hero, obviously based on Gardner, is concerned that his wife, Mina (short for Domina) is having an affair with his former boss, Hank Heyward. He finds some comfort in a bronze snail which he had acquired from somewhere and which had resurfaced in a drawer after several years.

When he was in the presence of any object of genuine antiquity he had a curious sense of complete familiarity with it, as though, through its medium, he could recreate the life which had surrounded it from its inception.[6]

He gradually drifted into a sleep which, to all outward appearances resembled a cataleptic trance. Inwardly he was able to re-live, in great detail, the most exciting part of one of his previous lives, as Kinyras, a citizen of Karpas, in Cyprus in the 15th Century BCE.

Kinyras, the hero through whose eyes the story is seen, and his brother Zadoug, are convinced that their land of Karpas, the north-eastern promontory of Cyprus, is in danger of invasion by the Khemites (Egyptians), who have already attacked the neighbouring kingdom of Aghirda, killing Damastes, the king, and capturing its princess, Dayonis. Some of the Karpasians, including Hange, argue against believing that the Khemites would invade, but Kinyras and others win the people round.

Kinyras, who saw in detail the plan of a fortified wall in a dream, sets everyone to work to build it in as short a time as possible. He also saw in a dream the design of a cross-bow ("Staveros"), which had the advantage of being capable of use by someone with little training and still have great strength and accuracy.

Meanwhile, Dayonis escapes from her captors and, after being found by Kinyras and helping him defeat an attack by the Khemites, is brought back to his house to rest.

The plot of the story is complex, with many attacks, counter-attacks, spying and other treachery. An attempted invasion by sea by the Khemites is defeated. Kinyras is married to Dayonis at a temple in her own land.

The climax of the book is set near Paphos, the site of Venus' legendary emergence from the ocean. Two religious factions are in conflict with each other. The Tamiradae, who were wool-merchants and owned dye-works, abhorred the sight of the naked human body and worshipped Hera. The worshippers of Ashtoreth, the more ancient goddess, loved nakedness.

Dayonis, having escaped capture a second time by diving naked into the sea, swam ashore where she was identified as Ashtoreth/Aphrodite. The Tamiradae were thus defeated.

Meanwhile, Hange is unmasked as a traitor. It is learnt that the Khemite king, Thothmes, is dead and the Khemite troops are withdrawn and return to Khem because it is seething with rebellion about his successor.

Back in the London of the 1930s, Heyward forces the snail from Denvers' grasp. Having slept for a fortnight, he wakes up, realising that Heyward and Hange are the same person. His wife, Mina, realises how much she loves him and wants to stay with him. The book ends with Denvers telling his wife about Steiner's theory of group reincarnation.

That, in outline, is the story. And it is a good one and an accomplished one for a first novel. But the important thing for us is to look at Gardner's references to witchcraft, how he saw it at that time, and other themes which would prove important in his later writings.

It becomes clear very quickly that Dayonis, the heroine of the story, is a witch. Zadoug, who had been finding out about her imprisonment, says "She passed most of the time at her witch-tricks."[7] and "It was well known that she was a true Cabire and had invoked these Lords [of Fate] and acquired mighty powers. I discovered that the Cabire were a secret witch cult."[8]

The use of the term "witch cult" is interesting, as Gardner uses it right through until *Gerald Gardner Witch* was published in 1960. It was, of course, the term which Margaret Murray used in *The Witch Cult in Western Europe*, published in 1921[9].

The existence of a secret society, another theme with which Gardner, with his Masonic background, was familiar with, is introduced by Kinyras:

"Princess, shall I make you one of us in brotherhood?" he whispered.

"If you so wish it," she murmured back.

"See, blood from this wound of mine mingles with that from your shoulder, and blood from your shoulder falls into this wound on my hand."

He moved so that it did so and bent his lips to her shoulder, sucking the wound, offering his hand for her to do likewise, which she did. Then he drew the rough outline of a sword on her brow with blood and another on her breast, over the heart, saying -

"Now you are my sword comrade, Dayonis, you are of the brotherhood of the sword."

"Now I am your sword comrade, Kinyras," she repeated after him with almost childish solemnity, for she had a child's delight and belief in rites of any sort. *"Now I am of the brotherhood of the sword and I swear loyalty to the death."*

"As a test of courage we all have to fight naked beside our sponsor. This you have already done and at a more convenient season I'll teach you the signs of the order."[10]

Later, he does give her the signs:

"... if you think only brothers are present the third and fourth fingers of the left hand are closed, the middle finger is held straight down, representing a sword, the index touching the thumb and

representing the sheath. Quietly done it is a most natural gesture, passing unnoticed though not to be used except when in the presence of brothers or if you are being tested. In such a case, give it first then draw your sword, holding it in the right hand upwards at full extent give the sign again. This is our royal salute, given only to our leaders, or at rites, or when being tested. ... You must never fail to help a brother and you will always be helped in turn ..."[11]

Nakedness is a frequent theme in the book, particularly of Dayonis. Whilst this may be an indication that Gardner was already familiar with, and active in, naturism during this period, it must not be forgotten that nakedness, particularly when fighting, was quite usual in the Mediterranean area during the period in which the book is set.

One particular passage is very striking, where Dayonis escapes from her captors on board ship:

For some brief seconds Dayonis saw a clear passage to the stern. It was now or never. She was naked, her hair was hidden and she had her sword for attack. If she sped lightly, in the rush she might escape recognition and it would be difficult to snatch at her naked body, which she had taken the precaution to oil well.[12]

The idea that it is difficult to capture someone in the nude whose body was well oiled, also occurs in *Witchcraft Today*:

... they found that the soldiers would usually let a naked girl go, but would take a clothed one prisoner. The slippery oiled bodies also made them hard to catch hold of.[13]

In *A Goddess Arrives*, Gardner attributes healing qualities to Dayonis and it is clear from the context that these are derived from her being a witch:

As she bathed with slow, rhythmic gestures she began to chant in a curious low croon, "Hail Hecate! Goddess, Ruler of the Night, Hail! Aid me, who thy dread secrets share. Help me staunch this flowing blood, banish pain - cool this fever with thy breath. By all the worship I have given thee, grant this man be made whole."

Kinyras listened with the utmost gravity as she chanted these words three times, unable to determine whether it was some magnetic quality in the slowly droned words, or some healing in the touch of her fingers which made the pain gradually leave him. The blood had stopped oozing and as he gazed the surface dried, looking like a healthy wound three or four days old.

"You must be a witch!" he exclaimed, making a snatch at her fingers, which she avoided, laughing in a teasing way.

"Well, cannot a witch have her uses sometimes?"[14]

Dayonis also says: "I have the gift of sight from the Old Ones."[15]

Later, she reveals other magical techniques to Kinyras, who in turn reveals his own techniques:

"I do nothing but leave my mind open for what will be put into it. I come and I go, up and down Time according to my need, sometimes without voluntary effort."[16]

She, by contrast, makes a dense smoke and the gods speak to her out of it. It is clear also that she makes sacrifices, both human and animal, as part of her magical workings. For example, she slaughters a jailer, not directly in order to escape, but as an offering:

"I knew that to obtain real power I must have a human sacrifice, but I always hated to do it. But when I was a helpless prisoner, and my country lost, it was another thing. And he was a beast of an enemy. So I did what was needful, and it worked, for the very next day Ammunz broke through the wall and led me to freedom."[17]

There is a vivid description of a ritual which Dayonis performed on board ship:

The great cabin in the ship's stern was cleared of furniture, only two chests being retained with which she prepared two altars. Upon these were placed several big, shallow bowls. She next drew a large circle upon the floor with red paint, setting the smaller altar with a brazier in the centre, the larger outside, and ringing the circle with little lamps set a foot apart. When the time drew near she summoned her assistants and the sacrifices were driven in.

"We must cast away our clothes," she announced in a hushed voice, as she slipped deftly from her one garment and her sandals.

Silently the two men obeyed her, while she took the sacred stone from her neck and laid it on the smaller altar. Prayer, in an unknown tongue, followed next and a command to her assistants to hold the black sheep. Midnight was now approaching and, with her sword in her right hand and holding a magic wand in her left, with one blow she severed each head from the animals, whose bodies were placed on the outer altar. The wand, the sword and a small figure of herself as enchantress, rested on the inner altar and her assistants were bidden to enter the circle with herself. Holding the two severed heads she marked both herself and the men on breast and forehead with blood, devoting them to Jask.

With the bloody necks of the slaughtered sheep she marked out a broad, inner circle round the celebrants and placed the heads on the small altar. Then, with a fire drill, she lit the lamps and kindled a fire, chanting all the while in her secret language and pacing the circle in antithesis to the progression of the sun. Next, lighting the brazier, she cast into it many roots and herbs. A dense, choking and stinging smoke arose while, unheeding its discomfort, the two men knelt clasping hands, one each side of her, with instructions not to lose contact until the ceremony was over. Dayonis then knelt between them with her arms on their shoulders, bidding them to support her body with their arms. So with the circle complete, she explained that, as she went into the trance she would bend over the smoke and breathe it in, bidding them breathe no more than was possible and to guard her from falling face forwards into the fire.

"Mark well what I say and lose not contact else shall I waken ere the magic be complete. Remember, every spoken word has its meaning."[18]

I have quoted this passage at length because, if one disregards the animal sacrifice, there are several factors which are later found in Gardner's own description of Craft rituals, including the ritual circle, nudity, sword, wand and incense.

The story could have been written without any reference to witchcraft whatever and would have been just as exciting. But it seems as if, by the time Gardner was ready to send the manuscript to the publishers (probably mid-1939), he had become sufficiently interested in witchcraft to have read Margaret Murray's *The Witch Cult in Western Europe*, since he uses the term "witch cult". Whilst the witches that he was later to meet (or perhaps had already met) would not have countenanced blood sacrifice and killing people for magical ends, we must remember that these were practices which were carried out in the period in which the story is set.

There are other references in *A Goddess Arrives* but I hope that enough has been quoted to indicate that Gardner was already sufficiently interested in witchcraft to give it a central role in the book, albeit in a rather different form to that which he was to write about later.

In this context, the date of publication of *A Goddess Arrives* becomes particularly significant. There is no date in the book and the records of the publishers (Arthur H. Stockwell Ltd.) were destroyed when their premises in Ludgate Hill, London were bombed during the war. The firm moved out to Ilfracombe in Devon and is still in existence.

However, the British Library received their copy on 6th December 1939. Under the Copyright Act 1911, publishers have to send copies of all new books published to the British Library, and this is obviously likely to happen shortly after copies have been received from the printers. According to Richard Price, the British Library's Curator of Modern British Collections, it was not unknown for publishers to omit the date of publication around the end of the year "so as not to make their work seem quickly out-of-date"[19]. This might well apply to *A Goddess Arrives*, particularly as it was being published not just towards the end of the year but towards the end of the decade as well. We can, I think, with reasonable confidence, give the date of publication as the very beginning of December 1939.

We have another clue. A review of *A Goddess Arrives* appeared in the *Christchurch Times* of 27th January 1940, presumably as the result of a review copy sent by Gardner. Assuming that the review copy was sent out shortly after Gardner received it and giving the reviewer time to read the book thoroughly (which he obviously did) the above publication date seems reasonable.

Gardner therefore probably submitted the book to the publishers no later than the summer of 1939, quite a time after his interest in witchcraft had been aroused as a result of his membership of the Folk Lore Society, but before his initiation into the Craft in September 1939.

Chapter 4
The Rosicrucians and the Crotona Fellowship

It was the end of the year; the naturist club which he had joined was closed for the winter, and he was thrown upon his own resources. On one of his long cycle rambles, Gardner came across a curious building in Christchurch. Cut in the stone the legend said: THE FIRST ROSICRUCIAN THEATRE IN ENGLAND. Later he was to find out what this meant. This was the discovery which led to his recruitment into the cult of the witches...[1]

Thus Bracelin tells the story of how Gardner took the first steps towards making contact with the witches. We will look at how it happened in a later chapter, but as Gardner claimed that it was through the Rosicrucian Theatre, it is important to look at how the Theatre came into being, the beliefs and practices of those who ran it, and some of the main personalities involved.

The Rosicrucians

Rosicrucianism does not reside within any one organisation. Rather it is a movement which forms part of the Western esoteric tradition. It has its roots in gnosticism, kabbalism and several other strands.

It really started with certain documents which were published in Germany at the beginning of the 17th Century. The anonymous *Fama Fraternitatis* explained how the Order of the Rosy Cross was founded by a mysterious figure known as Christian Rosenkreutz, who was born in the 14th or 15th Century and who lived to the age of 106. He is supposed to have gone on a long pilgrimage visiting the Middle East, Africa and Spain, then returning to Germany, where he started the Order, eventually dying and being buried in a tomb, which was re-opened after 120 years.

Two other works, the *Confessio Fraternitatis* and *The Chemical Marriage of Christian Rosenkreutz*, also appeared. None of these works gave a contact address but requested that those who wished to join the Order should make themselves known through published writings to enable the Fraternity to contact them. In fact, no one is known to have received an invitation to join the Order. Nevertheless, the movement spread throughout Europe, including England, and many have claimed that Francis Bacon (1561-1626) was a member. He was a philosopher and statesman, attaining the post of Lord Chancellor and being bestowed with the titles Lord Verulam and Viscount of St. Albans. But, apart from this, he was considered by some to have been a Rosicrucian. His book *New Atlantis* told of the discovery of a utopian society in an unknown land who sent out individuals to mingle with the inhabitants of the known world, which is a Rosicrucian concept.

There is a belief, popular particularly amongst Rosicrucians, that Bacon was the author of the Shakespeare plays. This idea had been popularised by F.W.C. Wigston in his book *Bacon, Shakespeare and the Rosicrucians* which had been published in 1888, and which attempted to show that the plays were full of Rosicrucian concepts. Christopher McIntosh[2] points out that Bacon was actually not very sympathetic to the occult and that his writing style was very different to that of Shakespeare.

There were probable links with Freemasonry from the earliest days, and certainly by the mid-18th Century there were specific Rosicrucian Masonic degrees. In 1865, the Societas Rosicruciana in Anglia (SRIA or Soc. Ros.) was founded, reputedly based on old documents found in Freemasons' Hall. Membership was limited to Master Masons, one of whom claimed initiation from German Rosicrucian adepts. The Order of the Golden Dawn was founded in 1887, largely the creation of William Wynn Westcott (1848-1925) and Samuel Liddell MacGregor Mathers (1854-1918). It combined a variety of sources, including the Qabalah, astrology, tarot, alchemy and the Rosicrucian legend. It differed from the SRIA in that it admitted women as well as men and openly claimed to practice magic. McIntosh says of it:

Mathers and Westcott, in concocting the Golden Dawn rituals, drew on many sources and managed to blend them so effectively that the ceremonial system they created has remained alive to this day.[3]

The Rosicrucian movement has never been limited to one organisation. Those which have flourished in the 20th Century have been largely American in origin, and include the Ancient and Mystical Order Rosae Crucis (AMORC) founded by H. Spencer Lewis and the Rosicrucian Fellowship, founded by Max Heindel.

George Alexander Sullivan

The existence of the Rosicrucian Theatre in Christchurch was overwhelmingly due to the vision and actions of one man: George Alexander Sullivan, who had been born on 24th September 1890 at 14 Elm Grove, West Derby, Liverpool, the son of Catherine Sullivan and her husband, Charles Washington Sullivan, a ship's steward.

What Sullivan had done in his early years is rather uncertain. According to a talk which he later gave to the Christchurch Post-War Brotherhood, he had travelled in Canada, through the United States, cruising among the West Indies and exploring the upper reaches of the Amazon, experiencing periods of privation, excitement and danger from natives, disease and hunger. All very exciting stuff![4] The first indication of any Rosicrucian activity is in 1911, when Sullivan was 21. In a pamphlet published in 1926, he gives a (tantalisingly brief) account of how he became involved:

I, George Alexander Sullivan, Founder and Head of the Rosicrucian Order Crotona Fellowship and the Rite of Egyptian Mysteries in which are incorporated the Occult teachings of the East and West, Declare that I have faithfully carried out the instructions given to me by my ancestor J.S. regarding the Re-establishment of an Occult Society in which the Rosicrucian Teachings might be taught to those willing to undertake such studies. Acting, therefore, on his instructions, I founded the "Order of the Twelve" in the year 1911, on the pattern of the old Rosicrucian Fraternity in the nature of a Society with Secrets.[5]

10. George Alexander Sullivan (1890-1942)

We have no further information about the identity of this ancestor, nor on the method by which the instructions were passed on. The Order was disbanded during the First World War when, as Howard[6] comments, many occult lodges and groups were forced to close.

In 1915 Sullivan got married. This was followed by unspecified adventures during the Great War (1914-1918) and a trip to Tibet. He writes about his "return from captivity in Germany in 1919", which suggests that he was a prisoner-of-war there. He goes on to state that, whilst in Germany, he "...became acquainted with other Rosicrucians and from them learned sufficient to convince me of the verity of that which had been given me by my ancestor." One would have thought that a prisoner-of-war would have had little opportunity to meet many native Germans, and it seems a remarkable coincidence to have met more than one Rosicrucian whilst there.

The Order was re-established in 1920 under the title of Rosicrucian Order Crotona Fellowship. It is possible that this may have had some link with the Order of the Temple of the Rose Cross, which was founded in 1912 by Annie Besant in connection with the Theosophical Society. It is understood, however, that this had collapsed in 1918.[7] In this connection, it is interesting that an organisation known initially as the Liverpool School of Mental Science and subsequently as the Liverpool College of Psychotherapy and Natural Therapeutics was also founded in 1920. The only leaflet produced by this group which I have seen was written by Sullivan and I strongly suspect that the whole organisation was set up by him.

By 1926, Sullivan was living at 11 Tynemouth Street, Everton, not too far from his birthplace, and during the period 1925 to 1928 he produced a journal entitled *The Rosicrucian Gazette*. Throughout the early 1930s, certainly from 1931 to 1935, he seems to have made his living as a journalist, still in Liverpool, ending up in 1934 at 22 Norwood Grove. For this, he took the name of Alex. Mathews, a name which he later used for all his plays.

'Alex', of course, was his middle name. It is pure speculation on my part, but I think he chose the name 'Mathews' because that had been a well-known name on the Liverpool stage. Moreover, there is a suggestion that he may have had a family connection, for his obituary in the *Christchurch Times* states: "He came from a family long associated with the theatre, his grandfather being well-known as a producer and theatre owner."[8]

Charles Mathews (1776-1835) was born into a family of booksellers in London but later entered the theatre and had a career spanning many years. His son, Charles James Mathews (1803-1878) was born in Liverpool and followed his father onto the stage. He was not only a talented actor, but also a playwright, performing in many of his own plays. There is a two volume autobiography, edited by Charles Dickens, which was published shortly after his death.[9]

I have not so far done the necessary research to prove the connection, but it seems likely that this famous actor/playwright, born in Liverpool, was the inspiration for Sullivan to adopt the name Mathews for his literary and theatrical life, particularly if he was, as Sullivan claimed, his grandfather. In this respect it is interesting that on his gravestone he is called "George Alexander Mathew Sullivan" whereas on his Birth Certificate he is plain "George Alexander Sullivan". This, of course, incorporates almost completely his stage name on his memorial.

The Crotona Fellowship

By the early 1930s, the Rosicrucian Order Crotona Fellowship, founded by Sullivan, was in full swing. It was named after the town on the east coast of Italy which became home to Pythagoras, an important figure in Sullivan's philosophy and teachings. The publications of the Order incorporate the cross on a five-pointed star background, which seems identical to that used by Max Heindel's Rosicrucian Fellowship, which was established in 1909. Indeed, it seems likely that Heindel was one of the main inspirations for Sullivan initially.

Many publications, most written by Sullivan, appeared during the early 1930s, initially originating from 27a Brunswick Road, Liverpool, which may have simply been a room associated with the Spiritualist Church at the same address. Sullivan had his own printing press, even though judging from the quality of the products, it was a fairly basic one. He used to turn out copies of the Fellowship's booklets under the imprint of the Bohemian Press, and by 1934 they were being issued from Sullivan's home at 22 Norwood Grove. Printing was important to him, and he is quoted as saying "The odour of learning and the smell of printing go well together".[10]

It is not clear exactly how the Fellowship operated. There were certainly meetings in Liverpool, an annual 'conclave', about which more later, and a Chapter in London, but much of its activity seemed to take place in the form of a Correspondence Course. The booklets are mostly very short, often only a single folded page in a coloured card cover. Each covers a single topic which students would probably study as a specific lesson.

The main influences seem to me to have been Rosicrucian tradition, Theosophical ideas and Masonic practices, together with Sullivan's personal contribution, often by means of inspired or guided writings which he issued under the name of 'Aureolis'. This is the middle name of Paracelsus (though sometimes spelt 'Aureolus'), a Renaissance medic and occultist, who was thought, certainly by Sullivan, to have been a Rosicrucian.[11]

There was a close if informal link with Co-Masonry. This can be seen, first of all, in the rituals which were carried out by the Fellowship, which are very masonic in content. Secondly, Mabel Besant-Scott, the head of Co-Masonry in Britain, brought with her several Co-Masons when she resigned from that organisation in 1935 and joined the Crotona Fellowship. We shall be looking at this in more detail in Chapter 7.

From 1935 onwards, the publications were issued from 7 Parkfield Road, a large house near Princes Park, south Liverpool, a much more prestigious address. It was the home at the time of Frederick Ellis Pritchard, LLM, barrister-at-law. It is likely that Sullivan never lived there, but he may have been provided with office space and accommodation for the printing equipment which he used to produce the numerous publications.

The Philosophy of the Crotona Fellowship

In the course of my researches I was given or otherwise acquired quite a range of the material produced over the years by the Crotona Fellowship. My intention initially was to try to summarise the philosophy of the Fellowship, but each time I tried to put something on paper my mind failed me. It seemed to wash over me. It was rather like intending to listen to the weather forecast and then realising that it was over and my mind had been wandering in other directions! Doubtless this is an inadequacy on my part, but I finally realised what was causing it. Quite simply, popular awareness of esoteric matters has changed markedly in the 60 years or more since most of the pamphlets were written. Much of what one might call the esoteric teachings of the Order are now so much part of general thinking, certainly among the pagan and New Age communities of which I am familiar, that one finds it difficult to formulate in modern language what is being said let alone realise the impact which such teachings had on a variety of interested individuals.

The fact that we are not just a physical body; that there is a part of us that survives physical death and is reborn; that our many lifetimes are periods of learning by experience; and that we are all potentially capable of great things, having esoteric faculties we can use and develop to help ourselves and others to make spiritual progress - all these are so familiar to most of us that it is difficult to realise the unfamiliarity with which most people would approach them in the 1920s and 1930s. In those days these things were genuinely new to many people and required a great change in their way of thinking and seeing the world.

In some small way, as we shall see, particularly through the Findhorn community and modern Wicca, some of the ideas of the Crotona Fellowship have not only survived but have, in their very success through unexpected channels, lessened their own impact upon a future generation.

Sullivan's Plays and Other Writings

If he indeed had a family theatrical background, it was perhaps natural that Sullivan would use the noble tradition of the theatre to express esoteric truths. He was not only an actor of some distinction, but also a playwright. His plays are not great drama, but it is worth looking briefly at them because they do help us to understand something of what the Crotona Fellowship was trying to do. They were not pure entertainment: they all had a moral to them, though one sometimes has to think what it is, which is perhaps, at least in part, the intention.

Pythagoras

Probably the most important play is *Pythagoras*. It is a full three-act play with 23 characters, so its production was a major undertaking. It was, perhaps, a particular characteristic of Sullivan's Rosicrucianism, this emphasis on Pythagoras. Indeed, the Crotona Fellowship is named after the town in Italy where Pythagoras lived and established a school of philosophy. It is perhaps therefore to be expected that some of the particular contributions of Pythagoras would be presented to the public by means of a play.

Pythagoras lived in the 6th Century BCE and was essentially the founder of a new religious philosophy as well as what might now be called 'science'. He actually seems to have invented the word 'philosophy'. Writing about the Pythagorean vision of the world, Koestler says:

"The essence and power of that vision lies in its all-embracing, unifying character; it unites religion and science, mathematics and music, medicine and cosmology, body, mind, and spirit in an inspired and luminous synthesis. In the Pythagorean philosophy all component parts interlock ..."[12]

The play starts with a Prologue which introduces the idea that a play can transform the words, deeds and lives of those who see it:

"Let this play, though humble in presentment,
Cast and diction, a lesson teach to all
Who have the will to learn of something more
Than every day's affairs ..."

The story starts with Pythagoras as a young man in approx. 570 BCE visiting Egypt to seek wisdom from its priests. They want to keep their own secrets, however, and plot to kill him. He is, however, rescued by the King, who engages Pythagoras in a discourse, which provides the opportunity for Pythagoras to confirm the reality of previous lives and of rebirth.

The next Act takes place 20 years later, at Crotona on the east coast of Italy, where Pythagoras is living. It includes a major oration to the citizens, incorporating much of his philosophy. He and Theano, the daughter of the Chief of Crotona, fall in love and are married. The tyrant, Cylon, asks to be accepted as a pupil in Pythagoras' School of Philosophy, but is refused because of his attitude.

The third Act is 18 years later. Cylon is plotting to kill Pythagoras. Pythagoras leaves the town, but citizens of the neighbouring settlements refuse or only give him temporary refuge because they fear reprisals from Cylon. In the final scene, Pythagoras dies from a 'spasm' but only after his daughter has pledged that she will continue his teaching and he has given an assurance that he will return, in a future life, when needed.

Henry VII

There was, quite naturally, as amongst any theatrical group, an interest in the Shakespeare plays. In addition, the Crotona Fellowship were, as we have seen, of the opinion that the plays had actually been written by Francis Bacon. There was, however, never a Shakespeare play entitled *Henry VII*. It may have been that Sullivan saw the opportunity to complete the series, but there is also the hint that, as a reincarnation of Francis Bacon, Sullivan saw himself as being the author of the other plays in the series.

The play is the story of Perkin Warbeck and Lambert Simnel, pretenders to the throne, and of the King's patronage helping Caxton to establish a printing press using metal type. According to the report of its first performance in the *Christchurch Times*, "in a colourful series of historical pictures and episodes, illustrative of the death of Richard III and the assumption of the throne by Henry VII, the tragic Lambert Simnel is shown to be an element of disruption and unrest". The report gave the opinion that the author showed "...how the heart burning for power can lead only to the awfulness of war. In this he succeeded admirably ..."[13]

Sullivan also wrote a series of one-act plays that were used as "fill-ins" or occasionally making up a programme on their own. *Mind Undying* is set in a country inn some time in the 1920s or 1930s which had once been frequented by Francis Bacon. A traveller, one Francisco Hogg, puts up there for the night and, in his discussions about the origins of the psychic ability, causes the landlord to realise that the traveller is none other than a reincarnation of Francis Bacon. *Out of the Depths* is set in 6th Century Ireland and tells of the coming of Christianity, with an underlying mystical theme. *As Ye Sow* tells in a humorous way of the dilemma of an author who is confronted with his own creations, in the form of disgruntled characters. And *The Window of Hudson's Pagoda* is described as a "thriller". It is a mystery play with the traditional criminal detective replaced by an investigator into psychic mysteries.

There was, however, more to the activities of the Crotona Fellowship than putting on plays, and this was encouraged by the move from Liverpool to the south coast of England in the mid-1930s, as we shall see in the next chapter.

Chapter 5
Activities At The Ashrama

The connection with Christchurch starts at least as far back as 1930. One enthusiastic member of the Fellowship was Catherine Emily Chalk. Her husband, Thomas Arthur Chalk (1861-1931) had been a Major in the Great War and, in 1924, they had had built for themselves a large house, known as Meadow Way, on Street Lane (later to become Somerford Road) in Christchurch. The house also had a considerable amount of land attached to it.

Catherine Chalk had been born about 1864 and, as well as being interested in esoteric matters, had become very knowledgeable about the theatre and particularly Shakespeare. Along with many esoterically-minded people of the period, she was convinced that the Shakespeare plays were written by Francis Bacon, and it was possibly through this belief that she initially made contact with Sullivan.

From 1930, a group of local Crotona Fellowship members, probably mostly recruited by Catherine Chalk herself and possibly including Luther William Newby Stubbs, the schoolmaster at Highcliffe, started to meet regularly at the King's Arms in Christchurch.

At about the same period, the annual 'conclave' of members was held in Bournemouth for the first time. Lectures were given and plays performed, interspersed with the usual sort of holiday activities for which the South Coast was ideal.

It was decided, probably in 1935, that the Fellowship required some permanent venue. Thomas Chalk had died in 1931 and Catherine had plenty of land (and, I suspect, money). She agreed to build in the grounds of her house a wooden building which became known as the Ashrama Hall. It was probably completed about 1936, although there is no record of any Building By-Law application being made for it.

11 & 12. The Academia Rosae Crucis 1937 Annual Conclave in the grounds of the Ashrama. Christchurch

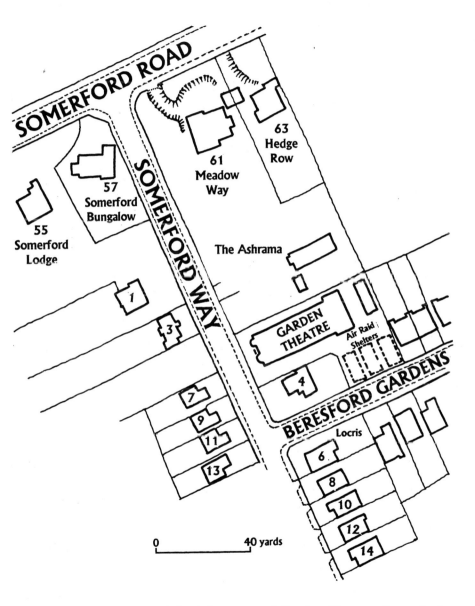

13. The Vicinity of the Ashrama and Garden Theatre, Somerford

This was approximately 60 ft x 20 ft in size - a single storey timber building with a pitched roof. It can be seen in the background of Illustrations 11 and 14. It included a private theatre. The *Christchurch Times* describes it thus:

The Ashrama Hall is actually a miniature and intimate theatre, completely fitted with stage scenery, and an auditorium provided with its tip-up seating, and comfortable auditorium.[1]

It was really the spiritual centre of the Order, where rituals were held, as were graduation ceremonies, performances, lectures and general meetings/discussions. Weekend gatherings and summer 'conclaves' were centred on this building, as was training in the various divisions of the Order.

Catherine Chalk also moved out of Meadow Way and into the smaller adjoining property of Hedge Row. This enabled Sullivan to move in to Meadow Way, probably in the Autumn of 1935.

The Activities of the Crotona Fellowship

The Fellowship's activities are set out like a prospectus and I rather suspect that this gives a rather grander picture than was the reality and that many things didn't quite work out in practice. The Correspondence Course, for example, is mostly on carbon copies rather than being duplicated, which tends to indicate that the number of students taking the course was somewhat limited.

The Academia Rosae Crucis

They called the branch of the society which contacts the public the Academia and I think they saw it almost as a University of the esoteric, albeit on a much smaller scale, but giving degrees, wearing academic gowns, as can be seen in Illustration 14. The Academia is described as being "devoted to the study of Mysticism, Comparative Religion, Philosophy, Drama and Elocution", and claimed that this range of topics was ancient in origin. Sullivan indicated that the Academia consisted of seven departments: Masonry, The Outer Court, Ordo, Ecclesia, Templum, Natural Therapeutics and the Theatrum.

Masonry

In Masonry the student is instructed in what is termed "Universal Symbolism". This wide subject, which concerns itself with architecture, the building art and archaeological lore, enables the student to view the Universe from the archaic to the present time. God has left a mark on all things and this mark constitutes a symbol which when read rightly reveals something of the plan and design of the Creator.[2]

Ordo

In the Ordo, or Order, the student reaches a higher level, and is prepared in an Outer court. Here he is furnished with an all round view of various subjects which help him to take a wide view of ... many subjects.[3]

14. The Academia Rosae Crucis Annual Conclave 1937 pictured in their academic robes outside the Ashrama, Christchurch

The Outer Court was the first contact an enquirer had of the Order. It basically gave an introduction to the Order's philosophy and work, through a correspondence course, pamphlets and lectures.

The usual sojourn in the Outer Court now-a-days is about twelve months, and after this period, if the student is found eligible, he passes into the Ordo. If not, he may make further progress in Free-Masonry, this further study may equip him for entrance into the Ordo later.[4]

Theatrum

The Theatrum was an important part of the work of the Order. The Players are "not only well grounded in elocution and dramatic art, but also receive a psychological training which helps them to speak verbatim on any subject they have studied. In other words, they acquire the art of oratory, which is something distinct from committing to memory a "part" and reciting it.[5] Each player must be a member of the society and each one is well and carefully chosen. He or she must have obtained the diploma of the society indicating that the student has taken at least one of the Academic degrees."

Students are taught the essential symbolism of the theatre and by studying and presenting the drama of the Tudor period, the most important in the history of the theatre, many things were made clear and many possibilities were opened up.[6]

The Theatrum also taught students to become proficient as public speakers, so that in their turn they should carry on the work and traditions of the Order as the ancient brethren had done before them.[7]

In 1937, they formed *The College of Drama and Rhetoric,* which would operate under the auspices of the Academia, for those who wished "to take up the stage, screen or platform work professionally".

The course has been devised to develop the individual character of the students and has the support of eminent members of the dramatic profession. The syllabus includes manuscript plays, reviewing modern and classic drama. Shakespearean plays are largely adhered to because it is considered that Shakespeare's works are supreme for the teaching of stage-craft, voice production and prosody.

The curriculum includes voice production, verse speaking, public speaking, reading and the grammar of elocution. Fencing (both for men and women) is included with gymnastics, dramatic exercises and deportment. The art of make-up is studied in the course dealing with stage craft and play production. Public speaking and the theory of elocution ensures good pronunciation and confidence before an audience.

Apart from the ordinary subjects which are taught under the heading of elocution and dramatic art, a special training is given in a psychology, which helps to build character and unfold the higher faculties, and is exclusive to the Academia.

All students are familiarised with the use of the microphone, gramophone recording and sound films.[8]

The Sunday Play Producing Society

They seemed to be short of people to act and otherwise help with the theatrical productions, so in January 1938 a new enterprise was announced: there was to be a new society affiliated to the Rosicrucian Players. The Christchurch Times reported that "Its membership provides for a whole series of most interesting Sunday evening productions (timed, of course, not to interfere with the church services) and whereby a member can become at once an active participator in a series of most original presentations. ... The fee is very small, a matter of five shillings for the whole year, and this includes not only indoor theatrical productions, but provision is also being made for a series of al fresco presentations in the summer months - for this dear little theatre stands in a garden."[9]

Natural Therapeutics

A member of the Brotherhood of Healers is trained in every system of natural therapeutics, and when proficient is examined in a number of selected subjects, and his ability to pass qualifies him to work as a Brother of Healing and so help to alleviate the pains and sufferings of his fellow men and always without fee.[10]

In the College of Natural Therapeutics, into which only few students pass, the subjects are technical and the student becomes a great observer of nature. Here he finds himself studying botany, dietetics, psychotherapy, light and colour therapy, chiropractic, and a number of other subjects which assist him to help his fellow men. Tests in sound, light and colour therapy are made in the college for the Order has many musicians and artists who contribute practical services to the cause.[11]

The name has echoes of the Liverpool College of Psychology and Natural Therapeutics, founded, probably by Sullivan, in 1920.

Ecclesia

In the Ecclesia, the student is trained to become a priest, one versed in the art of mental and physical healing ... tuition in comparative religion and ... in special occult and mystical subjects peculiar to the society which have evolved as the result of experience and application during the past 600 years.[12]

The Ecclesia ... is a training ground in comparative religion. The student in this department makes himself as much at home with Buddhism, Brahminism, Confucianism and Zoroasterism [sic] as he does with Christianity, and here a remarkable revelation would come to him, he would inevitably realise after a period that Christianity is actually the culminating point of all preceding religions.

In the Ecclesia, various Rites and Ceremonies are performed, and they portray in their presentment the atmosphere of the Religions of ancient Egypt, India, China, and other countries, and so one came to the Christian services which are taken in the little church on the estate, every Sunday morning.[13]

The Templum

The Templum, which is the next step after the Ecclesia, may be considered the higher church, for herein the student studies and practises the art of spiritual healing. He trains his mind and emotions to be subservient to the will and his thoughts are directed towards mankind. He does not allow his thoughts and emotions to run wild, but keeps both subject to a logical will. Those of the Templum become servants of mankind and offer their service to all willing to accept.[14]

The Archives

In the archives of the Order is a vast amount of knowledge available to the student and this knowledge is being added to year by year.[15]

In the archives of the society are thousands of lectures touching upon all branches of learning and also ancient manuscripts and books written by past members which are available to all students to assist them in their studies. The training is peculiarly mental and spiritual.[16]

We know something of what the archives contained, for in 1977 they were presented to the University of Southampton Special Collections Library, where they are still kept. They include two mediaeval manuscript books, one dating from the mid-14th Century and containing statutes of the Cistercian Order, and one from the late 14th or early 15th Century containing text by Bede. Where the Crotona Fellowship obtained these from is not known. There are also over 150 other volumes in the Crotona Fellowship collection, mostly relatively modern printed books. They include works by and about Shakespeare and Francis Bacon; esoteric and occult writers as varied as Eliphas Levi and Israel Regardie; together with books on such subjects as mythology, antiquarianism, Egyptology, Pythagoras, Rosicrucianism, Freemasonry and Theosophy.

Of course, we do not know whether this represents the complete archive of the Crotona Fellowship - probably not, but it gives us an idea of the range of interests which Sullivan, at least, possessed.

Members of the Crotona Fellowship

Membership of the Fellowship probably built up initially through word of mouth, newsletters, lectures, correspondence courses and the annual conclaves. I have studied the reports of theatrical performances, lectures etc. in the *Christchurch Times* and other papers for the 1936-1942 period and many names appear, which I give below. I single out some of the most prominent for special mention. Each, I am sure, is worthy of a chapter in their own right, but since the main subject of this book is the modern witchcraft revival, these characters are really only marginal to our main interest. Brief mentions, however, will help to build up a picture of what the Crotona Fellowship was like.

Ivy Veronica Keen was born in Prescot, near Liverpool on 26th July 1901, although her family later moved to Birkenhead. Her first contact with Sullivan is recounted by Bracelin, who says: "This lady had discovered at a Liverpool meeting that she had been the wife of "Aurelius" [sic] in a past life."[17] This would probably have been some time in the early 1930s. Certainly, she appears subsequently to have been very close to Sullivan, for she was living with him in Meadow Way after 1937.

His wife, Jane, and daughter, Brenda, stayed in Liverpool after he moved down to Christchurch and he left his property equally between his wife and Ivy Keen.

She took a major role in most of the theatrical productions of the Fellowship, where she was known as Francesca Keen. She was also the Grand Secretary of the Order. To quote Bracelin again: "*The High Priestess was there, too ... She had a keen business sense, ran the place, and had been Mary Queen of Scots in one of her incarnations.*"[18] This clearly shows how Gardner perceived her role. The use of the word "keen" is typical of his deliberate use of words to convey more than appears on the surface.

Peter Caddy gives another insight into her character and that of Sullivan. Writing about his marriage ceremony, he says:

After the ceremony, I invited him [Sullivan] *and Francesca Keen, the secretary of the Order, to lunch at a restaurant, where chicken and a bottle of wine had been ordered. Francesca was horrified but Doctor Sullivan silenced her protests - I did not know then that he neither ate meat nor drank alcohol. Since he had no wish to embarrass us, he consumed whatever was placed before him.*[19]

Sullivan left the house, Meadow Way to Francesca in his will and she continued to live there until her own death on 9th November 1972. Her body is buried in the same grave as Sullivan's. She is also commemorated in the names of the flats which were built on the site of Meadow Way after it was demolished in 1976. They are called Francesca Lodge, Francesca Court and Francesca Grange.

One of the most significant members of the Fellowship was **Mabel Besant-Scott**, known as 'Mabs'. Her role in our story is such that she has a chapter to herself - Chapter 7.

Ailsie D Hall was Secretary of the Fellowship and Assistant Manager of the Theatre until 1939.

15. *Mabel Besant Scott's Bungalow - Locris*

Edith Woodford Grimes was one of the stalwarts of the Fellowship, and we devote Chapter 9 to her story.

Luther William Newby Stubbs had been born in Cockermouth, Cumberland, in 1888. He seems to have chosen a career in teaching, as he became the Head Teacher of St. Mark's Church of England Infants and Junior School in Highcliffe in January 1923, retiring in 1932 at the early age of 44. He was certainly involved with the Rosicrucians as early as 1932 and possibly further back, helping Catherine Chalk in organising the meetings at the Kings Arms which started in 1930. He shared with her and with Sullivan an interest in the history of the theatre and spoke at Rosicrucian public meetings on the subject.

E. Marshall Harvey was a local barrister who lived at Branksome, Bournemouth. He ran the *Outer Court Correspondence Course* and was therefore, for many, the first, and perhaps only, point of contact with the Fellowship.

Ivor and Hilda Baker were well-known public figures in Christchurch in the 1950s and 1960s. They were local business people and were very active in the local Chamber of Trade. Ivor was a local councillor and Hilda was a J.P.

W. Martin Andrew was a solicitor and acted for many of the members. He and Cyril Barnes were executors of Sullivan's will.

Bracelin refers to David Brown, Rhona Perreau and Rene Lyon Clark indirectly when he says: "...quite a number of bungalows had been built, where the faithful could live."[20] I have no evidence that the building of bungalows was organised by the Order. I think it more likely that members wanted to live near the Ashrama and that when land immediately south of the theatre along Somerford Way was being developed those who wanted to bought plots or bungalows. Mabel Besant-Scott bought No. 6 Somerford Way, the bungalow on the corner of Beresford Gardens, and named it 'Locris' after the town in Sullivan's play *Pythagoras* of which she played a citizen.

Rene Lyon Clark lived at Ballard Lodge, New Milton, before moving here. She probably had some local connection as she wrote a series of articles for the *Christchurch Times* on "Literary Links with Christchurch". She bought plot no. 41. Building works for her bungalow took two years and were not completed until April 1940. I have not yet been able to identify which bungalow this is, but it was undoubtedly one in the vicinity of the Theatre. She was also a Druid.

David and Gladys Brown bought no. 12 Somerford Way (later renamed 'St. Clare') and **Rhona Perreau** bought no. 13.

Peter Caddy

It is perhaps fair to say that Sullivan and the Crotona Fellowship are remembered today not so much for their own sake but for the way in which they were influential in the development of other movements. Gerald Gardner and the modern witchcraft revival is the subject of this current book. Another movement, perhaps more noteworthy in terms of the more direct influence, is the Findhorn community, in Scotland, one of the founders of which was Peter Caddy.

Caddy was born on 20th March 1917 in Ruislip, Middlesex. His first job was working for J. Lyons, at that time the largest caterers in the world. At the age of 18, on holiday in Blankenberge in Belgium, he noticed a girl called Nora Meidling and instantly knew that he was going to marry her. She turned out to live in Ealing, not far from him, with her mother and sister. Peter got to know Nora quite well and also met her other sister, Elizabeth, who was married to Cyril (Jim) Barnes, a civil servant.

In discussions with Cyril and Elizabeth, Caddy realised that they followed Sullivan's teachings and went down to Christchurch most weekends. He was fascinated by the teachings and later met Sullivan in London. Shortly afterwards he was initiated into the "Francis Bacon Chapter No. 33" in London. In his autobiography, *In Perfect Timing*, Caddy refers to the Crotona Fellowship as "having chapters all over Britain". I think this is actually quite unlikely to be the case. Even by 1937, the annual conclave only consisted of some 36 individuals. The most that I can reasonably envisage is a surviving chapter in Liverpool in addition to the London one just mentioned. The "No 33" does not to my mind indicate that there were 32 other chapters around: the "33" I would have thought related to the number of degrees in, for example, certain Masonic traditions.

Peter and Nora attended the chapter meetings in London and later at Christchurch. They also attended at least one of the annual 2-week conclaves (or "retreats" as Caddy calls them). They married in December 1939 at a ceremony at the Ashrama presided over by Sullivan. This was followed by another ceremony on 30th December 1939 at St Matthew's Church, Ealing Common. By this time, Cyril and Elizabeth had moved down to Christchurch and were living in Somerford Bungalow, on the corner of Somerford Way and Somerford Road.

In his autobiography, Caddy gives a vivid impression of Sullivan:

He was a being of vast knowledge and seemed able to answer any question, but only if he felt it was right and appropriate to do so. He taught through lectures, drama, the church and Freemasonry, through fun and games, and by example. One had to remain alert during lectures and meetings so as to miss nothing, particularly the jokes. In spite of all his greatness, his wisdom and his love, he would appear to the average person as an ordinary human being. Doctor Sullivan was a humble person and I discovered that no job was too menial for him. He was the one who emptied the chemical toilets in his ashram. ... He slept only three or four hours a night and seemed to function on several different levels of consciousness simultaneously. ...one could enjoy an evening at the cinema with him, or a picnic to some historical place whose story he could 'read' from his inner connections. He said very little about himself; one had to get personal information through one's own intuition. We would often play table tennis together, as he always stressed the importance of coming back down to earth after his lectures. He maintained a careful balance in all aspects of his life.[21]

Other performers in the plays at the theatre whose names I have not mentioned elsewhere include Peggy Baker, Peter Brown, E.G.

Chalk, Leslie Davies, Archibald Deall, J. Donaldson-Palmer, Harry Dunn, Major C.F.J. Galloway, E. Gilholey, Dorothy Gray, Gavin M. Harris, Elza Irmgarde, Robert and Will Sawkins, Lea Shapiro, W. Lumisden Strange, A.C. Whitehorn and Eveline Wyatt.

Chapter 6
"The First Rosicrucian Theatre in England"

The first mention of a more permanent theatre is in September 1937. Mathews' play *'Pythagoras'* had just been successfully presented for the first time at the Ashrama Theatre. This, as mentioned previously, was fairly small and had clearly been full to overflowing. In a Press release it was stated that: *"We have been so encouraged ... by the appreciation which attended our presentation ... that something of a larger scope is almost forced upon us for next year."*[1] There were hopes at that time that the "private theatre" at the Ashrama would be enlarged and improved by the following summer. However, there was a subtle change of emphasis only a fortnight later: *"The Academia hopes to build a miniature theatre in Somerford ..."*[2]

PHONE:–
BOOKING OFFICE
CHRISTCHURCH 830.

GENERAL MANAGER.
G..A. SULLIVAN.

ASSISTANT MANAGER:
MISS A. D. HALL. /\

16. *Letterheading for Christchurch Garden Theatre*

The idea of a new Rosicrucian Theatre quickly seemed to take hold, because by November 1937 a Sale of Work was held to help raise funds for it. The new theatre, which it was hoped would be in existence by the following summer, was described as being "on a plot adjoining" and would be "larger and more lavishly equipped" than the existing Ashrama Hall. The plot referred to was to the south of the Ashrama, and was part of the original area of land owned by Mrs Chalk. It was some 70 feet in width and 180 feet in depth. The Sale of Work raised almost £50 but it is virtually the only fund-raising event for the Rosicrucians mentioned in the local paper, the *Christchurch Times*. Since we know from press reports that the theatre cost £4000 to build, it is evident that much of the money was raised in other ways, probably through wealthy benefactors.

By December 1937, the local Boscombe architect, R.H.F. Banning, had finished preparing plans for the new theatre. It was to be capable of seating an audience of 350, being 110 feet in length and 42 feet in width. The auditorium was planned to allow a comfortable view of the stage from all parts of the house and was built on a rake (or incline). The architect is quoted as saying: "a comfortable and well-spaced seated audience is an essential for effective presentation of stage plays"[3].

The building had all the usual facilities including a scene dock, property and wardrobe rooms and ample dressing room accommodation. The entrance to the auditorium was by a foyer from which cloakrooms led off.

Plans were approved on 7th January 1938, and building work commenced at the beginning of February, the builders being Messrs. W.J. Bryant of Christchurch. Mr. Bryant was a leading figure in Christchurch affairs and Captain of the local Fire Brigade.

The Laying of the Foundation Stone took place at 3 o'clock on Sunday 13th March 1938. This was an elaborate ritual, carried out in accordance with established Rosicrucian and Masonic principles. The Lord Mayor of Christchurch was present. It had been announced previously in the local press and a large crowd turned up to watch. Sullivan performed the opening ceremony and stone laying in his role as Head of the Order. A procession took place from the Ashrama Hall to the site of the new theatre, to the strains of the hymn "All People that on Earth do Dwell" played by the Town Band, and into the arena formed by the walls of the partially completed building.

The *Christchurch Times* reported the ceremony as follows:

Having made its entry by the south, the members stood in formation, whilst the Grand Master and his attendants examined the plans of the building and finally passed them to the architect. ... Then followed the singing of a Rosicrucian hymn, and the Grand Master, in a beautifully worded invocation, called for a blessing upon the work thus commenced.

17. George Alexander Sullivan laying the Foundation Stone of the Garden Theatre on 13 March 1938

To the great interest of the silent onlookers, the ritual observed at points of the compass included the scattering of corn to the accompaniment of the words spoken by the Grand Master. "Hereon let us cast corn, the symbol of Resurrection, to mark the East, whence all light cometh."

And to the West with the throwing of salt upon the threshold with the speech: "Salt the emblem of hospitality, friendship and fidelity, I cast in this Western place to mark the setting of the Sun. May it preserve this temple of learning from untimely corruption."

To the South with the sprinkling of wine: "He causeth the grass to grow for the cattle and the herbs for the service of man, that he may bring forth food out of the Earth and wine to make glad the heart of man".

Finally, oil was spilled to the North with the words: "...and oil to make his face shine ... the symbol of mortality ..."

And in conclusion the boldly spoken words addressed to all, "Peace to all good men and true".

"Various articles, documents and records were deposited in a cavity beneath the foundation stone, which bears the inscription:

This Foundation Stone
was laid by
Alexander Mathews
on March 13th, 1938
To commemorate the First
Rosicrucian Theatre in England.
Pax Vobiscum.

Upon the reverse side of the stone, at the moment of its "laying" the Grand Master inscribed with chalk the Holy Name in ancient Hebrew. The final words spoken to the assembly after this portion of the ceremony were: "May this undertaking, contrived by Wisdom, be executed in Strength and adorned with Beauty. So that it may be *a house of Peace and Harmony, wherein brotherly love shall perpetually reign. Peace be unto all beings."* Then followed a final Rosicrucian dedication.[4]

Various speeches were then made.

Construction of the theatre continued and, by the middle of April, the roof was on. The *Christchurch Times* reports on a remarkable occurrence in this connection:

"The assurance was made to the builders that fine and dry weather would attend their work and until the roof was in position, and this has been fulfilled in an emphatically marked manner. Not one small shower of rain has occurred during the past few weeks of building operations.

Now that the wide-spread span of the theatre roof is accomplished, the builders are declaring this as something that is more than unusual. From the day of digging of the foundations, to their last task on exterior work of covering in the big auditorium, they have worked under all sunshine conditions. On Thursday, when the roof was first completed, the barometer recorded its first fall, and promise of rain after 79 fine days."[5]

It is clear from this account that knowledge not usually possessed was being given and it is equally clear that we are dealing either with precognition or the working of magic. The unlikelihood of a 79-day rain-free period coinciding with the period from the start of construction to the roof covering being completed is such that magical working seems to be the only possibility. That such powers were not unusual within Rosicrucian circles will be confirmed later.

Opening

The Theatre was officially opened at 3pm on Wednesday 15th June 1938 by the Mayor of Christchurch, Councillor H.E.W. Lapthorne, when one of Sullivan's one-act plays, *The Master Beyond*, was performed. The first public performance, of Shakespeare's *The Merchant of Venice* was the same evening.

A Festival week followed in August with performances every day for a week, including a repeat of *The Merchant of Venice* and Sullivan's own plays of *Pythagoras* and *Henry VII* together with three of his one-act mystical plays. It was one of these performances of *Pythagoras* that Gardner attended, thus starting his acquaintance with the Crotona Fellowship.

The title of Garden Theatre caused a certain degree of confusion amongst some local people, who were under the impression that it was an open-air theatre. Sullivan had to write to the *Christchurch Times* in the following terms:

I'd be greatly obliged if you will kindly tell the burgesses of Christchurch that we have not only a roof but the most comfortably and properly seated auditorium in the district. Well heated and ventilated, and our garden is all outside the theatre - in its proper place.[6]

18. *The Garden Theatre, Somerford
Front View*

Unfulfilled Hopes

It soon became clear that the citizens of Christchurch were not flocking to the theatre in the numbers expected, as the *Christchurch Times*, in the kindest and most supportive terms, makes clear:

That the work of the Rosicrucian Players during their festival season at the Christchurch Garden Theatre has not been in vain, is judged by the enthusiastic, though small audiences, which have witnessed the plays.[7]

By the following month the paper was saying:

In consideration of the fact that the Christchurch Theatre is one of the most comfortable in the country, and the plays presented there of a most unique and artistic character, it is worthy of greater patronage.[8]

19. The Garden Theatre, Somerford Auditorium

By early October, the theatre was being let out on Sundays to the Methodists, who had decided to vacate their existing premises because of large repair bills. The following week, a cinema season was announced. Following a week in November, no further plays were publicised as taking place in the theatre - five months from opening to final performance!

In January 1940, Sullivan's play *The Demon Monk* was put on for three performances, not in the Garden Theatre, but in St. Peter's Hall, Bournemouth. This was the play in which Gardner took the part of a monk. Bracelin describes the play in vivid terms:

He acted the drunken monk in Liveda ("a devil" spelt backwards) when the play was produced in Bournemouth ... one monk corrupts others, and causes three of them to die. Their hearts are flung upon the stage. He prays to the devil, only for the ghosts of the monks to appear. Eventually he is sentenced to death by the abbot of their monastery.[9]

The *Christchurch Times,* in its report on 27th January 1940 states that Gardner played an ordinary monk, not the drunken one, so either the paper got it wrong or Gardner's memory was at fault. It should also be noted that *Liveda* is the name of one of the characters, not that of the play itself.

It seems as if, not only was the population of Christchurch largely unmoved by the presence of the Rosicrucian Theatre in their midst, there were also rumours flying around about the Rosicrucians themselves. An article in the *Christchurch Times* in May 1940 put it like this:

Recently, in a journal which enjoys a vast national circulation because of its "without fear or favour" order, a page was apportioned, what must have been to the uninitiated "amazing disclosures" ...[10]

The article went on:

As the man in the street bridles at the mention of "Masonic circles", secret societies and the like - the air of seeming aloofness created suspicion at the outset. The fundamental principle is a brotherhood which I would to God applied throughout the world today, where every effort is made to extend the knowledge culled from the learnings of centuries in such a way that it should find no fault, or interfere with any other religion whatsoever. By ancient usage Rosicrucians have sometimes conveyed their teaching by means of the drama, and the Principal or Grand Master at Somerford naturally expected Shakespeare would be an ideal medium with which to open the way.[11]

The article showed that none of the things that the Rosicrucians, in increasing desperation, put on at the theatre - Shakespearean plays, films, lectures, vaudeville and musical comedy - did the trick: the population stayed away in droves. And so, the Theatre closed.

Gardner parted company with the Crotona Fellowship, presumably after his performance in *The Demon Monk* in January 1940 and certainly after his initiation into witchcraft, as we shall see later. Bracelin tells the following story:

Christmas 1939 was the occasion of a prank which Gardner played upon the master. He gave a girl a bracelet to wear. A psychometrist was at once called, who said that the bracelet and its engraved characters were very old, had certainly belonged to an ancient Egyptian priest. Then Aurelius [sic] insisted that the characters were ancient Celtic. He pompously ended the discussion with the pronouncement: "It is ancient Celtic - older than anything you know".

Then it was revealed that Gardner had had the trinket made, and that the signs upon it came from Cornelius Agrippa's private code. Since he had once assumed this personality in his deathless existence, Gardner felt that Aurelius should have known this. In any case, this was the last time that he went to their meetings. A circular letter from the High Priestess is one of his memories, assuring her correspondents that there would be no war. It arrived on the day which war was declared. Aurelius had been more prudent; air-raid shelters were being prepared for him, though he also proclaimed the continuance of peace."[12]

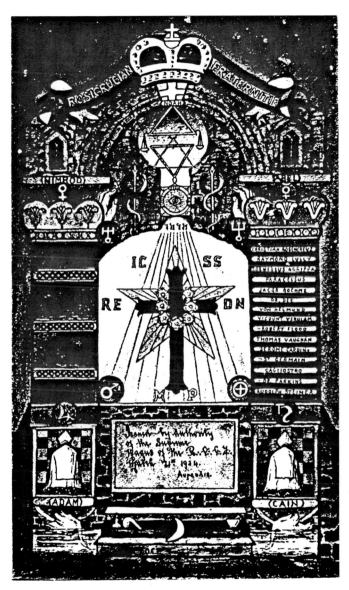

20. *Rosicrucian Plaque inside the Ashrama, Somerford*

Sullivan's Death

George Alexander Sullivan died on 3rd June 1942 at his home, Meadow Way. Cyril Barnes was present at his death. The death was certified by G. Maynard Brooks, MRCS and the cause of death indicated on his Death Certificate is given as Angina Pectoris, Coronary Artery Thrombosis and Myocardial Degeneration.

The funeral took place on the following Saturday at the Ashrama and his body was then interred in Christchurch Cemetery. The *Christchurch Times* reported it as follows:

At the Cemetery gates a long procession was formed of members and friends of the Order, the members in their robes of red and white, or brown, and led by the banner of the Order. An impressive service at the graveside concluded with the members filing past and dropping rose petals into the grave.[13]

The Cemetery is a fine wooded area, a haven in the midst of suburban Christchurch. Surrounded as it is by a high wall, it is like another world. There are some fine trees, including some exceptionally large pines, for which the area is famous. Sullivan's grave is in a particularly wooded part of the cemetery, close to one of the paths. It is a simple grave, but has the Rosicrucian symbol prominently displayed.

Gardner states that Sullivan claimed to be immortal. As Bracelin says:

Because people wondered why he did not grow old like them, he was compelled to slip away every few score years, to make another name in a fresh place. In the Ashram (temple) was a great plaque with the various identities under which he had lived through the ages inscribed thereon.[14]

I believe that Illustration 20 shows this. Certainly it includes the names of Cornelius Agrippa, Dr. Dee and others who are vital in the history of the Rosicrucian tradition.

Tillett, with striking understatement, says *"Sullivan's claim of immortality suffered badly as a result of his death..."*[15] And

Bracelin states quite bluntly: "*The movement foundered when the immortal died...*"[16]

But did Sullivan claim to be immortal? I think Gardner probably misinterpreted the claims of immortality, or they were being deliberately propagated by Sullivan for his own purposes. Sullivan had already confided to Peter Caddy the previous year that he knew he was going to die in 1942. As Caddy put it, "*...he reckoned he would be more useful operating on the 'other side' to combat the dark forces rolling across the world.*"[17] This was the impetus behind the "Soul Series" of lectures that so inspired Caddy.

It is clear that the Fellowship as a whole did not expect Sullivan to be immortal in the usually understood meaning of the term. Far from foundering it continued under the new leadership of Vincent Walter Brodrick-Bullock for some years. He had been introduced to the Order by Peter Caddy, but, inevitably, he could not replace Sullivan. As Caddy said:

Many members of the Order found it difficult adjusting to the change in style of our Supreme Magus. Walter Bullock lacked Doctor Sullivan's warmth and fun; I felt that his heart was not fully developed. He had great knowledge and hypnotic power, however...[18]

The Fellowship never really retained its brief pre-war level of popularity and by the early 1950s its centre of activities had moved to Southampton.

An organisation calling itself The Crotona Fellowship existed in South London during the 1970s, but this was really a revival rather than a continuation, and concentrated more on the life and teachings of Pythagoras rather than Rosicrucianism as such.

Perhaps an indication of the truth of Sullivan's approach to immortality is the inscription on his gravestone in Christchurch Cemetery, which reads: "From Life Unto Death - From Death to Immortality", which is far from a claim to the physical immortality which Gardner seems to be implying. It is really saying nothing more than that we will be reborn - a fact recognised by over half the population of the Earth and by the vast majority of those involved in esoteric circles, both then and now, including Gardner himself.

Chapter 7
Mabs and the Co-Masons

Mabel Emily Besant Scott, known to her friends as 'Mabs', is important in our story of how Gerald Gardner first met the witches. She wasn't a witch herself, but she brought Gardner together with those who were, so her story is worth telling.[1]

She was born on 28th August 1870, the daughter of freethinker, Annie Besant and her husband, Rev. Frank Besant, at Leckhampton, near Cheltenham, where he was the incumbent. Even at the time of her birth, her parents were not getting on personally and the great ideological differences between them began to surface. Frank had apparently hit Annie when she *"begged him not to force another child on her"*[2]

When she was only 8 months old, Mabel, who was described as 'delicate', contracted whooping cough and then severe bronchitis. Anne Taylor says:

Annie retreated with her into a makeshift tent before the fire where steam from a succession of kettles vied with coal smoke for the good or ill of Mabel's lungs.[3]

Her doctor gave her chloroform on a handkerchief to allay the severe coughing, apparently accepting the risks associated with that treatment because he believed she would not survive long. Probably as a consequence, she developed epilepsy, but she did survive, albeit as a frail child whose mother became overprotective towards her.

Annie left her husband in July 1873, taking Mabel and her elder brother Digby with her. Grounds for divorce at that time were limited to adultery, desertion and cruelty, whereas, as Anne Taylor says: "*Heresy ... was really the issue between the Besants ...*"[4]. In any case, they both had religious objections to divorce, so a "deed of

91

separation" was drawn up. This was permitted under the Custody of Infants Act, which had been passed earlier that year. It gave Annie the custody of Mabel, and Frank the custody of Digby, provided that each child spent a month every year with the other parent.

Frank Besant was never really happy with the arrangement, particularly when he obtained evidence that Mabel was not receiving religious instruction, in accordance with Annie's beliefs at the time. He petitioned the courts for the return of his daughter. The case hinged on whether Frank knew that Annie was not a Christian at the time he signed the original deed. The Court decided that Annie should give Mabel up to her father and, as a consequence, she spent the next ten years of her life at boarding school in Boston, Lincolnshire, living with her father in the holidays.

A campaign was fought against the decision. Anne Taylor writes of what this involved:

Portraits of the little girl in boots, short skirts, ringlets, and a simper were printed by the dozen with the caption 'Mabel Emily Besant, deprived of her mother, May 23 1878'. The National Reformer advertised a package of books - The Freethinker's Text Book, The Gospel of Atheism, The Fruits of Christianity, and the Law of Population - as 'works by Mrs Besant used in justification of taking away Mrs Besant's daughter'.[5]

However, by the age of 18, Mabel had started making clandestine visits to her mother, who by that time had become involved with Theosophy and was living at 19 Avenue Road, St John's Wood, and as Anne Taylor says:

Before she came of age she went to live there permanently. The law was on Frank's side had he chosen to claim her. Instead he banished her as he had his son.[6]

On 7th May 1892, Mabel married Ernest Scott. He was a reporter on the *London Globe* and had been born on 21st June 1867 in Northampton[7]. It is not clear how Mabel met him, probably in

London, although it is intriguing that it was Northampton where her mother campaigned to help get Bradlaugh, the atheist and freethinker, elected as its Member of Parliament in 1880.

They emigrated to Australia the same year, where Ernest had obtained a post with the *Melbourne Herald*. Their only child, Muriel, was born in 1893. Apparently at Mabel's insistence, they changed their surname to Besant Scott. Mabel continued the interest in theosophy which she had acquired from her mother, and Ernest also seems to have become involved, as on occasions he lectured on the subject as well as editing the *Austral Theosophist*.

The Australian Dictionary of Biography takes up the story as follows:

About 1896, however, [Mabel] was converted to Roman Catholicism and was estranged from her husband, although they continued nominal cohabitation. Scott abandoned theosophy. [Mabel] returned to England in 1909, taking their daughter ...

Scott went on to become Professor of History at the University of Melbourne, making a major contribution to the Cambridge History of the British Empire. He sounds an interesting person in his own right, emphasising "the capacity to understand and make good use of historical material" and advocating the use of primary sources. He died in December 1939.

The extent to which Mabel's involvement with the Roman Catholic Church was a continuing one after she returned to England in 1909 is not known. Nor is the extent to which she retained a link with theosophy, although she always remained a member. However, by 1921 she was certainly heavily involved with Co-Masonry and so it is perhaps appropriate at this point to look at Co-Masonry, with which both Mabel and her mother, as well as several other participants in our story, possibly including Gardner himself, were deeply involved.

Co-Masonry

Co-Masonry is a form of Freemasonry, the distinguishing characteristic of which is that it is open to both men and women, whilst still, strangely to my mind, referring to all members, both male and female, as "brothers".

It started in France in 1882, when Mlle. Maria Deraismes was initiated into a Lodge under the jurisdiction of the Grande Loge Symbolique de France, in Pecq, a small town outside Paris.[8] This was apparently not favoured by the Grande Loge and when, in 1883, after Dr. Georges Martin, a high ranking member of the Grande Loge, had tried unsuccessfully to persuade them to form a lodge for women, he approached Mlle. Deraismes and, as a result, a new lodge for both men and women was founded in Paris. It was called the Grande Loge Symbolique Ecossaise Mixte de France. In 1900, the Lodge established a Supreme Council to administer the Order and to take in the full 33 degrees of the Ancient and Accepted Scottish Rite.

Annie Besant, who had long felt that Masonry should be open to both men and women, on hearing about the French lodge, applied to be initiated, and subsequently obtained permission to form the first lodge in Britain open to both men and women. On 26th September 1902, a Co-Masonic Lodge was consecrated in London by officers of the Supreme Council in Paris, and it was given the title Lodge Human Duty No. 6, of which Annie Besant was the first ruler. The fact that Annie Besant was involved meant that there was a tendency towards an interest in esoteric and occult ideas amongst English members.

Certainly by the time Mabel returned from Australia in 1909, her mother was, and continued to be, heavily involved with Co-Masonry until her death in 1933. This would almost certainly have attracted Mabel as well. By 1921 she was ruler of the Lodge Maat, who met in Wimbledon. To reach that position would probably take several years, so it seems likely that her involvement started shortly after her return to England in 1909. Mabel, who was probably living in London during the 1920s and early 1930s (she was certainly living at 11 Christchurch Avenue, Brondesbury, London in 1937)[9], was actively involved in founding various lodges, including Lodge Beausant in Ladbroke Terrace, London in 1924; Lodge Amen-Ra (which is still active), also in Ladbroke Terrace, in 1925; Lodge Aurora in Harrogate in 1927 and Lodge Hypatia in Nottingham also in 1927.

She rose steadily in the organisation so that by the late 1920s she received the highest (i.e. 33) degree in Co-Masonry. She was appointed Deputy Supreme Council Representative in 1933 and in 1934, following the death of her mother, she was made Most Puissant Grand Commander of the British Federation, the top post[10].

To return briefly to Gardner, Bracelin claims that:

When the famous Annie Besant died, there was a split on the issue of the future leadership of the Theosophists. Some members wanted her daughter - Mrs. Besant Scott - others Bishop Leadbeater. The latter won. The unsuccessful candidate then took up co-masonry (female freemasonry) which Annie had started in England.[11]

This is in fact completely untrue. Annie Besant died in September 1933. Only two nominations for President of the Theosophical Society were received by the closing date in December 1933 - George Arundale and Professor Ernest Wood. Leadbeater died (on 1st March 1934) before the results of the poll for the new President were announced, in June 1934. Arundale won handsomely.

Not only was Mabel Besant-Scott not a candidate for the Presidency, there were no articles or letters by her in *The Theosophist* (the official journal of the Theosophical Society) during the period 1933 to 1939. In addition, there was no obituary or even mention of her following her death in 1952. It is reasonable to conclude, therefore, that, contrary to Bracelin's claims, whilst Mabel may have been a member of the Theosophical Society, she was certainly not an active one during that period.

Moreover, she did not take up Co-Masonry "on the rebound", so to speak. Her interest and active involvement with Co-Masonry predates those events by many years, as we have seen.

95

However, in 1935, Mabel resigned very suddenly from the Co-Masons, apparently for "personal reasons" and seems to have cut off all contact with them. The full story behind this remains a mystery, but, considering that by mid-1937, she was performing in the plays at Christchurch on a regular basis, it seems likely that her sudden split with the Co-Masons was occasioned by her enthusiasm for the Crotona Fellowship. How she came into contact with them is uncertain, although the Fellowship rituals appear to be very Masonic, and may have been based on those of the Order of the Temple of the Rose Cross, which Annie Besant founded in 1912.

Certainly by 1939 Mabel Besant-Scott was living in a bungalow very closely adjacent to the Ashrama [see Illustration 15]. She called it 'Locris' after the town in Sullivan's play, *Pythagoras*'.

Bracelin paints a picture of her:

Mrs. Besant Scott was a rather pleasant, sometimes uncertain old lady. She spent quite a lot of her time trying to remember a former incarnation as Queen Elizabeth. She had no occult powers, she told him, and neither, she admitted, had her mother.[12]

It is sometimes stated that Mabel was the leader, or joint leader, of the Crotona Fellowship. This is untrue, although she was a well-respected figure, who took an active and major role in many of the Rosicrucian Theatre's productions. She continued living in Christchurch until her death in a Folkestone nursing home on 22nd May 1952 at the age of 81. The role that she played, indirect but vital, in bringing Gardner in touch with the witches, is told in the next chapter.

Chapter 8
"The Most Interesting Element ..."

It is clear that by the time Gardner discovered it, the new theatre was complete. He mentions the foundation stone with the wording "The First Rosicrucian Theatre in England". He certainly doesn't mention the building as being under construction, which fits in as well, because the Theatre opened in June 1938 and Gardner probably moved in to 'Southridge' in July 1938.

Gardner says that he booked tickets for a performance of *Pythagoras*. This must have been on 1st, 6th or 12th August 1938, the only dates on which it was performed there. According to Bracelin, Gardner was not very impressed with the performance, and his wife even less so:

All the costumes were home-made, and not very professional. Many of the parts were rather badly acted. Pythagoras was played by a short, sturdy, black-haired individual. He was no actor, and the lines which he had to say were little better. Mrs. Gardner, who was an experienced amateur actress, hated it all, and said she would never go there again.[1]

Gardner, however, started to attend meetings at the Ashrama Hall, partly because he had learned a little about Rosicrucianism and wanted to find out if these people really knew anything. His first impression of Sullivan (the "short, sturdy, black-haired individual") was confirmed, as Bracelin recounts:

His ideas could be very puzzling. The first time he met Gardner, he asked him: "Do you remember the days when you were a noble Roman and wore a sari?" He also showed him a genuine African witch-doctor's wand with a devil's head knob on it - which Gardner recognised to be a Persian or Indian mace, and not an unusual one

97

at that. Among the claims made by the gentleman were that he had been the sage Pythagoras, the magician Cornelius Agrippa and Francis Bacon in past lives.[2]

His belief that the plays attributed to Shakespeare were actually written by Bacon was a familiar one to Gardner, since his own mother had held similar views. It is an intriguing thought, if nothing more, to wonder whether she may have met Sullivan at some meeting for devotees of the subject in Liverpool.

Members told Gardner more about Sullivan:

The chief of the Order was immortal. Because people wondered why he did not grow old like them, he was compelled to slip away every few score years, to make another name in a fresh place. In the Ashrama (temple) was a great plaque with the various identities under which he had lived through the ages inscribed thereon. ... Eventually Gardner was let into a great secret. They had part of an old (Dutch or Italian) lamp, hanging by chains from a ceiling. This, it was confided in him, was the Holy Grail...[3]

Nevertheless, Gardner continued to attend the meetings and, once he had been going for some time, he began to be aware of something interesting, as Bracelin records:

Now, at meetings, Gardner had noticed a group of people apart from the rest. They seemed rather brow-beaten by the others, kept themselves to themselves. They were the most interesting element, however. Unlike many of the others, they had to earn their livings, were cheerful and optimistic and had a real interest in the occult. They had carefully read many books on the subject: Unlike the general mass, who were supposed to have read all but seemed to know nothing.

Gardner always felt at home with them, was invited to their houses, and had many talks with them. The day came when one said:

"I have seen you before". Gardner, interested, asked where. "In a former life". Then all gathered around and agreed that this was so. What made it all remarkable to Gardner was that one of the

number proceeded to describe a scene "exactly like one which I had written in A Goddess Arrives, which was due to be published any day then, and which in fact came out the following week".

Then someone said, "You belonged to us in the past - why don't you come back to us?"[4]

In *The Meaning of Witchcraft*, Gardner reports them as saying: *"You are of the blood. Come back to where you belong."*[5]

"Now I was really very fond of them, and I knew that they had all sorts of magical beliefs" continues Gardner. "They had been very interested when I told them that an ancestress of mine had been burned alive as a witch at Newborough in Scotland about 1640; although I did not mention Grandfather. And I would have gone through hell and high water even then for any of them".

He felt sure that they had some secret, there must be something which allowed them to take the slights at the theatre without really caring. He still thought that they might be mooting Yoga, or something of that nature. He asked them why they were in this community, and whether they believed what Aurelius [sic] had to offer. They explained that they had been co-masons, and had followed Mabs (Mrs. Scott) when she had moved to this place; and added that they enjoyed the companionship."[6]

There are certainly various clues in this account which we can follow up to help find out who the members of this group were.

- they tended to stick together
- they had to earn their livings
- they had actually read a lot of books on the occult
- they had been Co-Masons
- they had followed Mabel Besant-Scott when she moved

Bracelin provides another clue when he says that the centre of Co-Masonry had been Southampton. This was not actually true, but it does suggest some link with that city, which is only some 25 miles from Christchurch. This led me to ask whether there had been any

Co-Masons in Southampton and, if so, whether any of them had connections with the Rosicrucians in Christchurch.

I found out that there was indeed a group of the International Co-Freemasons in Southampton in 1935-36, which is the right period[7]. The Chairman was Susie Mary Mason, and she lived with her brother, Ernest William Mason.

These two, together with their sister, Rosetta Fudge, appear as members of the cast for an earlier production of *Pythagoras* which was performed at the Ashrama Hall in August 1937[8]. I had found the connection!

Susie Mary Mason had also been the honorary secretary of the Southampton Lodge of the Theosophical Society from 1929 to 1934. She and Ernest lived at 1 Osborne Road, Portswood, a suburb of Southampton. Their sister, Rosetta, lived at 58 St. Mary Street, Southampton, running a drapery business with her husband, William.

I am certain that these are some of the group referred to by Gardner. They were members of the Crotona Fellowship, performed in their plays and were also Co-Masons living in Southampton. What had misled me was that Bracelin's account said that they "had followed Mabs when she moved to this place". I am clear now that this was not a physical move: they remained living in Southampton and Mabs had never lived there. It was a philosophical move from Co-Masonry to Rosicrucianism. Ernest never moved from Southampton, and Susie only did so after 1948, but they were certainly closely involved in the Crotona Fellowship from at least 1937, performing in their plays, Ernest in addition often acting as stage manager.

The Mason Family

"He was a witch, you know! The whole family were. They were mind control people. But he found the rituals too strenuous, so he couldn't do it any more."

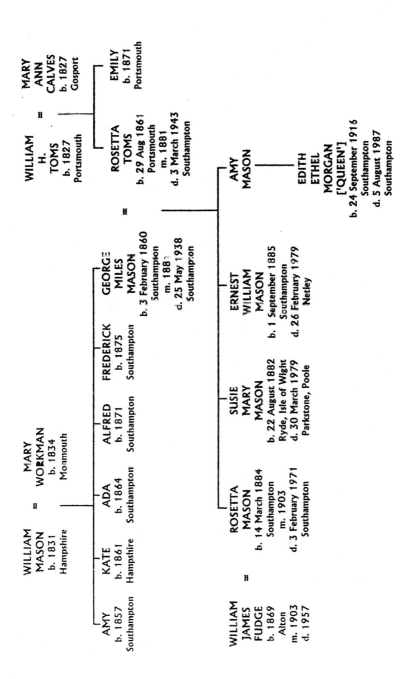

21. *The Mason Family Tree*

Bill Wakefield, my informant, was telling me about his friend, Ernie Mason. He and his brother, Colin, had known Ernie very well for some years before the latter's death in 1979 at the age of 93.

His statement was interesting. Could I have stumbled on a hereditary branch of the Craft that pre-dated Gardner and thus might well have been connected with how Gardner came into it? It certainly seemed worth studying the Mason family background to see what I could find out.

They seem to have been based in and around the Southampton area for almost 150 years. Illustration 21 gives their family tree as far as I have investigated it.

Let us start with George Miles Mason. He was born on 3rd February 1860 at 4 Winchester Street, Southampton. The Masons were certainly living in Southampton by that time. William, George's father, had been born in Hampshire and his mother, Mary, came from Monmouthshire. In early 1881 George is recorded as being an umbrella maker in Ryde, Isle of Wight, together with his sister, Kate. In this, he was following the family trade, as his father, William, is also recorded as an umbrella maker. George married Rosetta Toms, a servant girl working in Southampton, in 1881 and their first child, Susie Mary, was born in Ryde on 22nd August 1882.

Rosetta's parents were Mary Ann and William Toms, who lived in Landport, a settlement on the edge of Portsmouth. At the time of Rosetta's birth William was a seaman on *H.M.S. Excellent*. Probably most of the people living in the Portsmouth area, certainly at that time, had some connection with the Royal Navy or the naval dockyard. William had been born in Portsmouth about 1827 and his wife had been born in Gosport, over the other side of Portsmouth Harbour, in the same year. By the age of 54, William's sailing days were over, but he was still working for the Royal Navy, this time as a labourer in the dockyards.

To return to Susie Mary Mason, 'Susie' was the name given on her birth certificate, not Susan. This is perhaps the first sign of something slightly unorthodox, or it may simply have the same origin as marine painter, Harry Hudson Rodmell's first name: his father decided that it was pointless naming him 'Henry' since everyone would call him 'Harry' anyway!

By 1884, the family had moved back to Southampton and George had added "photographer" to the family business of umbrella making. But by 1891, he is shown on the Census returns as being a sculptor (artist). It is difficult to know whether he made a living from this: certainly he did not advertise in the street directories and Southampton City Art Gallery does not have any examples of his work. However, it seems as if he was able to make a good living

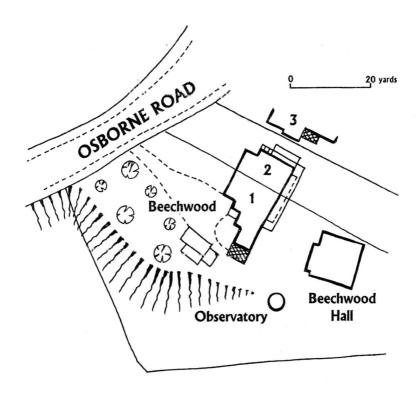

22. *Beechwood, Beechwood Hall and the Observatory*
1 Osborne Road, Portswood, Southampton

from some source, because between 1885 and 1900 the family occupied a series of houses, eventually moving in 1922 into No. 1 Osborne Road, Portswood. It was a large, detached early Victorian house, standing in its own grounds, which contained many mature beech trees, which probably suggested the name given to it - Beechwood.

By 1923, George was engaged in the business of lantern-slide manufacture, involving him in optics and photography, in which his wife, Rosetta and son, Ernest, played an active part. They had a shop at 14 Carlton Place, Southampton. George was what one might call an inventor. He was also an astronomer, having constructed an observatory in the large garden attached to the house.

This was the everyday, if somewhat unusual, side of the family. But there was another side - the esoteric, which linked anthroposophy, theosophy, Co-Masonry, Rosicrucianism and witchcraft into a lively mix.

Another daughter, Rosetta, named after her mother, had married William James Fudge in 1903 and was living in St. Mary Street, Southampton, running a drapery business with him. She had been born in 1884 (the same year as Gardner), and was interested in Rudolf Steiner's anthroposophy, possessing a copy of the first of his books to be translated into English, dated 1910, in a limited edition of 1500 copies.

In 1934, George Miles Mason had plans drawn up to erect a meeting hall within the grounds of the house. This was a substantial building, 30 feet by 20 feet in area. It had full height windows on two sides and had its own kitchen and lavatory. It is described on the 1948 Ordnance Survey map as a Church Mission Hall. Whilst one does not lightly criticise the Ordnance Survey, particularly in matters concerning its home town of Southampton, it was actually nothing of the sort!

It was known as Beechwood Hall and seems to have been used for meetings of the various esoteric groups in which the family were interested. It was completed some time in early 1935 and was probably used initially by the newly-formed local lodge of the

International Co-Freemasons. It is mentioned in the 1935-36 street directory but not in any other edition, earlier or later. So Bracelin may well have been right when he wrote: "*The centre of this was Southampton. Things seemingly did not prosper.*"[9]

George Miles Mason died suddenly in May 1938. He fell while attempting to board a moving tram-car in Portswood Road and died the same night from the injuries he received. His wife, Rosetta, died in 1943.

Susie Mary Mason

Susie seems to have been the organiser in the family. As well as being the Chairman of the Co-Masons in Southampton during their brief period of activity in the mid-1930s, she was also Hon. Secretary of the Southampton Lodge of the Theosophical Society from 1929 to 1934. During this time, she was living with her parents and brother at Beechwood.

Following the war, probably in 1946, she moved in with Rosetta and William at 58 St. Mary Street. She was still there at the end of 1948, but by 1950 she had moved to lodgings in Christchurch, at 190 Barrack Road. This suggests a continuing contact with at least some of the former members of the Crotona Fellowship, particularly Catherine Chalk, who left her £800 in her will. Apart from Martin Andrew, Susie was the only member of the Crotona Fellowship to be remembered thus.

Susie Mason died at Parkstone, Poole on 30th March 1979 at the age of 96, only four weeks after the death of her brother, Ernie.

Ernest William Mason

Ernest William Mason, commonly known as "Ernie", is not just a figure from the archives. Fortunately, I made contact with someone who had not only known Ernie Mason but clearly felt that he was the most remarkable man he had ever met.

He was born in Southampton on 1st September 1885. He told Bill Wakefield, my contact, that his "mind was open" from the month he was born and that he remembered being in his cradle and how he "couldn't stand the silly nonsense" of the way people spoke to him. Bill first met Ernie in the 1950s, when he was living in Beechwood with his brother, Alf. (I think that Alf could actually have been Ernie's uncle, though there was only a difference of 14 years in their ages, and they may have seemed very much like brothers.)

Ernie had inherited his father's interest in astronomy and was a founder member of the Southampton Astronomical Society. Following war damage, Ernie had reconstructed the observatory that George had built in the garden, with the help of members of the Astronomical Society.

The observatory contained an 18-inch reflecting telescope which Ernie had made himself - a remarkable achievement, involving working with mirror blanks, a grinding machine and plenty of carborundum to get a perfect finish; and a gearing mechanism to allow the telescope to keep pointing at the same part of the heavens as the Earth revolves. In fact, Ernie was awarded the honour of being made an FRAS (Fellow of the Royal Astronomical Society)[10].

His interest in optics was carried over into the activity by which he earned his living - lantern slide manufacture, a business which he had inherited from his parents. The slides were two and a half inch square sheets of glass which were projected by a 'magic lantern' which was fuelled by paraffin. As well as manufacturing slides for others (including, it is rumoured, copies of the famous Cottingley fairy photographs for Sir Arthur Conan Doyle to illustrate lectures), Ernie had a very large collection of slides on a variety of topics, the astronomical section of which was said to excel those of the British Astronomical Association. The slides were mainly in black-and-white, but some were hand-coloured, and others were mounted in a wooden framework and were capable of animation.

In fact, like his father before him, Ernie very much fitted the image of the 'eccentric inventor'. Before the war, for example, he was working on a method to produce good quality colour film. And he was, during the war, working at the request of the Government to see if he could provide the key to the release of "sonic energy", which was thought to be a better way of obtaining explosives.

Alf was a chemist and he taught Ernie how to make silver nitrate. Over his long life, Ernie worked a lot with both carborundum and silver nitrate, and his feet had become engrained with these materials: they looked so remarkable that when he went into hospital the medical people wanted to photograph them! But there was far more to Ernie Mason than the scientific side - there was another side, an esoteric side - one that only revealed itself if the circumstances were right. Bill had been attracted by the astronomy and had long talks with Ernie. One day, he asked him "Don't you ever think that there's something greater than us out there, something we might call "God"?" Ernie replied "Only a fool would deny that!" That was the opening, and from there on, Ernie used to teach Bill and his brother Colin about a wide variety of esoteric matters.

The Rosicrucian influence was strong and, just as with Peter Caddy, Ernie always acknowledged the influence of Sullivan as his teacher. And it seems as if Ernie Mason had taken on the mantle of the Crotona Fellowship with the demise of activities in Christchurch. He seems to have become custodian of the library and archives of the group (later donated to the University of Southampton), together with some of the Masonic regalia. But the main thing that Ernie had acquired was the Rosicrucian teachings, which he was able to pass on to others in a remarkable way - he was a Magus and a born teacher and he used to teach in parables and cartoons. He had a way of explaining things, and lawyers, doctors, academics and business leaders used to come to see him (some in Rolls Royces, Bill remembers!). He would never take a penny for all this, however.

To his students (including Bill and his brother Colin) Ernie would teach mental exercises. Nothing was written down and you weren't allowed to go on to the next exercise until you had mastered the current one, a technique he had learned from Sullivan. As Bill says, he was a hard taskmaster, but he used to go through things very thoroughly.

And yet, it was not just Rosicrucian teaching, but something coming through from Ernie himself. He certainly had remarkable abilities. Bill recalls a story that Ernie used to tell about an occasion when he was out in a boat with a friend (possibly in Christchurch Harbour) when he walked across the water. Sullivan, who was watching, merely commented "Why do you have to show off?" It was a salutary lesson.

We know that Ernie was actively involved in the Rosicrucians, as were Susie and Rosetta. In addition, Susie was involved with Co-masonry and Theosophy. Rosetta was interested in anthroposophy. Cyril and Elizabeth Barnes remained in contact with Ernie up to the time of his death, and they were also friends with his niece, Edith Ethel Finlay, née Morgan, commonly known as "Queen" (1916-1987). This name seems to have a semi-legal status as she is mentioned by that name in her grandmother's will of 1943. Whether she was involved in the Craft is not known, but it seems clear that she was in touch with prominent Rosicrucians throughout her life, and she it was who probably donated the Crotona Fellowship library to Southampton University.

After Alf died, Ernie continued to live in Beechwood on his own, although he seemed to have the ability to talk to those who had passed over, and Bill remembers him frequently talking to Alf. It was not practicable to heat the whole house adequately. There was no central heating and Bill recalls it as being freezing, particularly in the bedroom. The house had a dank, dark cellar inhabited by rats, spiders, etc. where Ernie kept his grinding machine. The two bottom rooms were used for testing optics, where an even temperature is important.

There was a large room upstairs, where the Rosicrucians used to have their rituals, including an 18ft square carpet in a black and white chequerboard pattern. The room had many books, and there were mice running around, but the only heating was a gas ring under Ernie's chair. As Ernie was somewhat disabled, he couldn't move very quickly, and Bill remembers one occasion when he had to rescue Ernie when his trousers caught alight.

23. Ernie Mason in Rosicrucian robe - June 1953

Ernie finally felt unable to cope any longer at "Beechwood" and spent his last years in a Nursing Home in Netley. He died on 26th February 1979 at the age of 93.

There are many other stories which make it clear that Ernie Mason was a remarkable person, but we must focus on his witchcraft, since that is what this book is about. If the whole family were involved, by which I would assume is meant at least his sisters, Susie and Rosetta and their parents, it is likely that we are looking at a hereditary tradition - something that has been passed down within several generations of the family, who have been in the Southampton and Portsmouth area for at least 150 years.

A Family Tradition

Whilst it was never as clear-cut as it sounds, the 'hereditary' tradition - that of passing down membership of the Craft within a family, or group of families, seems to have been a common way to help ensure the survival of the Craft. Patricia Crowther tells me that someone who knew Gardner and Dafo well has assured her that the coven which Gardner joined was a hereditary one, and this is confirmed by what Gardner has to say. This supports my claim that the tradition into which Gardner was initiated was passed down in the Mason family for many years.

Allen Andrews, writing in 1952 and clearly taking information from Gardner, states the following:

Hereditary witches, who have the lore handed down to them, form a proportion of the covens, whose average ages are rather high. They make up their numbers by inviting certain known enthusiasts to join them. These have made a wider study than the locals, and constitute the intellectual wing of a coven.[11]

I think Gardner is referring here to the group into which he was initiated in 1939. They were hereditary witches, their average age was rather high, and one of the "known enthusiasts" was clearly Gardner himself. He emphasises this when he says that:

110

> ... from an early date recruits were admitted only from people who were of the blood; that is, from a witch family. The various rituals of worship, secrets of herbal lore, and the Great Secret of what they call magic, have been handed down to what has become more or less a family secret society.[12]

Gardner states several times that the traditions were passed down in this way. He says, for example:

> ... there are very few real witches left, and those keep themselves very much to themselves. They are generally the descendants of witch families, and have inherited a tradition which has been preserved for generations. This is, indeed, the traditional way in which witchcraft was spread and preserved; the children of witch families were taught by their parents, and initiated at an early age.[13]

> The cult, whether in England or elsewhere, starts with several advantages. First, it obtains recruits very young and slowly trains them so that they come to have the sense of mystery and wonder, the knowledge that they have an age-old tradition behind them. They have probably seen things happen and know they can happen again ...[14]

It is clear by this emphasis that Gardner's experience was that of a witch family rather than a group of witches unrelated to each other. This gives further support to my contention that it is the Mason family that he is referring to.

The witches whom Gardner met were everyday practical people. For them, what was important was what they could do to help situations in the present. History, even family history, was much less significant. Some witches kept no written records for the simple reason that they couldn't read or write. But many could do so and did keep books, although certain important things were passed on by word of mouth. They had been told things verbally but a lot had been forgotten over the years, and they only had a very vague idea about the history of their own branch of the Craft. So, what history there is is couched in terms of direct or indirect personal memory.

Gardner writes that "unfortunately they had not preserved records of their family trees."[15] but does give some details of how far back living memory can take them. He says:

They know that their fathers and grandfathers belonged, and had spoken to them of meetings about the time of Waterloo ...[16]

Grandfathers and grandmothers have told folk still living of meetings they attended about a hundred and forty years ago, when the cult was thought to have existed from all time.[17]

Now, *Witchcraft Today* was published in 1954. 140 years previous to that takes us to 1814, which fits in with the comment about Waterloo, which was in 1815. I am guessing that Gardner would have met Rosetta Mason, as she did not die until 1943. Her parents were both born in 1827; and her husband's parents were born in 1831 and 1834. So, Rosetta and George's grandparents (whom I have not yet tracked down) would very likely have been of an age to have attended and remembered meetings which took place about 1815.

Toothill

But do we have any other evidence that the Mason family were involved in the Craft? Indirectly, we do. It is still inconclusive, but there is a piece of evidence which is very suggestive.

In 1965, a book entitled *Witchcraft, the Sixth Sense - And Us* was published. Its author was Justine Glass, an authority on nutrition who had written columns for the London *Daily Sketch*. She had studied psychology and ESP from her youth and had been commissioned by publishers Neville Spearman to write the book.

In researching the Mason family, I remembered one paragraph in Justine Glass's book where she is referring to traditional witch meeting places. It reads:

Gorse Hill, near Swindon, was another 'witch centre'; a coven which I am told is called the 'Moonrakers', meets there still. Avebury, the Rufus Stone ... in the New Forest, the Stype Stones in

Shropshire (which include the Devil's Seat), Toothill, outside Southampton are others.[18]

The reference to Toothill might, I thought, provide a clue as to where some of the Southampton witches met. But where did Justine Glass get her information? She says in a foreword that much of her material came from witches themselves, and that they preferred to remain anonymous. We know that Robert Cochrane provided a lot of information because she says so in the book, and this is confirmed by Doreen Valiente in Chapter 8 of *The Rebirth of Witchcraft*, who says that: "Cochrane pulled poor Justine Glass's leg unmercifully and shamelessly admitted to me that he had done so."[19] However, it is clear from the context that Doreen knew Justine Glass quite well, so perhaps the information came from her.

Anyway, the mention of Toothill interested me because of its proximity to Southampton and because it is one of only five sites mentioned. It seemed worth investigating further.

Toothill is situated approx. five miles NNW of Southampton city centre and approx. two miles SE from Romsey. It is in open country but close to the built-up area of Southampton, not far from the M27 motorway. And yet, it is in the sort of countryside which could be called "strangely remote". It is a hill, although not a very big one, and it is wooded. It has earthworks around its summit, the remnants of an Iron Age 'hill fort'. It is on private land and, although I am not averse to a spot of trespassing, I did not feel, on the occasion that I was in its vicinity, that I wanted to approach it more closely.

Could this have been one of the traditional meeting places of the Southampton witches? I thought I would not have been able to take it much further, when I had a look at the 1881 Census material which is now available on CD-Rom.[20] In 1881, Toothill was a hamlet nestling below the slopes of the hill itself: it still is. There were 72 people living there in 14 separate households. 16 of the individuals, in 3 households, shared one surname, and that surname, the most common in Toothill, was 'Mason'. Now, only 1 in 700 of the population of Hampshire had that surname, so I felt it was significant that there were so many Masons living under the slopes of Toothill.

I have still to establish whether there are any family connections, but I think it is worth commenting on at this stage.

Towards Initiation

So, Gardner made friends with the little group within the Crotona Fellowship, and I am reasonably confident that it would have included Susie and Ernie Mason and Rosetta Fudge. He would also have met their mother, Rosetta Mason.

It has been written on several occasions that the witches constituted some sort of 'inner circle' of the Crotona Fellowship[21] or that they used it as a "casting net" to gather in new recruits for their coven[22]. Neither is true to the slightest extent. There is nothing in the Crotona Fellowships writings or rituals to support the suggestion that witchcraft was associated with any secret inner core. It is clear from Gardner's comments that in any case they were on the fringe of the Fellowship, not an inner core in any way, and they had absolutely no desire for new recruits: Gardner had probably been the first for several years.

Anyway, at some stage (and, with Gardner's initial theatre visit in August 1938 and his initiation in September 1939, the traditional waiting period of a year and a day seems an intriguing possibility) they seem to have told Gardner to make himself available on a particular date, for Bracelin says: *"Gardner felt delighted that he was to be let into their secret."*

Bracelin tells us that Gardner was taken to a big house in the neighbourhood which was owned by someone they called 'Old Dorothy', and it was there, a few days after the war started, that he was initiated[23]. Clearly this is an important clue which we must follow at some stage.

But first there is one member of the Crotona Fellowship who needs a chapter to herself. She was a prominent and long-standing member of the Crotona Fellowship, taking leading parts in their productions, organising their elocution programme and issuing press releases.She became a very close friend of Gardner. She was also a witch.

Chapter 9
Dafo

The existence of a witch called "Dafo" has long been mentioned in witchcraft circles. One of the earliest references to her that I have found is in the introduction to June Johns' book *King of the Witches*, published in 1969. In it, she says:

Gardner was initiated into the first grade of the cult by a witch called "Daffo" in the New Forest ...[1]

This is interesting, not just in attributing Gardner's initiation to her, but that she spells the name "Daffo" with a double 'f', which is what one might do if one had heard the name rather than seen it written down. From the context in which it has been used, this obviously was, or became, her witch name, but it is interesting that, in the 1930s, naturists usually had pseudonyms of this sort as well.

We know from the identifying features given by Doreen Valiente in *The Rebirth of Witchcraft* that the witch who went by the name of 'Dafo' was a teacher of music and elocution and that her daughter married a dentist[2]. This, together with details given by Lois Bourne in her book *Dancing with Witches*[3] and with references by Cecil Williamson in one of the interviews he gave for *Talking Stick* magazine[4], is sufficient to identify Dafo and to give her everyday name of Edith Rose Woodford-Grimes.

We do not know when she first became involved with the Crotona Fellowship, but it may well have been in the early 1930s. For 15 years, between 1922 and 1937, she lived in the same street in Southampton as the Mason family, who were involved in esoteric activities during that period, and it is my guess that she became friends with them at some stage, perhaps after the Beechwood Hall was erected in 1935, and became involved in the Co-Masons and the Crotona Fellowship through them. As it is likely that

'Dafo' initiated Gardner, she probably became involved in the Craft during that same period.

Before we look at her early life, do we have any idea what 'Dafo' means? Not definitively, but 'Dafo' is the name given to the largest ancient sculpture of the Buddha in the world, which is 71m high and 28m broad and is carved into a cliff overlooking the confluence of the Minjiang, Qingyi Jiang and Dadu Rivers near the city of Leshan in China. It dates from the 8th Century CE[5].

There are, however, other possibilities. 'Dafo' is the name of a tropical hardwood (*Terminalia brassii*) which grows, among other places, in the Solomon Islands. In this context, it is interesting that Gardner's family firm were the largest hardwood importers in the world, though Gardner was not closely involved in its running and I can find no mention of the import of this particular species[6].

'Dafo' has other meanings as well, including being used as a personal name throughout North Africa[7].

Nevertheless, I think the most likely origin of Edith Woodford-Grimes' magical name of 'Dafo' is the name given in several instances to statues of the Buddha. Could this perhaps have been a name bestowed by Gardner, who, with his oriental knowledge might well have known of the sculpture? He might well have come across this name on the visit to China which he undertook in 1934. He certainly visited on route to China the Silver Pagoda at Saigon, which had eight thousand Buddha figures, the largest being eight feet high, in solid gold and encrusted with diamonds.

Gardner may well have bestowed the name 'Dafo' on Edith as something of a private joke, perhaps a comment on her appearance when meditating in the lotus posture, for it is likely that the witches he met were interested in and practised yoga. Then again, it may merely be a shortened form of 'Daffodil', employed by Gardner because of the connotations referred to above. At the moment, it must remain an open question.

But let us look at Dafo's early life. Edith Rose Wray was born in Malton in Yorkshire in the house now known as 5 Mill Cottages, off Castlegate, on 18th December 1887. Her mother was Caroline Wray (formerly Harrison) and her father was William Henry Wray, an implement maker at the local waterworks. The house is adjacent to the old Roman fort of Derventio and is also close to Lady Well, a natural spring which provided the town's water supply for many years. The waterworks where her father worked was established in the vicinity of the well. Efforts are now being made to renovate the well. It is surely significant that the woman who seems to have been one of the first High Priestesses of the modern witchcraft revival grew up so close to a spring dedicated to the Goddess of the Old Religion.

It may also be significant that the area of Yorkshire where she was born is one which is strong in traditions of witchcraft. I have been told of a tradition in a village not a dozen miles from Malton which survived at least into the 1980s and, for all I know, exists still. It is

24. Mill Cottages, Malton. Edith Rose Wray's Birthplace

not beyond the bounds of possibility that Edith was initiated into the Craft while she was still in the Malton area. Certainly those to whom I have shown her photograph have felt something unusual: it was described by one recipient as a 'psychic tingle'!

Edith was the eldest of what was quite a large family. She was apparently always the adventurous one, and possibly the only one that went away. Her astrological chart shows someone whose emotions are deep and strong, but kept hidden until you got to know her very well. She was also one who was attracted to adventure, new ideas and unusual ways of looking at things. At present, we can only speculate on what she did with her life until we next see her, at the age of almost 30, during the First World War. She was certainly intelligent, and may have gone to school in York, specialising in English, Drama and Music. She later became an Associate of both the London College of Music and the London Academy of Music.

In 1917 in the middle of the First World War, we know that she had her photograph taken by W. Hazel, a professional photographer of 116 Old Christchurch Road, Bournemouth, and this is reproduced as Illustration 26. The story of how I came upon this photograph is interesting. As part of my researches, I had tracked down her birth record and sent for a copy of her birth certificate to the Superintendent Registrar for the Ryedale District, which covers the Malton area. It turned out that Edith was her great aunt and that she had a photograph of Edith which she very kindly lent me. It is this kind of coincidence which keeps one going!

Anyway, I suspect that Edith was already living in the Southampton/Bournemouth area, probably teaching or possibly doing war work (nursing or whatever), for on 16th June 1920 she married Samuel William Woodford Grimes, who had been born in Bangalore, India in 1880. At the time that they married he was a Clerk in the War Pensions Office in Southampton.

Samuel William Woodford Grimes always seemed to indicate his surname as purely "Grimes". "Woodford" was merely one of his first names, although probably derived from one of his ancestors, as Woodford is a very common surname in the New Forest area, which suggests that one branch of his family may well have come from the area originally. However, Edith certainly preferred to use both as surnames, and by the time of her registration with the Teachers Registration Council in 1940, a hyphen had appeared, making the double-barrelled "Woodford-Grimes".

This may have been pure snobbery, or she may have felt that it sounded more elegant and exclusive - more befitting a teacher of elocution. She would also, being a musician, have undoubtedly been familiar with the work of Amy Woodforde-Finden, the sound of her name (and teachers of elocution are perhaps particularly sensitive to the effect of sound on mental impression) may have suggested the change.

Amy Woodforde-Finden (1860-1919) was born Amy Ward, daughter of the British consul in Chile. After studying music, she travelled to India and, in 1894, married Lieutenant-Colonel Woodforde-Finden, a medical officer in the Bengal cavalry. Returning to England, she wrote *Four Indian Love Lyrics*, of which the most famous is *Kashmiri Song*. These are settings of four poems from *The Garden of Kama* by Laurence Hope, actually the pseudonym of Adela Florence Cory, and they are described by the *Pandora Guide to Women Composers* as being full of violent and erotic imagery.

Although she had to publish these songs herself in 1902, they were a success and she followed these up by other song cycles, using poetry, to quote the *Pandora Guide*:

... set in the Middle East, Northern Africa, Japan or South America and drawing on elements of the music of these countries, always filtered through the Western ear.[8]

The *Pandora Guide* also calls Amy Woodforde-Finden "the composer of probably the most successful songs of the early 20th Century". It says that she "supplied passionate and exciting music, using harmonic inflections and other rhythmic and melodic touches to create a suitably exotic atmosphere."

This was just the sort of life that would have appealed to Edith, and it would have been to the fore at the time of her marriage, only a little over a year after Amy Woodforde-Finden's death at the height of her popularity. Calling herself Edith Rose Woodford-Grimes would have appealed to her. It is only speculation, of course, but I am sure the example of Amy Woodforde-Finden would have brought it to her mind.

After their marriage, Edith and William moved into what was then a brand-new semi-detached house, no. 67 Osborne Road in the Portswood suburb of Southampton and, just over a year later, on 30th June 1921, their only child, Rosanne, was born. This date was already familiar to me as the day on which Alfred Watkins

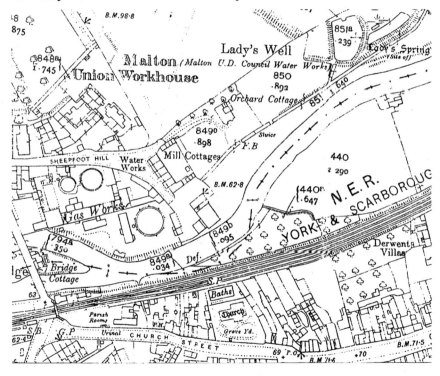

25. Mill Cottages and Lady Well, Malton
(extract from 1890 25 - inch Ordnance Survey map - reduced in scale)

26. Edith Rose Wray
February 1917
(photograph by W. Hazel, Bournemouth)

discovered those alignments of ancient sites across the landscape that we know as 'leys' and which have been an obsession of mine for nearly 40 years[9].

I have not so far been able to find out whether Edith had been teaching before she got married in 1920. It is quite likely, particularly with the war on, but it seems clear that she did no school teaching afterwards. Indeed, it was certainly the custom, if not a requirement of employment, for women teachers to resign their posts on getting married. In the early twenties, she probably had enough to do bringing up her daughter, but by 1924 she was working as a Tutor in English and Dramatic Literature to various student groups authorised by the Workers' Educational Association and the Extra-Mural Department of the University College, Southampton (now the University), and continued to do this for ten years. From 1928 onwards, she was also teaching Elocution and Dramatic Art at various Evening Institutes for the Southampton Education Authority. Edith also attended various

27. 67 Osborne Road, Portswood, Southampton
Edith Woodford Grimes' home from 1920 to 1937

London Academy of Music Teacher Training Vocation Courses between 1930 and 1934. She gained the Teacher's Diploma of the London Academy of Music, becoming an Associate in Elocution. She was also an Associate of the London College of Music[10].

Edith may have continued to live at 67 Osborne Road until as late as 1937. But by 1938 she had moved to Christchurch. She had bought one of the new bungalows being built in Dennistoun Avenue, Somerford, in the vicinity of the Theatre. Edith called her bungalow 'Theano', after Pythagoras' wife, the part she played in Sullivan's play of that name. It was the fashion of the time for most houses and bungalows to be given names rather than numbers, and these tended to change on change of ownership. So it is sometimes difficult to track down where any individual lived, but I have worked out that it is the bungalow now known as no. 16 Dennistoun Avenue.

At some stage, Edith became a private Teacher of Elocution and Dramatic Art, probably on moving to Christchurch in 1938, and certainly by 1940.

It is clear that her husband did not move to Christchurch with her. There is a report in one issue of the *Christchurch Times* that a "W. Woodford Grimes" took a part in one of the Rosicrucian productions. This might be a misprint (which was not unknown in the *Christchurch Times* of those days!) or it might be an indication that William had at one stage tried, or been persuaded, to take an interest in the Rosicrucian proceedings, but that really it wasn't for him.

I have heard from someone who knew Edith that she told him that her marriage was never really very successful. Certainly by the time of her daughter's wedding in August 1940, the marriage must have broken down completely, because the bride was given away, not by her father, which was customary, but by Gerald Gardner, who is described as "a close friend"[11]. We will look at Gardner's relationship with Edith in due course.

In August 1940, following their marriage, Rosanne and her husband, Cecil, moved into 'Theano' and, in her turn, Edith moved out to a substantial house known as Avenue Cottage, in Walkford, the neighbouring village to Highcliffe.

Edith was to become a close friend of Gardner's and to remain his friend for the rest of his life. There is a weight of evidence to suggest that she was a considerable influence on him and that what she told him had a marked effect on what he subsequently wrote about his experiences with the witches.

But before taking our story further, we must make the acquaintance of a character who looms large in Wiccan folklore - 'Old Dorothy'.

Chapter 10
Dorothy St. Quintin Clutterbuck

Dorothy Clutterbuck is remembered today as the High Priestess of the New Forest coven who initiated Gerald Gardner into the Craft. Such claims were never actually made by Gardner, at least in his writings, but he does implicate her, so I thought it was important, before looking at this statement in more detail, to accumulate the necessary background information in order to be able assess it properly. By finding out what I could about 'Old Dorothy' and about the house where it has been claimed that Gardner was initiated, I had hopes that I could shed some light on the extent of her involvement.

She is a figure who has, of late, caused much controversy within the Craft, with such figures as Fred Lamond[1], Lois Bourne[2] and Ronald Hutton[3] arguing that Dorothy was never involved at all and that Gardner used her name to divert attention away from Edith Woodford-Grimes.

It was clearly important to me to find out what I could. Gardner had told Doreen Valiente and a few others that Old Dorothy's surname was Clutterbuck, and Doreen did us all a good service when, in the early 1980s, in order to disprove Professor Jeffrey Russell's statement that there was no evidence that Old Dorothy ever existed, she demonstrated not only that a lady named Dorothy Clutterbuck had very definitely existed but that she lived in the same village as Gardner at the same time that he did and that other details given seemed to correspond[4]. Not that she demonstrated that Dorothy Clutterbuck had any connection with the Craft, but then that was not her intention at the time.

Valiente ends her essay *The Search for Old Dorothy* with the statement: "For the time being, my search was ended."[5] This has

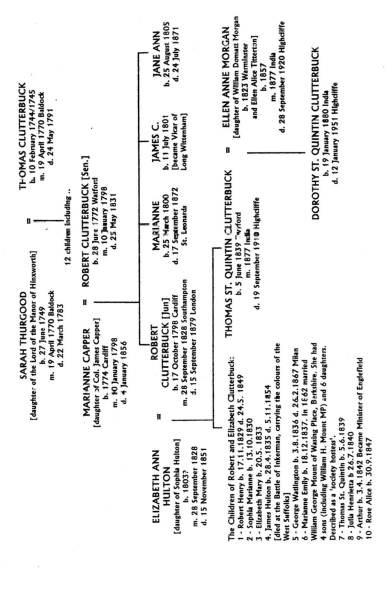

28. *The Clutterbuck Family Tree*

always seemed to me an invitation to find out more, and I began to realise that it had fallen on me to take up the challenge.

The Clutterbucks

According to such a worthy source as *Burke's Landed Gentry*, the Clutterbucks are said to be of Dutch origin, settling in the Gloucestershire area as early as the 15th Century. There are still far more Clutterbucks in Gloucestershire than anywhere else.

The earliest recorded relatives of Dorothy's on her father's side date back to 16th Century Bedfordshire and Hertfordshire. Her great-great-great grandfather was born in Gloucestershire in 1707, but was married in Great Gaddesden in Hertfordshire, which remained the focus of the family for many years.

Dorothy's great great grandfather was Thomas Clutterbuck of Watford, Hertfordshire (1745-1791). He married Sarah Thurgood, of Baldock in the same county, and reputed to be daughter of the Lord of the Manor of Hinxworth and on 28th June 1772, she gave birth, in Watford, to Robert Clutterbuck.

This was Dorothy's great grandfather (1772-1831) and he is mentioned in the *Dictionary of National Biography* as being a local historian and topographer, a county magistrate and a Fellow of the Society of Antiquaries. His most famous work was a 3-volume book entitled *The History and Antiquities of the County of Hertford*, which appeared between 1815 and 1827. Whilst writing this great work, he lived at the 15th Century Hinxworth Place, near Baldock, presumably inherited from his mother.[6] Hinxworth Place is reputed to be one of the most haunted houses in Hertfordshire. Robert later lived at Watford House, Watford, a prestigious address in the High Street, right in the centre of the town. It was built about 1775 by his father, Thomas Clutterbuck, and was a typical three-storey detached Georgian house, with six windows across the frontage and a pedimented porch. It was approached by a carriage-drive and was sheltered from the High Street by a line of mature trees and shrubs. It also had a fine garden. The grounds of the house (amounting to 1239 acres in 1880) ran eastwards to what is now the west coast main railway line.[7]

Williams writes of the Clutterbucks:

"This excellent family were residents at Watford for many years, and took very great interest in all that concerned the well-being of the town and its inhabitants, endearing themselves to every one who knew them."[8]

In 1798 Robert married Marianne, daughter of Colonel James Capper, of Cathays, near Cardiff. They had two daughters, Jane (1805-1871) and Marianne (1800-1872), and two sons, James (born 1801) and Robert (1798-1879), who was Dorothy's grandfather.

I have been unable to find out what Robert Clutterbuck (jun.) did for a living. He is described on some of his children's birth certificates as 'Esquire', a term which I take to be the equivalent of the later used 'of Independent Means'.

Robert married Elizabeth Anne Hulton (supposedly a minor, with the consent of her mother, Sophia Hulton, although her birth date is uncertain) at St. Mary's, Southampton on 29th September 1828. They had ten children, five boys and five girls. They lived in the Bevois Hill, Portswood area of Southampton (possibly in the house of that name) from their marriage for at least five years.

By 1837, and the birth of his sixth child, Marianne Emily, Robert was living at The Frythe, near Welwyn, in Hertfordshire, a large country mansion in its own grounds.

Robert was back in the Southampton area, living in Twyford, a village three miles south of Winchester, by the time Thomas St. Quintin Clutterbuck (their seventh child and Dorothy's father) was born, on 5th June 1839. We do not quite know where the 'St. Quintin' part of Thomas' (and subsequently Dorothy's) name originates. The St. Quintins are a long-established family originating in the East Yorkshire village of Harpham, the birthplace of St. John of Beverley. I have not been able to find any direct family link between the St. Quintins and the Clutterbucks. However, Arabella Bridget [born 1772], the widow of William Thomas St. Quintin [1770-1805] of Scampston, the East Yorkshire seat of the St. Quintins, died in Southampton on 26th January 1841. There is a memorial to them both in Harpham church. Robert and Elizabeth Clutterbuck had lived in Southampton at least from 1828 to 1833 and were still living near Southampton at the time when Thomas was born. I am willing to speculate that they knew Arabella and named their son Thomas St. Quintin after her late husband as a mark of respect.

A portrait of the three sons of Robert Clutterbuck was painted by Sir Martin Archer Shee, probably in about 1838. This was immediately before Thomas was born. The three sons concerned would have been Robert Henry, James Hulton and George Watlington Clutterbuck. This portrait was bequeathed in Dorothy's will to Arthur Stuart Beazley and is now believed to be on display in the Town Hall at Watford. Archer Shee (1769-1850) was President of the Royal Academy, and his portraits included members of the royal family, including Queen Victoria. He was regarded as rather old-fashioned by the early Victorians, but was still much in demand, and a portrait by him of one's family would indicate a certain standing in society.

Robert died on 30th September 1879, by which time he was resident at 8 Great Cumberland Place, Hyde Park, London.

Thomas St. Quintin Clutterbuck

Thomas was destined for a career in the Indian Army. By 1860, at the age of 21, he had become an Ensign and he was a Lieutenant before his 23rd birthday. He had become a Captain by 1869. In 1871, he was Officiating Wing Officer with the 29th (Punjab) Bengal Native Infantry (late 21st Punjab Infantry) with headquarters at Jhelum.

It was probably about this time that he met Ellen Anne Morgan. Her father, William Domatt Morgan, was a Captain in the 22nd Regiment of the Bengal Native Infantry (E.I.C.S.), and it seems possible that Thomas met her through his friendship with William, who was more of Thomas' age. In any event, Thomas and Ellen married at Lahore on 7th November 1877 and, on 19th January 1880, their daughter, Dorothy, was born. She was baptised on 21st February the same year at St Paul's Church, Umbala. By this time, Thomas was a Captain in the 14th Sikhs. Later that same year he was appointed a Major, and in 1886 he became a Lieutenant Colonel.

It seems that Thomas retired from the Indian Army in January 1889, the year in which he attained the age of 50. Certainly he is not mentioned in the Army Lists after that month until he appears, in January 1893, in the list of Officers Retired from the Indian Army. It is my guess that on his retirement Thomas returned to England. Dorothy would have been nine years old, and whilst it is possible that she and her mother may have moved to this country before Thomas' retirement, she would at the latest have moved at an age when she was still capable of adapting to the English way of life. And yet, was she, as was the custom in India at the time for daughters of Army officers, waited on hand and foot? And, if so, did this have a subconscious effect on her attitude to others? I am here reminded of Mary Lennox in Frances Hodgson Burnett's *The Secret Garden*[7].

Dorothy's Early Life in England

I have not yet managed to plot out clearly where Dorothy was living during the early part of her life, but it seems to focus on the county of Oxfordshire. In her diaries she mentions Ditchley, a stately home near Charlbury in Oxfordshire. It was the home of Harold Arthur, Viscount Dillon (1844-1932), Curator of the Armoury at the Tower of London, President of the Society of Antiquaries and a Trustee of the British Museum. He knew Thomas Clutterbuck well enough to be present at his funeral. They probably met in India, as Dillon was stationed there in the 1870s before returning to Oxfordshire in 1874. It is obvious from her diaries that Dorothy spent a lot of time at Ditchley during her childhood, and it is possible that Dillon may even have offered a home for Dorothy and her mother until Thomas retired in 1889. Certainly Ditchley made a great impression on Dorothy. Writing about the portrait of Queen Elizabeth there, she says:

"As a Child, and for years I looked at her. On many a happy night when her dim outline like a Ghost shewed pale in the candle light. For by the soft light of candles Always we used to dine.

And what a lovely light they made on flowers and Fruit and Wine.
Touching the gleaming silver the crystal of the glass
Flickering on soft and shining gowns Ah! Happy days all past.
Past but not gone for ever yet For they are memories gold
Ditchley most beautiful of houses, what stories could be told.
Of Christmases and Easters such lovely ones spent there
The Chapel on Easter mornings with lilies white and fair
And at Christmas with holly shining Old Banners Hanging High
The flame of great log fires Cedars against a snowy sky
And of those two for whom it made so perfect and true a frame
Such love for both of them we had It had no words or name.
[entry for 31 December 1942]

Incidentally, from November 1940 onwards, Ditchley was the venue of many of Churchill's full moon weekends, as his official country residence, Chequers, was too obvious a target for bombers.[10]

There seems to have been some connection with Henley-on-Thames, also in Oxfordshire. Dorothy's uncle Edward, from her maternal grandfather's second marriage, was born there in 1875, and, in her will, Dorothy's mother, Ellen, states: "I enjoin on her [i.e. Dorothy] to have my body cremated and the ashes deposited where she chooses, here [i.e. Highcliffe] or at Henley." Ellen's husband Thomas's body is buried in Highcliffe churchyard, and the above seems to indicate either a certain coolness towards the idea of having her ashes deposited with her husband's remains or, more likely, an affection for Henley as a result of long acquaintance, possibly from living there between 1889 and 1908 - almost 20 years. Further research needs to be carried out.

Dorothy's great uncle, Rev. James C. Clutterbuck [born 1801], was vicar at Long Wittenham in Berkshire, very close to the River Thames, which formed the boundary between Berkshire and Oxfordshire. He was an expert on the construction of dewponds and I wrote about him in my book *Mirrors of Magic*[11], long before I found that he was related to Dorothy.

And Dorothy's uncle, Rev. Arthur Clutterbuck [born 1842], was Officiating Minister of the parish of Englefield, also in Berkshire.

In 1922, in a legal document prepared in connection with Dorothy's lease of Mill House, Dorothy's address is given as The Panelled House, Whitchurch, Oxfordshire. Whitchurch is a small village on the opposite bank of the Thames to Pangbourne, and in the 19th Century was included in Berkshire. In 1881, Elizabeth Slatter, who was to become Dorothy's companion, was living in The Rectory, Whitchurch, with her mother and her father, John Slatter, who was Rector of Whitchurch. Whilst Dorothy obviously had lived there at some stage, the language of legal documents, certainly in those days, was such that, because she had no legal title to Mill House, her previous address was given, even if she left it years previously.

In one of her diaries, Dorothy included a long poem entitled "Father Thames", which is a poetic journey from the source of the river (which, interestingly, is given as Seven Springs, near Cheltenham) down to its mouth. The section of the river from Goring and Streatley past Pangbourne and Henley is particularly detailed and clearly suggests local knowledge.

Much remains to be discovered, but I think that I have demonstrated that for a substantial part of the time between 1889, when she was nine, and 1922, when Dorothy took on the lease of Mill House, at the age of 42, she was living in the Oxford area, probably at Ditchley, Henley and Whitchurch.

Chewton Mill

In 1908, Thomas was 70 years old, and, for whatever reason, was looking for somewhere to live near the Hampshire coast and within easy reach of the New Forest, which he may well have remembered from his youth. He stayed temporarily in Gilpin's Cottage, in the village of Boldre, probably as a base to explore the area, in the course of which he spotted Chewton Mill House, which had closed as a working mill and was on offer to lease from the Hon. Edward James Montagu Stuart Wortley of the Highcliffe Castle estate.

The Mill House is situated in the steep-sided and wooded Chewton Glen which carries the Walkford Brook, which rises at the southern edge of the New Forest, down to the sea near Highcliffe. It is the first building you come across in the glen itself on walking up the footpath alongside Walkford Brook from the sea shore. The significance of this spot as a landing place has long been recognised, as Olive Samuel points out:

"When England was apprehensive of invasion by the Spanish Armada in 1588, Chewton was defended by 200 men ... as opposed to Christchurch being allotted only 165 men for its defence. Chewton was considered a more likely landing place than Christchurch."[12]

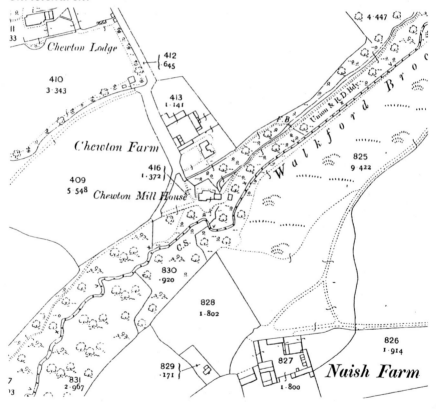

29. *Chewton Mill House and the Walkford Brook (extract from the 1893 Ordnance Survey 25-inch map - reduced in scale)*

In later years, this same quality made it an attractive spot for smugglers. The wooded nature of Chewton Glen plus the presence of quicksands at the mouth of the Walkford Brook made it an attractive smuggling route on dark nights (and they would be very dark in the days before street lights) for those who knew the 'lie of the land'.

There was thus established a well used smuggling route up Chewton Glen from the coast, along the evocative 'Froggy Lane', across to Chewton and Cranemoor Commons to the Cat and Fiddle Inn, which seemed to act as a distribution centre to such places as Burley, in the heart of the New Forest. Being the first building on this route, the mill was sometimes used for storing contraband, although Naish Farm, up on the plateau, was actually used more, because a good look-out could be kept from there. There are legends of a secret tunnel up to the farm.

30. Chewton Mill as a working mill

Captain Frederick Marryat (1792-1848), the naval writer and novelist, wrote his most famous book *The Children of the New Forest*[13] the year before he died, while he was living at Chewton Glen, a large house (now a hotel) overlooking the Walkford Brook not half a mile further up from the Mill House.

There are records of a mill in Chewton Glen as early as the 13th Century, when one is recorded being in the ownership of Christchurch Priory. The present building dates from the early to mid 18th Century, although there was an earlier mill which stood on more or less the same site. There is a depression in the ground to the north of the present house, which is all that remains of the mill pond.

The mill continued working until 1908, when Thomas and Ellen Clutterbuck moved in. It was clear that certain alterations and building works were going to be necessary before the Clutterbucks

31. Chewton Mill House following alterations about 1910 with a figure who may be Thomas Clutterbuck

32. Chewton Mill House about 1910 with a figure who may be Dorothy Clutterbuck

would have a house which would be to their requirements and expectations of comfort. These were largely in brick, some of which was rendered, including a substantial two-storey extension, a new porch and complete re-roofing, including a dormer window. I do not know whether such alterations were carried out by Thomas or by the estate prior to his moving in, but Illustrations 30 and 31 show the Mill House before and after these alterations.

Ironically, the first rent payment fell due the month of Thomas' death, in September 1910. On Monday 19th September, he was returning from taking Dorothy to the station (my guess is that she was on her way back to Oxfordshire after spending a weekend in Highcliffe) when he was seen to collapse at Sea Corner, on Lymington Road, Highcliffe. He died very quickly thereafter and the inquest confirmed that he had died from a blood clot in the pulmonary artery. Earlier that day, his groom had announced that he intended to resign without notice, which may have contributed to Thomas's condition.[14]

Whilst a relative newcomer to the village, Thomas took an active interest in village events and was associated with the Highcliffe Stuart-Wortley Scouts, probably one of the first Boy Scout troops in the country, since the first scout camp had taken place only three years previously, on Brownsea Island in nearby Poole Harbour.

Dorothy's mother, Ellen, continued to live at Mill House for another ten years until her own death in 1920. She had a gift for poetry and passed on to Dorothy not only her own volume of verses but also the ability to write in a similar vein. Her verses are full of love for and awareness of nature and we will be looking at some of them in the next chapter.

The Mill House Players

Elizabeth Slatter was described locally as Dorothy's 'companion' and went by the name of 'John'. She was born in 1853 and was therefore some 27 years older than Dorothy, in fact older than Dorothy's mother. At what date she started living at Mill House is unclear, but she remained living there until her death in 1933 at the age of 80. She may originally have been Dorothy's mother's companion, as she witnessed a lease document in 1917.

Dorothy had inherited enough from her mother to become what was described as "a woman of independent means". She took over the lease of Mill House in 1922 and, in 1924, bought the freehold outright, with the help of a £2500 mortgage. The mortgage document was drawn up by a firm of Oxford solicitors and the mortgagor was a resident of Oxford.

Dorothy did not fit easily into the category of 'lady of leisure', however. After her mother's death, she took out the old mill wheel and converted the mill room so that it could be used as a rehearsal room for what would be a major interest of hers for the next 15 years or so - the Mill House Players. This room was known as the Music Room, and had a first floor gallery, which, I imagine, would have been very useful in rehearsals.

33. *Orpheus, on the exterior of the Music Room Mill House*

A statue stands on the outside wall above the window and has the inscription: *"Orpheus - Designed for this Music Room by RMD - Feb 1924"*. The identity of 'RMD' is not known.

There is also a plaque with a verse on this 1932 extension which reads as follows:

THE LITTLE STREAM

BELOW MY CASEMENT WIDE, A LITTLE STREAM
MURMURS AND RIPPLES IN A HAPPY DREAM
WINDING ITS WAY AROUND EACH MOSS GROWN TREE
THREADING A FAIRY PATH TOWARD THE SEA

D.C.S. JUNE 1927

The poet is probably Dorothy. The initials D.C.S. should therefore read D.S.C. I suspect that this was a mistake that was either not spotted or not considered important enough to re-make the plaque. The date is about five years prior to the extension to which it is fixed. This suggests either that it was originally situated on the end wall of the original building and then moved to its current location or, more likely, the date relates to the composition of the verse.

Amateur theatricals were far more popular than they are today, as we have already seen with the Rosicrucian Theatre. Dorothy had obviously been involved previously in something of the sort and enthusiastically formed a group of players in Highcliffe who specialised in musical performances, particularly Gilbert and Sullivan. Reg Kitcher gives his memories of the period:

"... when I was 18 years old I was invited to join a group at Highcliffe in 1928 called the "Mill House Players". They were a bunch of local amateur singers and players both young and middle-aged from around the area and they intended to put on the Gilbert and Sullivan opera "The Mikado". We were all happy to meet down

at the Mill House, Chewton Glen, to learn and rehearse every night of the week and on Sunday afternoons for about three months, previous to putting on the show for a week of evenings at Highcliffe and one night stands at Christchurch, Boscombe, Milford, New Milton, Brockenhurst and Lymington. We were conveyed to these halls by taxi and various private cars all arranged and financed by Miss Clutterbuck of the Mill House. We did one opera each year for about four years. It was through these shows that I met the girl who was to be my wife ..."[15]

Sheila Herringshaw adds:

"Principal singers were hired from Bournemouth but many local people took part, including Harry Lee, a local butcher, Herbie Hann, the manager of Misselbrook and Westons, ... and Ken Whitcombe, the Parish sexton."[16]

One notable production was that of "*The Yeomen of the Guard*" in 1929 [see Illustration 34]. A tambourine has survived which was presented to Dorothy by the members of the cast, inscribed "To Elsie [the character played by Dorothy] January 7th-16th 1929 From The Mill House Players", and signed by them all. Apart from those mentioned above, the signatories on the tambourine included William Pelly, Lawrie Macfarlane, William Keeping, George Stone, John Pelly, S.H.M. Hatton, F.A. Tuck, M.C. Gill, C.O.S. Hatton, Gerald Kaye, Philip Taylor, Nan Tuck, Margaret Hann, Nancy Tugwell, Lottie Whitcombe, Irene Harper, Ruth Whitcher, Evelyn Joyce, Irene Rickman, Doris Bailey, R.K. Knight, Dorothy Forrest, Helen Harrison and Ruby James.

Rupert Oswald Fordham

As the 1930s dawned, things were about to change for Dorothy, in terms of her relationship with a man whom she would later marry. By this time, Dorothy was in her fifties. Whether there had been earlier relationships I do not know - perhaps with young men who had died in the Boer War or the Great War, as was so common in that generation. There is certainly a poem in her diary, which is highly poignant, though this may have been about a brother:

34. The Mill House Players in a performance of "The Yeomen of the Guard" in 1929. Dorothy Clutterbuck is the figure in the centre.

Alice's Blucbell Wood near Bowerwood - *in memory of AJC*
I used to think bluebells and skies had made the colour of your eyes
As long as bluebells still I see, then always you'll come back to me.
[entry for 4 May 1942]

Anyway, Dorothy met Rupert Fordham, who was 18 years her senior (how often that difference in years seems to come up - possibly something to do with the moon's nodes, which circle the zodiac completely in that period).

The Fordhams were a noted family having estates at Odsey and Ashwell on the Hertfordshire-Cambridgeshire border. They had been brewers in Ashwell since the early 1800s. Rupert's father, Edward King Fordham (1810-1889) was a prominent landowner and a Justice of the Peace for the Counties of Hertford, Cambridge and Bedford and was Deputy Lieutenant for Bedfordshire, and

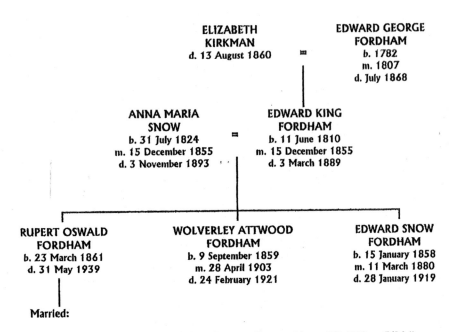

35. The Fordham Family Tree

High Sheriff in 1884. His memorial in Ashwell churchyard states: "*A noble character of the highest moral courage, he lived an active life, devoting great energy to the happiness and improvement of those around him.*"

Edward, together with Rupert's uncle Herbert owned the family brewery business which was based in Ashwell. The brewery business was a thriving one, and Sheldrick writes that "...*the pleasant aroma of malt still drifted over the village and lorry loads of Fordham's ales went out to quench the thirst of folks in at least four counties until World War Two ..."*[17] The brewery was subsequently taken over, closed in 1965 and demolished in 1973, apart from the office, stable block and maltings, which have been converted into dwellings. It is commemorated in a new estate road called Fordham Close.

Rupert Oswald Fordham was born on 23rd March 1861. By 1881 he and his brother Wolverley are described as "brewery pupils". They both obviously had a share in the business and Rupert is always later described as being of "independent means", i.e. he didn't have to work. Like his father, he became a Justice of the Peace.

In 1893, Rupert married Caroline O'Malley, widow of Sir William O'Malley, and in June 1894 acquired Broom Hall, a stately home and grounds near Biggleswade in Bedfordshire, only a few miles from Ashwell. Caroline died in 1900, leaving almost £30,000 in her will.

Rupert married again in 1905. This was to Janet Elizabeth, daughter of William Durning Holt, of Liverpool. The Durning Holts were a prominent Liverpool family, involved in Liberal politics. Janet died in 1913, leaving over £40,000 in her will.

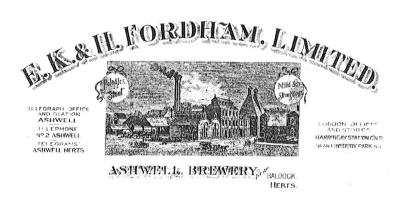

36. Letterheading from Fordham's Ashwell Brewery

Rupert had some cottages of interesting architectural design, in random stone and eyebrow roofs, erected in her memory in the village of Broom. A plaque on the cottages reads: "*In memory of Janet E. Fordham, whose wish was to do good to others. Go thou and do likewise. 1913.*"

Rupert married his third wife, Julia Blanche, in 1916. She was the daughter of Colonel George William Cox of the Indian Army. At some stage, she became mentally ill and was cared for, at home and in a nursing home, for the rest of her life. She died in 1955.

Rupert had met Dorothy, probably in late 1930 or early 1931. We don't know how they met, but Dorothy's great-grandfather, Robert Clutterbuck, lived for many years at Hinxworth Place, in the neighbouring village to Ashwell, and I suspect that down the years there were local contacts between their families, which Gardner characterised as 'county'.

37. *Broom Hall, Bedfordshire*
Rupert Fordham's home from 1989 to 1932

In her diary Dorothy includes a verse dated August 1931 entitled *"The Cornfields of Ashwell"*:

A Song before Sunrise - A Day at the Dawn
The dew on the Meadows - The Light on the Corn.
Golden Cornfields, near Ashwell
For ever will be - Beloved. For your sake
Like Heaven to me.

I am surmising that this is a love poem directed towards Rupert and that it was written not long after they met. I suspect that they must have fallen in love and decided to live together. Dorothy was obviously the more determined because by April 1931 she had had a self-contained extension to Mill House approved, and I am guessing that this was intended to provide some independent

38. Latimers, Highcliffe
Dorothy Fordham's home from about 1935 until her death
in 1951

accommodation for Rupert. He obviously moved in to Mill House by Autumn 1931 or Spring 1932 because he appears on the 1932 Electoral Register as living there. In any case, his Broom Hall estate was put up for sale by auction in September 1932. Also, on 1st February 1935, Dorothy's mortgage on Mill House was paid off, presumably by Rupert.

Latimers

Whilst the living accommodation at Mill House was quite adequate, Rupert was clearly used to living in more comfort and space, and he was looking around the neighbourhood for something more suitable for a gentleman in his position. In 1933, he found what he was looking for. Donald Stuart Baynes, the owner of a large house in Station Road (now Hinton Wood Avenue) known as Latimers, had died in 1931, and his wife Annie, finding herself unwilling or unable to continue living there, put it up for sale. Rupert bought it at the auction which took place in December 1933.

Latimers seems to have been built some time in the 1870s. It does not appear on the 6-inch Ordnance Survey map revised in 1867, but there are residents there in the 1881 Census, albeit just a married couple, George and Louisa Oxford, the gardener and housekeeper respectively. By 1885, the property had been acquired by Dame Sarah Emily Amphlett, who had a house built in the grounds for the gardener and his wife. She sold Latimers in 1903 to Donald Stuart Baynes.

The house itself was not over-large, but it had three impressive southward-facing gables looking over the ornamental garden. From the look of the photograph accompanying the 1933 sales document and subsequent photographs, it would appear that Rupert added fake half-timbering to the whole of the south elevation of the house, making a striking alteration in its appearance, to say the least!

The grounds were over four acres in extent and included a lawn, ornamental pond, kitchen garden, paddock and two cottages. The Friar's Rest was a sort of pavilion which Rupert and Dorothy had erected in the grounds of Latimers where they could entertain guests in an informal way away from the main house. Dorothy includes a poem in her diary which gives a clear idea of its character:

Quaint little house in the garden alone
Standing demurely there, all on your own
Black and white walls, and its Norfolk reed roof
It's a fairy tale house if you're telling the truth...
[6th July 1942]

It is illustrated by a small watercolour by Christine Wells which, to move ahead in our story for a moment, bears for me a striking resemblance to the 'witch's cottage' which was later to feature prominently in Gardner's life.

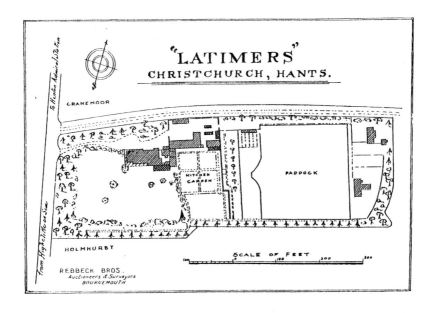

39. *Plan of Latimers accompanying 1933 sale document*

Rupert and Dorothy

On 8th August 1935, Rupert Fordham and Dorothy Clutterbuck went through a marriage ceremony at the Kensington Registry Office in London. At the time, Rupert was still legally married to his third wife, Julia Blanche, who did not die until 1955, so his marriage to Dorothy was not valid under English law. I do not know why they went through with this ceremony which they must have known was legally invalid. It was certainly not to lead people into thinking that they were married, because it was carried out with little fuss and no publicity. (There is no report or mention of it in the *Christchurch Times*, for example.) Certainly local people in Highcliffe assumed that they were living together without being married. Everyone knew, for example, that Hudson, Dorothy's chauffeur, was sent up every week to the home where Blanche Fordham was living, with fresh fruit and vegetables for her.[18] And it is certainly true that the *Christchurch Times*, which reported regularly on the activities of the Mill House Players, was referring to Dorothy as 'Miss Clutterbuck' up until early 1935[19]. By 1936 she was being referred to as 'Mrs. Fordham'[20]. She is also referred to as Dorothy Fordham in the Electoral Registers compiled in that and subsequent years. There were results leading from this which would not surface for several years, as we shall see.

Anyway, soon after this, Rupert transferred to Dorothy about £100,000 worth of brewery securities, the equivalent of many millions of pounds in today's money. Dorothy thus became a very wealthy woman.

Despite Rupert's purchase of Latimers in 1933, it was to be another three years before he, Dorothy and the servants are indicated on the Electoral Register as living there. I think it likely that they kept both houses on and that it was only gradually that the "centre of operations" so to speak focused on Latimers.

The Staff

Dorothy and Rupert were of a class and lived in an age when domestic servants were to be expected. Before Rupert came to live at Mill House, Dorothy had three servants. This increased to five in 1934, six in 1935 and seven in 1936. After Rupert's death and during the war years, this figure went down again to six and after the war down to four. Several of the staff had been with Dorothy for many years, such as her cook/housekeeper Aronica (Annie) Williams, and Frances Cox, her maid, to both of whom she left £1000 in her will.

In her diary for December 1942, Dorothy gives brief portraits in verse of each of her staff. These included her chauffeur, Hudson, whom she calls "The Wise Man"; her gardener, Griffin, of whom she writes "Here's to a Wizard with a Wand! who makes the stoniest of ground to blossom like the Proverbial Rose"; to her Chef, Aronica Williams; and to many others, including 'Curtis the Willing', of whom she says:

> *"Twenty years must it be, and more,*
> *Since first He saw The Mill House Door.*
> *For Groom to "Frollo", Then was He.*
> *But what completely puzzles Me,*
> *Tho' years have gone by, by the Score*
> *How He can still look 24!!"*

Dorothy's dogs - Don, Boris, Rufus and Ranchi - and her white pony, Kitty are given equal space!

Their Role in Society

After moving into Latimers, Dorothy and Rupert took an active part in the social affairs of Highcliffe, Christchurch and beyond.

Dorothy was a Conservative - a very keen Conservative, encouraging membership of the party in what was one of the safest Conservative seats in the country. She obviously did this from inner conviction, and was elected President of the Highcliffe Conservative Association in January 1939. What Rupert felt is not known, although he supported her. However, traditionally, the Fordhams had been Liberals.[21]

The grounds of Latimers and, in case of inclement weather, the Friar's Rest, were used for innumerable Garden Parties to raise

> Thursday December 31st
> New Years Day
> The Writer, and The Artist are bidding you Adieu.
> They've done Their best To Please You, in 1942.
> They wish You every Blessing.
> As Through The Year you Go.
> And Sign Their names, beneath This Verse,
> So They Can Tell You So
>
> Dorothy St Quintin Fordham.
> Christine M. Wells. also.

40. An extract from Dorothy's Diary for 1942

money for the local Conservative Association and the other organisations which Dorothy supported. These included the Boy Scouts (continuing the support which her father gave in the early years); the Royal Victoria and West Hants Hospital, for which Dorothy organised an annual street collection for many years in the 1930s; the Highcliffe and District Horticultural Society, of which Dorothy was elected President in January 1940; and the NSPCC (National Society for the Prevention of Cruelty to Children).

Other organisations represented at Dorothy's funeral, which would suggest that she gave them her support, included the RSPCA (Royal Society for the Prevention of Cruelty to Animals); the Highcliffe Missions to Seamen; Highcliffe Guides; the Red Cross; the Highcliffe British Legion; the Hampshire Association for the

*41. Dorothy St Quintin-Fordham in about 1950
(copyright Ian Stevenson)*

Care of the Blind and the Bournemouth and District Bee Keepers' Association.

But Dorothy and Rupert also took part in another, more campaigning public action. The cliffs from which Highcliffe takes its name had long been a favourite place for locals and others to stroll and admire the view along the coast and the panorama from Hengistbury Head to the Isle of Wight. The problem was that the coast was eroding and that the former right of way had been extinguished as a result. In 1937, the cliff owners enclosed part of the land, denying public access, and planned to build bungalows on it.

A public meeting of 200 residents was held which urged the Council to acquire the land as the only way of preserving it for the public, but Council representatives pointed out that they had limited finances. At this stage, Dorothy and Rupert came into the picture, offering £2,500 towards the purchase of the cliff-top land. As Dorothy explained in a letter:

...we are both very anxious that the cliffs should not be further enclosed or built upon, but remain an open space for the benefit of the residents of Highcliffe for ever. We wish to do this in memory of my father and mother and Miss Slatter, who loved the cliffs very much, and for the regard and affection my husband and I have for the people of Highcliffe.[22]

In the end, the asking price for the land was too high, but war intervened before any development could take place, and the post-war Town and Country Planning system put paid to any renewed attempts to build.

The Latter Years

On Friday, 6th January 1939, Rupert and Dorothy, and their chauffeur, Hudson, were involved in a serious accident on the road between Alton and Winchester, when returning to Highcliffe from London. Their car was following a heavy lorry at normal speed, when suddenly, a car coming the other way collided with the lorry, was hurled up over it and landed on the Fordhams' car, crushing the bonnet. Rupert, who was sitting next to the chauffeur, had, according to the *Christchurch Times*: "...*his legs thrust through into the engine, and the pipe he was smoking was smashed, leaving the stem still in his lips.*"[23] Both he and Hudson were trapped in the wreckage and had to be freed. Dorothy, sitting in the back seat, suffered no worse than a twisted ankle.

Rupert, who was 78, never really recovered from the accident, and he died on 31st May 1939. Dorothy went into the customary six months' mourning, which traditionally involved avoiding social engagements.

In August 1939, following Rupert's death, Dorothy covenanted to "provide for the maintenance and comfort of Mrs. Blanche Fordham" after her death and she started to send monthly cheques for Mrs. Fordham's maintenance.

Rupert died intestate (i.e. without making a will) but Dorothy, claiming to be his widow, was granted Letters of Administration on 11th October 1939. These were challenged by Rupert's son by his first marriage, Rupert Granville Fordham. The challenge was upheld in the courts and an Order was made in the Probate Courts on 13th January 1941 revoking the Letters of Administration which had been granted in 1939 to Dorothy, and granting them to Rupert Granville Fordham, Rupert's only son. Costs were awarded against Dorothy.

Later that same year, and presumably as a direct result of this case, Dorothy changed her name by Deed Poll. On 7th November 1941, she: "... *did thereby absolutely renounce and abandon the use of her surname of Clutterbuck and in lieu thereof assumed as from the date thereof the surname of St. Quintin-Fordham.*"

According to Gareth Medway, it was in 1943 that Dorothy acquired a house in London, no. 17A Thurloe Place, Knightsbridge, which she named Amberwood House, after Amberwood Farm, which she owned. There may have been earlier links with Thurloe Place, since Dorothy and Rupert both gave their residence as the Rembrandt Hotel, Thurloe Place, on their marriage certificate in 1935. Dorothy obviously had a lot of social contacts in London at the time (some possibly originally acquaintances of Rupert's) and she must have felt that a house in London would be useful. It was, of course, the middle of the war and I suspect that she may have been able to acquire it relatively cheaply (not that she needed to economise!).

It is uncertain what happened to Mill House during the War. Dorothy's diaries, which we shall be examining in some detail in the next chapter, certainly suggest that she was dividing her time between Mill House and Latimers, although no-one is indicated on the Electoral Register there from 1937 to 1945. Olive Samuel states that during the War, Mill House was subdivided into three dwellings, although I have not seen any other reference to this. In 1946 and 1947, Alfred Lay, Dorothy's gardener, and his wife Gladys, are indicated as living there. In 1950, Dorothy leased Mill House to the Hon. Violet Stuart Wortley, who had given up Highcliffe Castle and needed somewhere to live.

On 12th January 1951, Dorothy died. Her death certificate indicates that she died of a cerebral thrombosis, in other words, a stroke. She was just a week short of her 71st birthday. She left an estate worth £60,000.

Violet Stuart Wortley continued to live in Mill House until her own death in 1953. Mill House was then put up for sale by auction on Tuesday 21st April 1953. The present owner, John Ferguson, bought the property in 1963. After a spell as a Rest Home for the Elderly, it is now again a private house.

It may be worth quoting from the brochure for the sale of Mill House in 1953. Describing the garden, it refers to:

"... a mixture of forest and ornamental trees, also flowering shrubs and rhododendrons. There are flower and herbaceous beds, small pond with fountain and central figure; ornamental brick and flagged terrace. Delightful walks through undulating woodlands intersected by the running Mill stream wending its way to the sea and crossed by a small rustic bridge.

In the spring the whole of the Grounds present a very colourful and beautiful sight with the profusion of bulbs of many varieties."

Chapter 11
Dorothy's Diaries

If we were looking for evidence of involvement in the Craft, an examination of Dorothy Clutterbuck's life, as outlined in the previous chapter, would not go very far towards providing it. However, in the early 1980s, over 30 years after Dorothy's death, some writings came to light which could, potentially, shed considerable light on the proceedings.

Helen Bassett had taken a job in 1982 as a Secretary at a local firm of solicitors in Highcliffe. Like most solicitors' offices, there was a store-room with racks lining the walls piled high with the papers from previous cases, all tied up with the ubiquitous pink tape. It was part of Helen's job to file things away and, one day, three books caught her eye, all alone on a shelf. They appeared to be hand-written diaries, illustrated by small but most attractive watercolour sketches. Two of them had embroidered covers. Someone had obviously spent many, many hours in making them.

Helen asked the solicitor where they had come from. "I really don't know anything about them" he said. "They've been here as long as I have, which is getting on for 20 years now." During her spare moments of calm during a busy office day, Helen looked through the diaries and thought how attractive they were. She found that they were by a certain Dorothy St. Quintin Fordham, and were for the years 1942 and 1943.

At the top of the first volume, Dorothy has added, after it was completed "To Mr and Mrs Lawrie, Nance and Kit". These were her near neighbours, Arthur Gavin Wallace Lawrie, his wife Edith Mary Lawrie, Anne Eliza Oldmeadow and Katherine Louise Oldmeadow, who all lived at Glen House, at the corner of Mill Lane and Lymington Road. The diaries may have ended up with Katherine Oldmeadow's solicitors when she died in 1963. There is no mention of them in her will.

Thursday December 3rd To Hudson. "The Wise Man"
See The Wise Man's Cars, all shining! its Elbow grease & Punctual Timing.
Every Morning, wet or fine, They always get Their daily Shine!
And what about His many Clocks? They've got to make Their Ticks & Tocks,
All Strike just with The B.B.C. or very Angry He would be!
Always Cheerful, always Willing, Every Second with Jobs filling.
Never once, has He been late, To The moment at The Gate.
To The moment he'll come round round, Tho' ice & Snow are on The ground.
Such Comfort to His Master He. Which makes Him all The More to Me.
"Mr Tomy" Chose His name. As "Wise Man" She knows to fame,
So many Things He knows
You See, no better name could ever be.

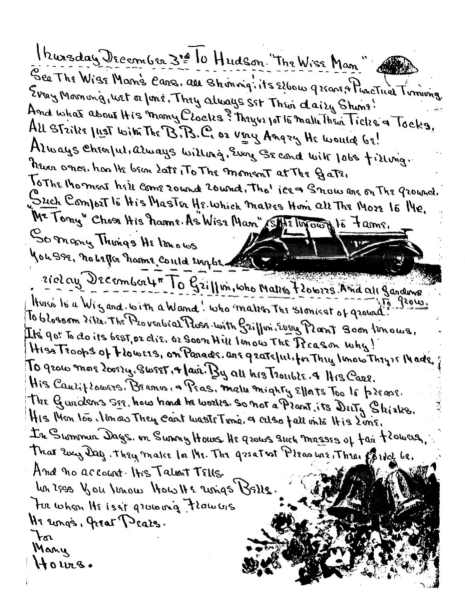

Friday December 4th To Griffin, who Makes Flowers. And all Gardens
Here is a Wig and, with a Wand! who makes The stoniest of ground. To grow.
To blossom like. The Proverbial Rose with Griffin, every Plant soon knows,
It's got To do its best, or die, or Soon Hill know The Reason why!
His Troops of Flowers, on Parade, are grateful, for They know They're Made,
To grow more Lovely, Sweet, & fair. By all his Trouble, & His Care.
His Cauliflowers, Beans, & Peas, make mighty efforts Too to please.
The Gardens See, how hard he works, So not a Plant, its Duty Shirks.
His Men too, know They can't waste Time, & also fall into His Line.
In Summer Days, in Sunny Hours He grows such masses of fair Flowers,
That every Day, They make to Me. The greatest Pleasure, There could be.
And no account. His Talent Tells.
For yes you know How He rings Bells.
For when He isn't growing Flowers
He rings, great Peals.
For
Many
Hours.

42. An extract from Dorothy's Diary for 1942

Several years later, some time in 1985, the solicitor was inspired to do some 'spring cleaning'. He came out of the store room with the diaries in his hand, saying "I think we've had these long enough. They'd better be thrown away!"

"That's a shame!" commented Helen. "I've always thought they were so attractive!"

"You might as well have them, then" replied the solicitor and gave them to Helen, who took them home with her.

Both her mother and Helen's friend, Kenneth Harvey-Packer, were fascinated with them. Indeed, Kenneth felt that they were well worthy of exhibiting and arranged to have them displayed at the Lansdowne Library in Bournemouth, with a different page being open each day. They were later displayed at the Bishopsgate Institute in London, in April 1986, with the encouragement of Alison Carpenter and David Webb, who worked there. They were also exhibited in Christchurch Library in Spring 1988. Several people suggested that they would be worthy of publication, comparing them favourably with Edith Holden's *Diary of an Edwardian Lady*. Several publishers were contacted, and one came very near to agreeing, but in the end nothing came of it.

The first thing to say is that to call them 'diaries' is really a misnomer. These were in no sense recording Dorothy's secret thoughts, to be locked away, or even a chronicle of each day's events. Rather than diaries in the usual sense, they were more properly a vehicle for Dorothy's 'thoughts for the day', reflecting her interests and attitudes to life. Here were no secret diaries: they were clearly meant to be displayed and admired by visitors and one can imagine Dorothy leaving them out for guests to look through. Indeed, to be fair, Dorothy did not call them 'diaries' but 'calendars', a term we would probably not use today for what was essentially a work of art. They have also been called 'commonplace books', though that also is not quite right.

Anyway, for convenience, we will continue to refer to them as diaries.

They consist of three volumes of what are basically ordinary hard-backed exercise books of lined paper. The first volume, which contains the entries for the whole of 1942, has a page size of approx. 9 inches high x 7 inches wide. The second volume, which contains the entries for 1st January 1943 to 25th September 1943, is somewhat bigger, having a page size of approx. 12 inches x 7 inches. The entries are more spread out, as each day's entry is on a separate page, with a watercolour sketch opposite. This pattern is repeated in the third and last book, which is "long and thin", being approx. 12 inches high x 4.5 inches wide. This contains the entries for 26th September to 31st December 1943. There is evidence within the diaries that these were the only ones ever produced: in other words, none have gone missing.

There is an entry for each day for the two years. Usually it is a verse or verses written by Dorothy specially for the occasion. It is also illustrated with small watercolour sketches by her friend, Christine Maud Wells (1885-1969), who was an Associate of the British Watercolour Society (ABWS). She was a pupil of Sickert at the R.A. and, whilst she had lived at Dorchester at some time in her life, she was, in the 1940s, living with her father in New Milton. She was known as a painter of watercolours of all aspects of the New Forest, and of painting large houses on commission, such as Walhampton, near Lymington. She was also an etcher and illustrator of children's books. She taught at local schools.[1]

Whilst the verses were clearly composed by Dorothy, they were usually copied into the book by Christine Wells, who had a readable, flowing, cursive style of writing. There are sections, however, presumably when Christine Wells was away or otherwise indisposed, where it is written by Dorothy herself, who had a very distinctive writing style, somewhat angular, which someone familiar with it has described as "witchy". Certainly her capital "D" is very characteristic and is in effect a moon symbol. [See illustrations 40 and 42]

In this chapter, I shall be looking at the various topics which Dorothy covered in her diaries and what they tell us about her life, interests and attitudes. One of the first things to say is that, even for a 'lady of leisure', as Dorothy might reasonably be described, the diaries are a remarkable achievement, with an entry, and usually a substantial one, for every day for two years - 730 days in all.

Dorothy always has at least one eye on the calendar and uses specific dates as a prompt for her verses. Thus we have saints' days such as Valentine's, Patrick's, Swithin's and Cecilia's; traditional festivals such as Lady Day, April Fool's Day and May Day; festivals marking the church year, such as Palm Sunday, Easter Day, Trinity Sunday and All Saints' Day; such vital markers of the country calendar as the beginnings (and endings!) of Grouse, Partridge and Pheasant shooting; and assorted patriotic anniversaries such as Trafalgar Day.

Birthdays are also frequent features, both of her own friends and those of national figures such as the Royal Family, together with a selection of writers, actors and composers that she obviously admired.

The presence of the War is never far away, both in patriotic sentiments (There are no fewer than ten entries entitled "To the RAF and Victory" in the first eight months of 1942 alone) and in humorous references to the deprivations and ingenuities of living in wartime, ranging from making bricks out of coaldust for burning on the fire, to dried egg, the lack of ingredients for pancakes on Shrove Tuesday, and economical recipes like "Sprouts au Gratin"!

There are also frequent pieces expressing some aspect of personal morality or philosophy including extolling the virtues of hard work, noticing and taking advantage of opportunities, and making things happen by actually doing something and doing it now! The importance of modesty, sharing, extra kindness and laughter, doing ordinary things extraordinarily well, the importance of gratitude, and that we see what we are looking for, are all included.

One aspect of this moralising which is emphasised quite strongly is that of keeping secrets, something which has always been regarded as important for the magical practitioner, as summed up in the phrase "to know, to dare, to will, and to keep silent", the last being by far the most difficult.

There are at least five separate entries on this theme, and to quote from some of them:

> *Mind you keep your Promise, for it is a Trust*
> *It must be just like a Rock, and not a bit of Crust*

[21 July 1942]

> *A Bird who was old and very wise*
> *For silence was given the first Prize*
> *He lived in an Oak and never spoke*
> *And he found it such a lovely Joke!*
> *To pretend to be Deaf when he went at all*
> *So all his neighbours great and small*
> *Told him everything that they knew*
> *And soon, a very wise Bird he grew!*

[15 September 1942]

> *Words all have Wings*
> *Once said, they fly for ever*
> *And when they're spoken*
> *We can recall them never.*

[28 November 1943]

Dorothy had perfected the technique of using a quotation, perhaps just a few lines, as the inspiration for her daily entry. In this way she quotes from a wide variety of poets, novelists, playwrights, politicians and others, including Kipling, Byron, Emerson, Chesterton, Schiller, Goethe, Burns, Dickens, Kingsley, and, of course, Shakespeare. Whilst we cannot discount the judicious use of a convenient *Dictionary of Quotations* (and theoretically work out which one it was!), Dorothy was obviously in any case a well-read and cultured woman.

The two main clues to understanding Dorothy as she was in 1942-43 is in her writing about Nature on the one hand and religion on the other. Of course, as a pagan I would make no distinction between the two, but Dorothy was living in a very different environment and social milieu and would naturally express things in different ways.

Let us first look at her orthodox religious references. There are frequent references to God, praying, angels, blessings and Heaven, and less frequent or individual references to God's great Grace, Pity and Mercy and Charity Divine, Hope and Faith, Saints (particularly Michael and Francis of Assisi), and Our Lady's Robe: an impressive array of religious devotion.

And yet, is there not something missing? No mention of Jesus throughout the two years of writing! Very strange for one who was supposed to be a devout Christian. There are three references, and three references only, to Christ and Christianity. One is a plea to Hitler: "The Prayers of all the Christian Earth against you ...". One recounts the story of the building of Christchurch Priory:

> *"This Church, apart from any other*
> *Its Legend tells, was made*
> *Fashioned and made by Christ's own Hand,*
> *And for that reason named."*

[11 July 1943]

And the third is a quotation from a Latin inscription on the walls of Ely Cathedral:

> *On its outer walls is a*
> *motto, which a*
> *Fordham Bishop made here*
> *Centuries past it was graven*
> *But still to read is clear*
> *"Christus Turris, Fides Telum"*
> *"Christ our Tower, Faith our Spear"*

[14 March 1943]

In the first case, it is almost as if she is an outside observer; in the second she is reporting a well-known local legend; and the third is really an item of family history.

And that is all!

There is a series of verses, one for each Sunday starting at the beginning of 1943, on the Cathedrals of England, illustrated by some of the finest watercolours by Christine Wells in the whole of the diaries. But these are no professions of Christian faith: they are rather word sketches of the places themselves, including some historical facts and Dorothy's memories of her visits there.

We see the emphasis even more strongly when we look at Dorothy's diary entries for the main Christian festivals of the year. To quote just a few:

Easter Day 1943
The Loveliest of Seasons Fair
Now Reigns once more on Earth
Easter, whose silver voice again
Sings to us of New Birth.

Christmas 1942
Then with a flash of Scarlet
Sweeping across the snows
Comes Christmas, Radiant Creature!
She's laughing as she goes. The shining holly fills her lap
Blue pages hold her train
Dear Time of lovely memories. So you are here again
There stand the glittering Christmas Trees
The Fires flame and glow. Soft fingers tapping on the pane
Are fairies, made of snow.
The Bells ring out
The Carols Mount
All the old songs are dear
The First Most Sacred Festival
The best of all the year

Christmas Day 1943
> *Once more a flash of scarlet*
> *And there, in the frosted air*
> *Shines the same Radiant vision*
> *Christmas once more is Here*
> *Her mantle made of Holly Leaves*
> *Fringed round with Berries Red*
> *And, her own Christmas Roses*
> *Set like Stars around Her Head.*

Whit Sunday 1942
> *The Sunday that comes in the time of the May*
> *With its crown of white blossoms for this sacred Day*
> *The Essence of this Day - The Spirit of Prayer*
> *Brings to us those loved Spirits who used to be here.*

Just where one would most expect a reference to Jesus and to the Christian significance of the festival, we get instead a divinity which is expressed through and found in the local landscape, and the legends and spirits associated with it.

There is a word for this, and that word is Pagan.

And of what day did Dorothy write:

> *"Of all the days of the wonderful year*
> *This is the day of all days most dear."*?

Not Easter, nor Christmas, nor any of the Christian festivals: she was writing about Midsummer Day.

It is abundantly clear that Dorothy's main inspiration is Nature. She was acutely aware of the cycle of the seasons and of the birds, animals and flowers that marked it. And, whether to be interpreted literally or not, the pages of her diaries are liberally scattered with accounts of fairies and a nameless being whom we can only identify with the Goddess.

Indeed, it is no exaggeration to say that much of Dorothy's verse would not look at all out of place in any of today's Pagan journals.

To give a few examples:

> "...Each Pilgrim of Life has had at least
> Just one enchanted day
> When the forest of Arden and Arcady
> Took our Hearts to the Heart of a Wood
> And there, with the one we loved best upon Earth
> In silence, complete, we stood
> Just gazing up in the branches
> Hearing the song of the birds
> For love, when its true is an extasy
> That goes Far too deep for words."

[9 July 1943]

> Evenings of July
> "Who does not know these evenings
> Quite divine
> So Rare and Perfect, just about this Time
> The flowers drowsy from the Day's Hot Sun
> Lifting their scented goblets
> And flinging Incense warm upon the breeze
>
> The deep Blue Sky, just shot with Silver Gleam
> Where, behind clouds, there rises the night's queen.
> Sending Her Fairy Light across the flowers
> Oh! what Enchantment lies
> In these rare Hours."

[12 July 1943]

The White Shepherdess
(In memory of the Knole, above Down Farm at Rockbourne in Wiltshire)

165

Among the May Trees White
But, e'er I could get close to her
She vanished from my Sight
A Shepherd's Crook was in Her Hand
Her Dress was Purest White
Her Curls were Blowing in the Wind
She was the Fairest Sight
T'was on a Soft Green Wiltshire Down
In the Gay month of May
I tell you, for some Time perhaps
You too might go that Way
But, I think She was a Vision
Just a Vision of Delight
For each Time that I came
Close to Her
She Vanished from my Sight
[20 September 1943]

In this context, it is interesting that Patricia Crowther informs me that in ancient Greece, one of the names of the Goddess was The White Shepherdess.

The Vision of the Beech Woods
The day I saw you dancing
In that gold October wood
I thought you were a fairy
In your little scarlet hood
I thought the swaying beeches
Made your floating golden hair
And that rose pink spindle berries
Had dyed your cheeks so fair
To your tiny mouth that scarlet hips
Their colour they had lent
All this I thought, while in your dance
You swayed, and turned and bent.
And then I thought "I'll go quite close
And look in to her eyes"
They were purple Autumn violets

And, at once, they made me wise
I knew you were a vision
The loveliest ever seen
But I also knew that you were Real
And of my heart, the Queen.
[27 October 1943]

May Blossom
It snowed last night along the way, it snowed great masses of white May
There never was a sight more fair, there never was a scent more rare
Enchantment fills one with delight to gaze on such a perfect sight
There's just one tree we used to pass, deep in the forest, near the grass
It looked just like a Bridal Veil covered with snow white blossoms frail
We always halted every May to see it in its fair array.
[2 May 1942]

The Dawn Wind
I pass by your Window
When the Fair Dawn is Breaking
My Feet on the Green Turf
Fall softly and Light
The Moonlight grows Paler
The Birds are all Waking
I am the Dawn Wind
I end the Long Night

If you open your Window
And carefully listen
You'll hear my Feet passing
I'm calling the Sun
Aurora is coming

The Night Sky is breaking
With Rose and with Amber
The Day has Begun.

In her Chariot of Fire
On the Wind she is Riding
The Day's Golden Banner
Is Flying Unfurled
A Spear from her Armour
The Night Sky is Breaking

And a Bright Golden arrow
Is tossed o'er the World
[28 August 1943]

There are other Pagan themes as well:

And I will build an Altar to God in every field
And the fragrance of the flowers
The Incense of my Prayers
An open church, where everyone can roam
And the Sky, so blue above, shall be the Dome.
[28 June 1942 - the night of the Full Moon]

The March Hare
Mad as a March Hare, what a shame
That you should have so cruel a name
I love your antics and your Dance
It's Spring - and I shall with you Prance!...
[27 March 1943]

Dorothy expressed some interest in herbs, not always the most obvious ones, which suggests some knowledge of herbal remedies:

Basil and Rosemary, Valerian, Rue
Ready to cure all the ills for you

> *Cowslip, Marigold and Dittany*
> *Such a wonderful Litany!*
> *They're all good, tho' they are old-fashioned*
> *And all of them free and none of them rationed.*
[9 July 1942]

Dorothy also wrote frequently about fairies. I don't know whether she actually saw them, whether she felt that they ought to have been there, or whether they were the means by which she felt best able to express her feelings about Nature. Chewton Glen reminds me very much of Cottingley Glen, in Yorkshire, where in 1917 two cousins, Elsie Wright and Frances Griffiths, claimed to have seen and photographed fairies. They later (over 60 years later!) admitted they faked the photographs, but were always insistent that they had really seen fairies, as had others at the same place.[2] Indeed, I would say that if there was anywhere that one would see fairies, that place would be Chewton Glen. And perhaps Dorothy felt this as well.

Indeed, Dorothy goes further and some of her writing is really a vivid description of the Goddess, albeit under another name. One poem starts with an adaptation from Tennyson's *Maud*:

The Red Rose cries "She is here" "She is here!" The White Rose cries "She is late"

> *I am waiting for my Lady*
> *For, down the pathway shadey*
> *I think I hear her footfall light*
> *My heart beats wildly with delight*
> *But No! its just a Squirrel leaping from tree to tree*
> *She's late! How can I bear it - wherever can she be?*
>
> *I cannot wait - the minutes drag*
> *Just when I'm in despair*
> *Dear Heaven! She is coming! And now She's here! She's here!*

[30 July 1942]

43. Mill House and the stream

It is interesting to note that this is the entry for the day before Lammas Eve.

And what is this next poem but an emotional description of the Goddess?:

> *Of all the Ladies that I know*
> *There's only one can please me so*
> *That all her Looks and all her Ways*
> *Make Music for me all my Days.*
> *For Life, I love her, and adore*
> *I only saw her once - not more*
> *But once I saw her, as I say*

> *But once she crossed my Path, my Way*
> *For Ever. She will be my Queen*
> *Where did I see her? - in a Dream.*

[21 June 1943]

It perhaps comes as no surprise to learn that the Moon features prominently in the diaries:

> *The Forrest now is Silent*
> *No Bird's voice sounds a note*
> *A Hush is over Everything*
> *The Snowflakes Downward Float*
> *The Branche's Frozen Feathers*
> *Like a Silver ostrich Plume*
> *But the most Radiant Vision*
> *Is the Bright December Moon*
> *It Floods the Woods*
> *With its Soft Light*
> *And turns Them*
> *To a Palace Bright*

[26 December 1943]

As a semi-public document, it is clear that the diaries could not be too explicit about Nature Religion, but it is clear that the deepest emotions present in the diaries, apart from those which quite clearly relate to personal relationships, are engendered by Nature, and the expression is equally clearly pagan in content if not openly in terminology.

Dorothy's mother, Ellen, wrote poetry in much the same way as Dorothy and it is clear from the style that Dorothy learned much of her technique from her mother. Ellen also incorporated strong imagery into her poems, which also have a very pagan quality. Dorothy includes several of her mother's poems, taken, as she said, *"from my mother's Book of Verses, written at the Mill"*. For example, take just one line from a lullaby which Ellen had written for Sir Edward Goschen: *"The old world keeps spinning - round the bright Moon"* [Dorothy quotes this on 19 May 1943]. There are quite a lot of implications in that, the main one being that the

Moon would appear to have had just as much significance to Ellen as it did to Dorothy.

> The Debutante
> *This Day*
> *dawned not upon the Earth*
> *As other days have done*
> *A Throng of little virgin clouds*
> *Stood waiting for the Sun*
> *Till the herald winds alined them*
> *And they blushed and stood aside*
> *As the marshalls of the morning*
> *Flung the Eastern Portals wide*
> *So Nature let her Playhouse*
> *For the Play, that May begins*
> *And the stems of all the flowers*
> *Sawed like little violins*
> *In the Dawn, there was a whisper*
> *Of a Presence that was new*
> *For slender spring was at the Wings*
> ......
> *The World was all Attention*
> *And the Pine Trees stood arow*
> *They wear the selfsame colour*
> *Through the summer, through the snow*
> *While the day, below the hillside*
> *Tried her colours one by one*
> *In the clouds experimenting*
> *Till the coming of the Sun*
> *In the vines about my window*
> *Where the sparrows all convine*
> *They were practising a chorus*
> *Which should usher in the Queen*
> *But the sod-imprisoned flowers*
> *The Greatest Secret knew*
> *That Blue-eyed Spring was at the wings*
> *And waiting for her cue*

[1st May 1943]

> The Wishing Well
> [from my mother's verses written at the Mill 1918]
> *"...A' wishing at the Wishing Well*
> *As wise folks should*
> *I saw a sudden Brightness*
> *In the deep green Wood*
> *And something drifted by me*
> *Where the honeysuckle blows*
> *As softly as the petals of a pale wild Rose. ..."*

[17th June 1943]

There are further hints in the diaries which are somewhat difficult to assess. For example, it is clear that, not only were roses Dorothy's favourite flower but she was obsessed with them. She brings in references to them throughout the year, and not just during their flowering season. Moreover, there is a lot of rose imagery in the diaries, often to my mind rather forced or not obviously appropriate:

> *"When the apple and the almond blossom float in rosy rain"*

[17 May 1942 - 2 days after New Moon]

> And then, at Old Lammas, 3 days after New Moon:
> *"Rosey is the West. Rosey is the South,*
> *Roses are her cheeks. And a Rose her mouth."*

> *I sent a Valentine to you*
> *Of Roses, bathed in morning dew*
> *Roses to West, and North and South*
> *A Rosebud like your tiny mouth*

[15 August 1942]

This is an interesting piece as, whilst it follows Dorothy's pattern of a quotation followed by her own verse on the same theme, this is different in that the quotation is not identified. In fact, it is from Tennyson's *"Maud"*. Also, to my mind, it would not seem inappropriate as a circle invocation. The mention of Valentine is interesting. St. Valentine's Day (14th February) is, of course, Old Candlemas and the directly opposite time of year to Old Lammas. The following month, three days after the New Moon, we get, also from "*Maud*":

> "*Her Feet had touched the Meadow and left the Daisies rosey*" Maud

> *Her tiny feet upon the Daisies danced a Minuet*
> *And that is why, on every flower, a rosey stain is set.*
[12 September 1942]

I am struck by the spelling 'rosey'. Now, Dorothy was not very good at spelling, consistently getting words like forest and incense wrong, but certainly nowadays, 'rosy' would be the more usual spelling. It does, however, remind me that in Gardner's Book of Shadows there is a phrase "by thy rosey love", which is very curious. The Farrars comment on it[3] and change it in their version of the ritual, but I suspect that it may be one of the oldest phrases in the Book of Shadows. It is also interesting, in view of the date of the entry in Dorothy's diary, that it is included in the ritual for the festival of Lammas.

Celebration of the "Old" festival dates comes about because when Britain changed from the Julian to the Gregorian calendar in 1752, eleven days needed to be missed out in order to adjust to the seasons as they then were. Many traditional people, seeing how seasonal events such as the opening of the May blossom had not also adjusted, kept to celebrating the Old festivals, so that Old May Eve was on 12th May, Old Hallowe'en on 11th November, and so on.

There is some indication that Dorothy was at least aware of this, for, as well as the extract given above for Old Lammas 1942, her entry for Old Lammas the following year (14th August 1943) referred to the death of William Rufus, which traditionally occurred at Lammas.

Having noticed the amount of rose imagery in Dorothy's diaries, I wondered what its significance might be? An obvious thought is that it has something to do with the Rosicrucians, to whom the image of the rose was highly significant, as we have already seen (Chapter 4). But the rose was also a tantric symbol and the symbol of Venus, the goddess of erotic love. Andrew Chumbley, in writing about one tradition of the Craft, refers to the 'Family of Roseblood'. He doesn't say anything about it, but it is an evocative phrase and there could be some connection.[4] A Roman legend states that the rose originates in the blood of Venus when wounded by Cupid's dart. The rose is also associated with secrecy, and the phrase 'sub rosa' (under the rose) is used when a matter is being dealt with secretly. But we will probably never know whether there was anything in Dorothy's mind beyond a love for and enjoyment of roses for their own sake.

Dorothy was obviously very aware of previous threatened invasions of this country, presumably because of her near-coastal residence and that in 1942-43 the very real threat of invasion was a recent memory. She has a piece about Drake's Drum, which I quote in Chapter 13 and there is an unusual piece which draws attention to the fact that it was on Michaelmas Day that Queen Elizabeth heard of the defeat of the Spanish Armada.

T'was on this Day that Drake himself (who was a Devon man)
Was busy playing bowls on Plymouth Hoe.
And when the news was brought to him
He went on with his game.
And merely said "The Spaniards They must Go"!

And when He'd swept the Seas quite clean
He sent a message to his Queen
Now Elizabeth, at Kenilworth
In Warwick's lovely county
Was at a Banquet of Roast Goose
Served by Lord Warwick's bounty
"Now on this glorious Day" cried she
"Let Goose forever eaten be"!

And then the Queen called for a glass of Burgundy's red wine
"My Lords and Ladies, Rise" she said "and drink before you dine"
"To Drake and all his gallant fleet
who've made the Spaniards' winding sheet"
[29 September 1942]

Dorothy adds: "*For many years this toast was given to Queen Elizabeth and the Armada on this day by the host at the Fordham Houses, and drunk in Burgundy, at Michaelmas Lunch ... of Roast Goose*"

There is much more in the diaries which is worthy of close scrutiny. I very much hope that it will be possible at some stage to have them published, not just so that this research material can be made more widely available, but because of their intrinsic qualities and beauty.

What conclusions can we draw from an examination of the diaries? Well, I would submit that they do not answer the big question in many people's minds: "Was Dorothy a witch?" In asking such a question, we need to be quite clear that they are far from being secret diaries: they were meant to be looked at by visitors and consequently any evidence of the Craft would not have been too obvious.

Nevertheless, we might expect hints and I would suggest that they are there in abundance. The almost complete absence of Christian imagery and observance, and the presence of a strong and deeply-felt pagan expression seems to me so clear that I could not reasonably ask for anything more. It is clear from the diaries that Dorothy was a pagan in all but name, and so was her mother. To answer the question as to whether she was also a witch we need to look elsewhere.

In the interim, and having 'set the scene', we are now ready to look again at Gardner's initiation in the light of what we have learned of Dorothy and Mill House.

Chapter 12
Initiation

In one sense, the event described in this chapter represents the heart of the book - Gardner's claim to have been initiated into a surviving witchcraft tradition. Yet this is the very event that we have most difficulty in finding out what happened. Perhaps this is as it should be, for initiations are to this day secret rituals.

Let us see what has actually been written, and again we rely largely on Bracelin, who tells the story as follows:

Gardner felt delighted that he was to be let into their secret. Thus it was that, a few days after the war had started, he was taken to a big house in the neighbourhood. This belonged to "Old Dorothy" - a lady of note in the district, "county" and very well-to-do. She invariably wore a pearl necklace, worth some £5,000 at the time.

It was in this house that he was initiated into witchcraft. He was very amused at first, when he was stripped naked and brought into a place "properly prepared" to undergo his initiation.

It was halfway through when the word Wica was first mentioned: "and I knew that that which I had thought burnt out hundreds of years ago still survived".[1]

One wonders from this how much Gardner knew of what was going to be happening. Bracelin says:

He felt sure that they had some secret, there must be something which allowed them to take the slights at the theatre without really caring. He still thought that they might be mooting Yoga, or something of that nature.[2]

So he knew that he was to be 'let into their secret' but he claimed afterwards that he didn't know what it was. He was amused, and therefore presumably surprised but accepting, at being stripped naked, and it was only half way through the proceedings, when the word 'Wica' was mentioned, that he realised what was going on. I think it shows something of the trust which he put in those whom he considered to be his friends that he went along with all that might happen. It is also, it must be said, a rather different approach to initiation than that which would usually be taken nowadays, when it would be made very clear in advance to anyone what it was that they were being initiated into.

We do not know the exact date, but Bracelin does say "a few days after the war had started". This happened on 3rd September 1939, so we may assume that it was some time during that month. Patricia Crowther suggests that it may have been on the night of the new moon, which was Wednesday 13th September.

There is an inconsistency of chronology in Bracelin's account. In Chapter 8, I mention that one of the witches told Gardner that they had known each other in a previous lifetime, and that another of them described a scene exactly like one in *A Goddess Arrives*, which was not published until the following week.

If Edith Woodford-Grimes had been helping Gardner with the book, it would be easy enough for her to have told them about the scene in advance, suggesting that Gardner's surprise may have been because the Masons and Edith did not acknowledge each other openly at Crotona Fellowship meetings.

Leaving aside this point, the incident is certainly reported as having taken place before Gardner's initiation. Now, if, as I believe I have demonstrated, *A Goddess Arrives* was not published until early December 1939, Gardner could not then have been initiated in the September.

I point this out as an inconsistency, for which there are several possible explanations, the most obvious being Gardner's memory of the sequence of events after a gap of 20 years or Shah's misinterpretation of what Gardner told him.

One interesting thing about that account, however, is something else. It has been stated numerous times that Gardner was initiated by Dorothy Clutterbuck ("Old Dorothy"). I want to point out that nowhere in the above account does it say so. It merely says that he was initiated. Indeed, the wording used suggests strongly to me that Dorothy wasn't actually present. Note the wording - "the house 'belonged to' Old Dorothy; She 'invariably wore' a pearl necklace".

Whilst one might refer familiarly to someone as "Old so-and-so" one wouldn't be introduced to them in that way. "Old Dorothy" is just the sort of epithet that one applies to someone who is not actually there. I submit that if Dorothy had been present, the book would have said something like: "He met a lady called Dorothy Clutterbuck ..." and would then proceed to give his impressions of her. It seems clear to me that Gardner's friends were talking about someone who was known to them but a little bit distant - not one of their regular companions. Also there is the implication that she was a senior figure in some way, both in age and in rank - "old" in experience and knowledge and one who was entitled to considerable respect. And "Old Dorothy" is a convenient way to refer to someone without giving too much away.

Bracelin does not give Dorothy's surname. When *Gerald Gardner: Witch* was published, it was only nine years since Dorothy died, and a certain degree of caution was probably felt desirable. Indeed, it was not for another 24 years, in 1984, when the Farrars' *The Witches' Way*[3] was published, that her surnames of Clutterbuck and Fordham were made generally known.

It has been pointed out that Dorothy was only some four years older than Gardner and only slightly older than some of the others whom he met. This, however, is, in my opinion, no bar to her being referred to as "old". From my own experience, friends who are 20 or even 30 years younger than me seem to be closer to my age than those who may be only two or three years older, who often appear to be of my parents' generation. It is my guess that this applied equally in Gardner's day.

Then again, Bracelin says that the house "belonged to" Old Dorothy. If she was actually there, living in the house, one would be unlikely to use that phrase. You'd probably just say something like "He was taken to meet Dorothy Clutterbuck. Her house was a big one ..." However, if the owner was not present, the phrase "belonged to" might well be applied. Also, the phrase, "she invariably wore ..." suggests to me hearsay - what Gardner had been told - rather than direct experience of her. But it may be that Gardner's original words were different and that Shah has introduced subtleties not present in the original account. I merely point out that Gardner never said, certainly in his published writings, that he was initiated by Old Dorothy.

Leaving this aside for the moment, and taking Bracelin's account at face value, where exactly was Gardner initiated? Dorothy owned three houses in the Highcliffe neighbourhood - Mill House, Latimers and Amberwood Farm. I think we can discount Amberwood Farm. Whilst it was owned by Dorothy, it was let as a working farm and the relationship seems to have been a purely financial one. Referring to Latimers, Ronald Hutton writes: "... this was apparently the big house at which Gardner claimed to have been initiated into witchcraft."[4]

Hutton does not present any evidence to back Latimers rather than Mill House. In objective terms it is, or rather was (it was demolished in about 1969 or 1970) not much bigger than Mill House. And it is Mill House whose photograph appears in Janet and Stewart Farrar's *The Witches' Way* under the caption "The house on the edge of the New Forest where Dorothy Clutterbuck initiated Gerald Gardner."[5]

I suppose I had first read Gardner's *Witchcraft Today*[6] in about 1959 and followed it up with *The Meaning of Witchcraft*[7] in the early 1960s. In them, I had read of Gardner's claims to have been initiated into the Craft. As we will see, he gives very little detail, but it is generally acknowledged that one of the joys of reading is the way in which our imagination seems to conjure up images for us. And so, when reading and thinking about Gardner's initiation, an image regularly came to my mind of a fairly large house with a secluded garden, a rectangular room with windows looking out

44. *Mill House in 1998*

onto the garden along its longer dimension. The room seemed to be sunken in some way, as if one went down into it, and it had seating around the edge with a clear area in the middle for dancing. There was an open fire on one of the shorter walls. I didn't pay any particular attention to this image, thinking of it merely as one of those scenes which naturally spring up when one is reading stimulating material.

On one of my research trips, it had been arranged for me to visit Mill House and to meet the present owner and his family. It was something I was very much looking forward to. On my previous trip, I had merely walked down as far as the entrance gate and taken the obligatory photograph from the same angle as that which appears in *The Witches' Way*. Now, I was to cross the threshold!

As I entered the porch I felt enveloped by a warm and comforting

45. The Porch, Mill House

*46. Mill House.
The room where Gardner may have been initiated*

feeling, which seemed to be physical, mental, emotional and spiritual all at the same time. It felt welcoming and also gave me the same sort of feeling that I get at certain old places, both buildings and natural sites, which have an association with witchcraft. It was also the same feeling which I often get in rituals where what Evan John Jones calls "The Hidden Company"[8] - those members of the Craft who have gone before us - turns up to witness our rites. And it was very much the same feeling which I get on reading the passages in Gardner's writings where he is telling us what the witches that he met believed, felt and did. It was really a feeling of pure joy.

The feeling was so strong and unexpected that I do not think it was engendered by my expectations on entering a house that was reputed to have played an important part in the history of the Craft. So I was in some changed state of consciousness as I entered the house itself, into one room, which felt like a sort of ante-room, and then down a short flight of steps and I was in the 'sunken room' with the open fire at one end and the windows looking out onto the garden: it was the room of my imagination!

I knew at that instant that here was where Gerald Gardner was initiated. Whether 'Old Dorothy' was involved was a separate issue which could be tackled separately. Now, this may not mean anything or be at all convincing to anyone else, but the experience of being in Mill House certainly made me absolutely convinced that it was here that Gardner was initiated.

And, of course, Mill House has ghosts. The present occupants tell of several experiences of this sort - nothing unpleasant, but adding to the atmosphere of the place. Indeed, it would have been mildly surprising if they had said they had not experienced ghosts in that place. They invited me to stay overnight in one of the bedrooms where ghosts had been experienced. I'm sorry to report that, apart from having a very good night's sleep, I didn't feel anything out of the ordinary!

However, a Wiccan Priestess of my acquaintance tells me that when she first visited the Mill House, she clearly saw the ghost of a young man dressed in early 20th Century clothing, before anyone had even told her that the house was haunted.

What do we know of the initiation ritual which Gardner went through? Actually, very little, from his writings. Let us see what he says:

He was very amused at first, when he was stripped naked and brought into a place "properly prepared" to undergo his initiation. It was half way through when the word Wica was first mentioned ...[9]

...I soon found myself in the circle and took the usual oaths of secrecy which bound me not to reveal any secrets of the cult.[10]

And that is it!

However, we can tell something from this. It was clearly not obvious that witchcraft was involved until half way through when the word 'Wica' was used. Now, this is not true of the ritual given by Gardner in his novel *High Magic's Aid*[11], nor of the ritual commonly used nowadays in Gardnerian covens. 'Witch' and 'witchcraft' are mentioned early on: conversely, 'Wica' or 'Wicca' are not mentioned once.

This, in itself, is enough to make it clear that Gardner was not, in *High Magic's Aid*, merely using the initiation ritual by which he himself was initiated.

I suspect quite strongly that the initiation that Gardner went through consisted of a few traditional elements plus material that was either spontaneous or specially made up for the occasion. We have to remember that Gardner's first impression of the Craft was of something in decline. It may well be that his was the first initiation in that particular group for many years. If, as I suspect, nothing was really written down, then it would only be the strongest traditional elements, and the things that were done rather than said that would be most likely to be remembered and used again.

Being undoubtedly in a state of excitement, Gardner would not have remembered all the details of the initiation, though I suspect that, as soon as he could after the ritual, he would have written down what he could remember. It is quite possible that, with one exception, he was the last ever to be initiated into that particular group, which may have held no further meetings following the momentous 1940 invasion ritual.

What else does Gardner say about his initiation?:

... I was half-initiated before the word "Wica" which they used hit me like a thunderbolt, and I knew where I was, and that the Old Religion still existed. And so I found myself in the Circle, and there took the usual oath of secrecy, which bound me not to reveal certain things.[12]

Gardner also writes that the witches used to talk of 'belonging', without ever adding to what, and they used to talk about being 'inside', meaning the same thing. Initiation was seen as 'bringing someone in'.

In fact, the main point which Gardner makes about initiation is not about details of ritual but the whole purpose of it, which is the passing on of power. He refers to this in the following passage:

The witches tell me: "The law always has been that power must be passed from man to woman or from woman to man, the only exception being when a mother initiates her daughter or a father his son, because they are a part of themselves." (The reason is that great love is apt to occur between people who go through the rites together.)[13]

I suspect that it is the actions rather than the words of the initiation that Gardner would have remembered most clearly. In *Witchcraft Today*, he says: "At her initiation a witch is always received into the circle with a kiss on the mouth."[14] He gives a more detailed account in *High Magic's Aid*, and it is so distinctive that it strikes me as being genuinely old:

... going behind him she blindfolded him, then clasping him from behind with her left arm around his waist, and pulling his right arm around her neck, and his lips down to hers, said: "I give you the third password; a kiss." So saying she pushed him forward with her body, through the doorway, into the Circle. Once inside she released him whispering. "This is the way all are first brought into the Circle."[15]

Bracelin writes of Gardner:

Until then his opinion of witchcraft had been based upon the idea that witches killed for the purpose of gaining or raising power, and he had thought the persecutions of them fully justified. [16]

That this was indeed Gardner's view is supported by the text of *A Goddess Arrives*, some of which I quote in Chapter 3. So, the witches contradicted Gardner's pre-conceived ideas on the Craft, and this was far from being the last occasion on which they had to do this.

Bracelin gives the only other written details of Gardner's initiation, when he quotes him as saying: "*It was, I think, the most wonderful night of my life. In true witch fashion we had a dance afterwards, and kept it up until dawn.*"[17]

Now, I have come to know Highcliffe quite well during my various research trips for ths book, and there are few houses where one could have a dance going on until dawn without drawing any attention, and one of these is Mill House. Olive Samuel says of it: "*It is hidden from sight of roads and properties nearby and is situated in seclusion surrounded by trees on the banks of Chewton Bunny.*"[18]

Having examined what material we can, we are still left facing a very misty image when trying to look at Gardner's initiation. Perhaps this is as it should be - it was, after all, a secret ritual, as initiations still are today. Should Gardner's be any different because of the role which he was to play in the survival of the Craft? I have already indicated the venue and several of those who may have been present. Perhaps the veil should be allowed to remain.

Chapter 13
Old Dorothy - High Priestess or Red Herring?

We now have at least some of the facts about Dorothy's life and know what Gardner is supposed to have said about her. And we can now ask the question as to whether she was a witch, someone who let the witches use her house, or someone who had no connection with the Craft at all but whom Gardner implicated for reasons best known to himself.

She is the only one Bracelin mentions by name, so let us see what he has to say about her. He mentions 'Old Dorothy' just three times. We have already seen her referred to as the owner of the house in which Gardner was initiated. The second reference is as follows:

He [Gardner] found that his friends, after following Mabs to her settlement, had discovered an old Coven, and remained here because of that. "I found that Old Dorothy and some like her, plus a number of New Forest people, had kept the light shining."[1]

The last sentence, the one about 'Old Dorothy', is in quotation marks - those were the actual words which Gardner used, so they can legitimately be given due weight. The question of whether there was anything which could reasonably be called 'the New Forest Coven' is something we will be looking at in the next chapter. But for the moment all we need to note is that this statement unambiguously pronounces Old Dorothy's involvement with the Craft - one of only two statements in Gardner's own words to do so. I take that very poetic phrase 'kept the light shining' to imply that Dorothy had been true to the spirit of the Craft through difficult times and that she had therefore been involved for quite a few years.

I think we have to take these statements of Gardner's seriously. In my experience in researching this book, he was not someone who made up complete stories - the essential facts are likely to be true. But if it is true, then where and when did Dorothy become involved in the Craft? In India? Oxfordshire? Or, indeed, in Highcliffe? Was there a family link with the tradition that the Masons espoused going back to the 1830s, when Dorothy's grandparents lived in Southampton, or to the 1840s and 1850s, when Dorothy's father was a child in the Southampton area?

The link with Southampton back to the 1830s is an intriguing one, suggesting that the Clutterbucks themselves could have been part of the same hereditary Craft tradition as that within the Mason family, who were living in the same area at the same time. Much more investigation is clearly needed.

The third quotation from Bracelin is in the context of the proposed magical working to stop the threatened invasion in 1940:

Old Dorothy called up "covens right and left; although by Witch Law they should not be known to each other".[2]

We shall be looking at this in detail in Chapter 16 but for the present purposes we need to note that Gardner is stating here that Old Dorothy was the one who was calling up the covens. There is therefore the clear implication that she was 'in charge', whether she used the term 'High Priestess' or not. There is also the implication that she knew of the existence of at least two other groups which would generally not be known to each other, which implies a long acquaintance with such matters and with the local area. Sybil Leek has referred to four covens in the New Forest area and Gardner also spoke of other covens, though it is, of course, quite possible that the "covens right and left" might have been located quite a distance from the New Forest.

Gardner spoke frequently about Old Dorothy to those who knew him. Patricia Crowther remembers that when she first knew Gardner, in the late 1950s, he used to refer, rather mysteriously, to "Aunt Agatha" and that it was only later that he began to talk more openly about Old Dorothy. She is quite clear in stating that

Gardner told her that Old Dorothy had been the High Priestess[3]. Doreen Valiente says that Gardner often used to talk to her about Old Dorothy.[4]

There have been those who have been dismissive of Gardner's story ever since *Gerald Gardner: Witch* first appeared in 1960. The criticism that Old Dorothy never existed was clearly countered by Doreen Valiente in her Appendix to the Farrars' *The Witches' Way*, published in 1984. But more recently there have been suggestions that Dorothy was never involved in the Craft at all and that Gardner used her name in order to draw attention away from 'Dafo'.

This argument does not really stand up to serious scrutiny. First of all, it was only in 1960 that mention of 'Old Dorothy' first appeared in print: this was well after the press investigations that took place in the 1950s. Surely, if Gardner had wanted to draw attention away from Dafo, he would have done it then. Despite his liking for publicity in some aspects of the Craft, Gardner was always very careful to protect the identity of the witches that he knew. To state that someone was a witch who in fact had nothing to do with the Craft would not only be out of character for someone like Gardner who took his religion seriously, but would also hardly achieve the objectives attributed to him.

Gardner's own statements and the statements of those who knew him well must be given due weight, but is there any independent evidence which would enable us to assess Dorothy's role in the whole thing. We need to be asking two questions. Is there anything inherently unlikely in Dorothy being involved in the Craft? And is there any independent evidence for such involvement or which would make such involvement more likely?

I have only really begun to scratch the surface of evidence about Dorothy. I am sure that there is a wealth of information waiting to be discovered.

All I can attempt here is to address a few of the more obvious points whilst fully appreciating the inadequacy of the material presented.

Dorothy's Character

What sort of person was Dorothy? She was certainly someone who was sensitive to her environment, noticing subtleties and oddities, communicating her feelings effectively and without effort. The most obvious manifestation of this is, of course, the Diaries.

Dorothy also liked to be the centre of attention, possibly originating in her early life in India, but certainly illustrated by her central role in the Mill House Players, as producer, director and lead actor in the proceedings. There is a tale told by those who lived in Highcliffe at the same time as Dorothy, that she used to arrive in her chauffeur-driven car outside the local shops and sit there waiting for the shopkeeper to come out and serve her. Perhaps this only happened on one occasion, and perhaps she was incapacitated in some way at the time, but this sort of story seems to indicate a common attitude to her in later life. In other words, that she put on airs, and was living somewhat above her true station in life.

She could certainly be secretive when she wanted to be. The whole business of her marriage to Rupert illustrates that, and I am still not clear why the marriage ceremony took place. One interesting thing in connection with it, however, is that, on the marriage certificate, Dorothy gave her age as 42 years: in fact, she was 55. Now, I know that women of that period were apt to "adjust" their age a bit, but an alteration of 13 years on a legal (though invalid!) document shows that she was quite capable of being less than truthful if she had the mind to.

Dorothy was also someone who might swing suddenly between her normal state of passivity and, on rare occasions, losing her temper so that others would certainly know about it.

She could also be quite determined and decisive. One example of this is the case of Charles Edward Byron Du Cane (1910-1996). He was in the R.A.F. during the war and it is obvious from Dorothy's diaries that she had got to know him very well indeed before he was sent abroad to India. In her will dated July 1949, she left him £5000, plus paintings, silver and her cars. In a codicil dated January 1950, she revokes this completely. The reason for this action is not known: he obviously displeased Dorothy in quite a serious way. One can only speculate.

There is a post-script to this. When Dorothy's diaries were on display in Bournemouth and there was some publicity in the local paper, those who were exhibiting them received a telephone call from a Mr. Du Cane, who said that they were "as green as grass about Mrs. Fordham" and that the best thing they could do with the diaries was to burn them.

There are many other aspects to Dorothy's character. I hope that the chapter on her Diaries has given some impression of her, but she seems to me to have been a complex person, and I suspect that she only really revealed her true character to those who got to know her well.

Dorothy's Relationship to the Church

In the 19th Century it was expected that suitable professions for men setting out on a career would be the army, the church and, probably, very little more. So it is hardly surprising that Dorothy's great-uncle, uncle and cousin all became clergymen. And her companion, Elizabeth Slatter, was also the daughter of a clergyman. This did not, of itself, imply a specially Christian family.

On 23rd January 1939, Dorothy Fordham sent her apologies to the St. Mark's Church and Vestry meeting[5]. This seemed to be the equivalent of an Annual General Meeting, where an account of the Church finances for the year were given and officers were (in most cases) re-elected. I have looked through copies of the *Christchurch Times* for 1935 through to 1942 and, though I may well have missed some, I can find no other reference to Dorothy in connection with the Church. There are plenty of references to her role in the Conservative Party and the local Horticultural Society, but this is the only one I have found in connection with the Church.

The thing to note about that particular meeting is that, as the equivalent of an A.G.M., it would be open to all members of the Church to attend. Not only did Dorothy not have, as far as I have been able to find, any formal post in the Church, but the only time she is mentioned is to send her apologies (probably the result of her car accident earlier that month). Dorothy was undoubtedly a member of the Church, but on the basis of the evidence not a particularly enthusiastic or committed one.

I think we need to understand what society was like in an English village before the last war. People went to church. It wasn't so much that they were expected to and would be frowned on if they didn't, as that it never occurred to them not to do so. It was just something that one did: one's personal beliefs didn't really enter into it.

Rupert Fordham's gravestone is an impressive feature in Highcliffe churchyard. It is a Celtic cross, at least ten feet in height, on a large base stone on which the following inscription is given:

> IN EVER DEAREST
> AND MOST BELOVED MEMORY OF
> RUPERT OSWALD
> DEEPLY LOVED HUSBAND OF
> DOROTHY ST. QUINTIN FORDHAM
> WHO PASSED AWAY MAY 31ST 1939
> AGED 77 YEARS
>
> AND THEY SHALL BE MINE SAITH THE LORD OF
> HOSTS IN THAT DAY WHEN I MAKE UP MY JEWELS
>
>
> O LORD SUPPORT US ALL THE DAY LONG OF THIS
> TROUBLOUS LIFE UNTIL THE SHADES LENGTHEN AND
> THE EVENING COMES THE BUSY WORLD IS HUSHED THE
> FEVER OF LIFE IS OVER AND OUR WORK IS DONE THEN LORD
> IN THY MERCY GRANT US SAFE LODGING A HOLY REST AND
> PEACE AT THE LAST THROUGH JESUS CHRIST OUR LORD

47. *Rupert Fordham's Gravestone*
Churchyard, St Mark's Church, Highcliffe

Ronald Hutton calls this "*one of the longest and most impassioned affirmations of faith in salvation through Jesus Christ which I have ever read upon any funerary monument*"[6], imputing such sentiments to Dorothy.

The latter part is a prayer which is adapted from 'Wisdom and Innocence' in *Sermons Bearing on Subjects of the Day (1843) no. 20.* by John Henry Newman (1801-90), the English theologian, leader of the Oxford Movement and later Cardinal. It is incorporated into prayer books and has become one which regular churchgoers would have been likely to know by heart. I don't think it can really be called an "affirmation of faith", as it seems more like a rather evocative view of the closeness of divinity throughout life. In any case, I think it is wrong to assume that these were necessarily Dorothy's own feelings: it was Rupert's gravestone, and if she chose the wording it was surely something that she knew he would have liked and been familiar with, even if they had not agreed it beforehand.

The first two lines are different - they are from Malachi 3.17 [7] and are also quoted on Dorothy's mother's gravestone, so I think they are very likely to be Dorothy's choice. The main point about the evidence of gravestones, however, is that it is reasonable to suppose that they do not represent the beliefs of the one

*48. Thomas and Ellen Clutterbuck's Gravestones
Churchyard, St. Mark's Church, Highcliffe*

commissioning the stone so much as what they think the one who has died would want.

Dorothy bequeathed £1000 to the Reverend Henry Brownlow, Vicar of Highcliffe. Some have seen this as indicating a close friendship between them, but I think it really needs to be put in context. She also left £500 to her doctor, £200 to her bank manager, a cottage to her solicitor and £5000 in trust for his children. To each of her staff she gave bequests, two of £2000, two of £1000 and several of between £300 and £500. The point is that it was not so much that Henry Brownlow was a close personal friend, but that Dorothy thought it right to leave a legacy to the vicar in the same way as she left them to her doctor, solicitor, bank manager and all her staff. I don't think it meant anything more than that.

The name "Brownlow" interested me initially in that Cecil Williamson claimed that Mrs. Woodford Grimes had sent a "Mrs. Brownlow" to the Isle of Man to negotiate with Williamson over some documents. However, Henry Brownlow was not married and I have been unable to find any connection with him.

Dorothy expressed a desire in her will for her body to be cremated and for her ashes to be buried in Rupert's grave, and I have no reason to doubt that this was carried out. There is, however, no gravestone to her, or any addition to Rupert's gravestone, nor any other monument or memorial. It seems very strange that one of the most prominent members of Highcliffe society should have no memorial. It is true that Dorothy had no close family, but it seems unusual that none of her friends, nor any of the organisations that she supported, none of those to whom she left relatively large sums of money, not even Henry Brownlow, should have felt it appropriate to add a simple inscription or stone to Rupert's grave. Indeed, Dorothy's bigamous marriage to Rupert in a Register Office strikes me as being unexpected for a committed member of the Church of England.

The Evidence of the Wrist-Watch
In her will, Dorothy left to her former nurse, Eliza Kirtley, £4000. She also left her furs, etc. and a diamond wrist-watch, engraved "August 5th, 1935".

Now, this is interesting as the date is three days before 8th August 1935, the date of her marriage ceremony. It is very strange that it should be three days before, and some have speculated that it could have commemorated a witch 'handfasting' followed by the legal ceremony three days later.

Gareth Medway has another explanation, which he admits is a rather wild speculation:

"... supposing they first got together in 1931. Then they might have decided on a 'year and a day' marriage, which in Gaelic custom could be done at Lughnasadh, 1 August (though sometimes 31 July). If they decided to renew their contract annually this would take them up to 5 August 1935, though they could perhaps not get the registry office for the exact day."[8]

Now, what he did not know when he wrote that piece is that Dorothy and Rupert did indeed get together in 1931. However, despite this, I have to say that I think the most likely explanation is a legal clerk's typing error and that the wrist watch actually had "August 8th, 1935" engraved on it. In the absence of the watch itself, we will probably never know.

The Evidence of the Museum Displays
We need to jump forward a bit, to the early 1950s, when Gardner was Director of the Museum of Magic and Witchcraft in the Isle of Man.

One of the museum showcases (No. 1) had the following inscription:

"A large number of objects belonging to a witch who died in 1951, lent by her relatives, who wish to remain anonymous. These are mostly things which had been used in the family for generations.

Most of them are for making herbal cures ... She had a very fine ritual sword, which for many years was lent to the Druid Order which holds its annual Midsummer ceremony at Stonehenge, because it fitted exactly into the cleft in the Hele Stone."[9]

It was this, re-read by Doreen Valiente many years later, that enabled her to find Dorothy's death certificate, for Dorothy did indeed die in 1951.

For many years, there has been little doubt expressed that the caption referred to, and therefore by implication the contents of the display had belonged to, Old Dorothy. However, Gareth Medway has drawn my attention to the existence of an earlier caption. This was mentioned in an article by Daniel P. Mannix, who visited the Museum and interviewed Gardner in about 1959. He wrote:

I saw a large wooden box looking somewhat like an overgrown vanity case, which was opened to show a miscellany of vials, charms, talismans, and tiny knives with cabalistic signs inscribed on their blades. Below the box was a sign reading:

"As a tribute to Aunt Agatha, one of our most outstanding witches, this collection of paraphernalia which she used is affectionately dedicated. Presented by her family in loving memory, 1951".[10]

Gardner also told Mannix:

"Aunt Agatha" also had a very fine ritual sword, but we've lent that to the Druid Order for their annual midsummer ceremony at Stonehenge because it fits exactly into the cleft of the Hele Stone."

Now, this is very interesting because of how the earlier version differs from the later one. Note, for example, that it gives the former owner a name, albeit a pseudonym, whereas the later version does not. (It may be that, on searching round for a pseudonym, Gardner picked on the character of "Aunt Agatha", who appears in P.G. Wodehouse's *The Inimitable Jeeves* (1923), a formidable figure with which Gardner was doubtless familiar.)

Also, she is described as "one of our most outstanding witches" whereas the later version merely calls her a witch. The use of the word "our" and her description as "outstanding" both suggest that she was someone known to the caption-writer (presumably Gardner) well enough to be able to use those terms.

Perhaps one of the most significant differences is that there is no mention of her year of death in the earlier version, merely a date, which could reasonably be interpreted as the year when the collection was presented to the museum. It is indeed quite possible that the "paraphernalia" had been kept by her family for several years before they decided to donate it to the museum, which opened in 1951.

Any museum attracts to itself a large number of donations of material, and whilst it could be that the box and its contents had no direct connection with Gardner at all, this is actually unlikely in this case for the reasons noted above. We have also already noted that when Patricia Crowther first met Gardner, he used to refer rather mysteriously to "Aunt Agatha".

The most likely owner of this paraphernalia was Dorothy Clutterbuck. She did not have any family at the time of her death who could have made such a donation, although it has been suggested that the "family" referred to was in fact her "witch family" rather than a family in the usual sense of the term.

One family which I have suggested was involved in the Craft was the Mason family, and it is possible that "Aunt Agatha" was Rosetta Mason (29 August 1861 - 3 March 1943), the wife of George Miles Mason, and the mother of Ernie Mason, Susie Mason and Rosetta Fudge. Another possibility is Anne Eliza Oldmeadow, whom I discuss in the next chapter. She certainly had a family who may have been involved in the Craft, she did die in 1951 and she was a close friend of Dorothy's.

The Evidence of the Diaries

My conclusion to the previous chapter was that, judging from the material in her diaries, Dorothy was a pagan in all but name. It may be worth emphasising that my evidence for this consisted of two elements - a record of deep spiritual experience through Nature and, conversely, the lack of a conventional Christian interpretation of the annual festivals, including a total absence of any mention of Jesus.

There are, however, certain very interesting and specific items in the diaries which are very suggestive of possible involvement in the Craft, if nothing more.

Let us look at Dorothy's diary entries for the very end of 1942. She calls Wednesday 30th December "The Last of This Year's many Days", and she calls Thursday 31st December "New Year's Day". Why should she make what appear to be obvious mistakes? Could it be an allusion to the fact that in older teachings the festival traditionally starts at sunset on the previous day? As Gardner says: "It is noteworthy that, being a moon cult, they [i.e. the witches] celebrate the night before the day of the festival."[11] So Dorothy, writing in the evening, could write what she did perfectly correctly.

On Thursday 21st January 1943, Dorothy wrote what might be called a fairy tale in verse entitled "The Snow Princess". It tells of how a prince and princess are turned into trees by a being variously described once as a 'wicked fairy' and twice as a 'wicked one'. Now Dorothy liked fairies - she wrote sympathetically about them - and yet in this tale she wrote about a 'wicked fairy'.

Might there have been anything that stopped her from using the word that has (wrongly) been universally applied in fairy tales to such a wicked being - the word 'witch'?

It has been suggested that the use of the phrases "Wise Man" (for her chauffeur, Hudson) and "Wizard with a Wand" (for her gardener, Griffin) in Dorothy's diaries may have been a subtle indication of their involvement in the Craft. The page of her 1942 diary which relates to them is reproduced as Illustration 40. At present we really do not know enough to make any kind of judgement about this, but it remains an intriguing possibility.

There is a lot more evidence in Dorothy's diaries which could, with close examination, be drawn out, and I hope to produce a more detailed analysis of them in due course.

The Evidence of Mill House

Is there anything in Mill House which might suggest Dorothy's involvement with the Craft?

I have already recounted the experience which convinced me to my own satisfaction that Gardner had been initiated at Mill House. But it was the atmosphere there which struck me - not something

49. Ram's Head Chimneypiece, Mill House

that would have been retained from one meeting. In some ways it was like the atmosphere you get in an old church, where it is the repetition of worship and devotions over perhaps hundreds of years which builds up the strong sense of presence. I got the definite feeling that Mill House had been used for witch rituals on numerous occasions, and it was the feeling that these had generated which I was picking up.

It is clear that some time between the compilation of the 1936 and 1937 Electoral Registers, Dorothy and Rupert and the staff moved their 'centre of operations' from Mill House to Latimers. This left Mill House empty, though it is likely that at least one of the staff, probably Walter Lloyd, was kept on there for maintenance and gardening purposes. Dorothy's diary entry for 5th December 1942 is entitled "*To Lloyd of the Mill*":

> *For Years and Years, with Heart and Will,*
> *Lloyd has worked daily at the Mill.*
> *With all His Heart, He loves the Place,*
> *With all its most enchanting Grace.*
> *It's always been just His "Own Place"*
> *And dearly does it love Him too.*
> *For always to it He's been True*
> *And all Day long when He's not here,*
> *We see Him with his Flowers Fair.*
> *Tho' for a Time, He's now away,*
> *The Mill will see Him back one Day.*

Presumably, Lloyd had gone away on military service, but there is no evidence to suggest that he ever did return.

The absence of any residents at the Mill House and its relative isolation made it ideal for both indoor and outdoor rituals. I am not suggesting, and I do not think it would be possible, for such rituals to have taken place without Dorothy's (or, indeed, without Lloyd's) knowledge.

Mill House (now a Grade II Listed Building) is an interesting historic building which has been altered and added to over the years, as we have seen.

Ronald Hutton tells the story of the chimney piece which was said to have a carving of a goddess between two goats' heads[12]. They were in fact a cameo of a woman's head with a ram's head at either end. Nevertheless, they are very striking (as can be seen from Illustration 49). This in fact is in the 1931 extension that Dorothy had built prior to Rupert moving in to Mill House. The room is somewhat separate from the rest of the house, having an attached toilet and access only via the Mill Room. It is wood panelled in cedar and is clearly not intended as a Sitting Room for the self-contained accommodation above, for that has one of its own. The chimney piece is, according to the 1953 sale catalogue, in cedar, is probably Victorian and must therefore have been moved from somewhere else, possibly from Broom Hall, Rupert's previous house. In fact, ram's head decoration would be particularly appropriate for Rupert, whose birthday on 23rd March means that, astrologically, his Sun would be in the sign of Aries, the ram. The rams' heads are very striking and, together with oak leaf and acorn decoration on the pilasters, would form a focal point which I would imagine that most pagans and witches would think highly appropriate for a ritual temple.

Some have commented that the circular bay window which Dorothy had added, and which is a prominent feature in most of the photographs, could act as a sort of 'lookout post', but that it would also enable a magic circle to be cast within the adjacent room. The bay does have an internal diameter of 9 feet, which is the standard size which witches now use.

It has been pointed out to me that there is a low brick wall and adjacent concrete surface behind the garage building which would make a fine and secluded ritual area.[13]

Others have commented on the poem on the wall that I quoted in Chapter 10 and have noted the similarity in style between this and the poem found by Gardner in a witch's book which seems to be an adaptation of a poem by Aleister Crowley.

Conclusion

I posed two questions in this chapter. To attempt to answer them, I would say that there was nothing in Dorothy's way of life that would make it inherently unlikely that she was a witch. Indeed, to the contrary, there is a significant body of evidence in her diaries, and intriguing hints elsewhere, to suggest a philosophy of life in harmony with that of the Craft.

I have found nothing which would contradict Gardner's statement that Dorothy was a member of the Craft, but neither have I found the unequivocal independent evidence that she was. It is my opinion that Dorothy would have to have known about what was going on and have been sympathetic to it, if she let them use Mill House. But on the basis of the evidence presented so far, I have not so far proved to my own satisfaction that she was directly involved at the time Gardner was initiated, though she may have had some family connection. But this is only a tentative conclusion and I am always open to new evidence which might prove me wrong!

And yet, the name 'Dorothy Clutterbuck' sounds like a witch's name! Her handwriting has been described as 'witchy' and her capital D's are like moon symbols and very striking. Her house and garden in the glen are all that a witch's house should be. So, it is not unlikely that she might have been considered a witch by local residents. Indeed, if she wasn't a witch, then she certainly ought to have been! Then again, she might actually have been one!

Time, and further research, I am convinced, will tell.

Chapter 14
The New Forest Coven?

One of the elements of the 'myth' of modern witchcraft is that Gardner was initiated into what has become known as "The New Forest Coven".

Did this ever exist? And, if so, what do we know about it?

As we have seen in the last chapter, Bracelin states clearly that the witches that Gardner got to know "had discovered an old Coven and remained here because of that". It may well be that the witches themselves did not use the word "coven", which was only used traditionally in Scotland. It was only following the publication of Margaret Murray's *The Witch Cult in Western Europe* in 1921 that the word gained a wider currency. It is likely that Gardner, telling the story in 1959 or 1960, used it because it had by then come into common use.

If I am right, we can identify the witches that Gardner met as being the Mason family and Edith Woodford-Grimes. And if we take Bracelin's story at face value, the Masons and Edith met some members of an old coven, or long-established group of witches. We don't know how they met them, but witches often talk of a spark of recognition when they meet another witch and, without introduction, can know that they are also members of the Craft.

Bracelin then quotes Gardner's own words when he writes: "I found that Old Dorothy and some like her, plus a number of New Forest people, had kept the light shining."

There are three categories of individual mentioned - Old Dorothy herself, 'some like her' and 'a number of New Forest people'. Bracelin states that these were members of a coven which, by implication, was in existence before the Masons and Edith Woodford-Grimes had established contacts in the Christchurch area, and was therefore in existence as a separate tradition to the family tradition that the Masons practised.

And who were the "some like her" to whom Bracelin refers? The implication is that they were people of a similar social standing to Dorothy and that, in contrast, the 'number of New Forest people' were more like ordinary working people who had their roots in the local area.

One possibility might be near-neighbours of Dorothy's - a family she knew well, well enough, indeed, to give her diaries to when she had finished writing them. They were Katherine and Anne Oldmeadow, their sister Edith and her husband, Arthur Lawrie.

Dorothy was very close to them all, which is natural in that they were in fact virtually her nearest neighbours. They lived at the Glen House, situated at the junction of Mill Lane with the main Lymington Road, and they had all lived there since at least 1922 and possibly since 1913.

Katherine Louise Oldmeadow (10th June 1878 - 8th July 1963) and her sister, Ann Eliza Oldmeadow (30th May 1875 - 17th July 1951) were the youngest of nine children of George and Annie Oldmeadow. They were born and lived in Chester, where George ended up as Deputy Chief Constable. Arthur Lawrie was married to Edith Mary, an older sister of the Oldmeadows.

Dorothy gave her diaries for 1942 and 1943 to them. At the top of the first page of the 1942 diary has been added the words "To Mr. and Mrs. Lawrie, Nance and Kit" in Dorothy's own handwriting, and the entry for 20th June 1943 describes Chester Cathedral and starts:

> Chester, well beloved I know
> By some who this Book will own

Katherine Oldmeadow was a children's author. Between 1919 and 1958 she wrote and had published over 20 books, with titles such as *Madcap Judy*, *Princess Pat*, *The House in the Oak Tree*, *A Strange Adventure*, *The Three Mary Anns* and *Three Corners Camp*. She also contributed stories to girls' annuals, including one entitled "*The Witch of Whitestones*".[1] Whilst on the surface it appears to be a fairly unremarkable story about a schoolgirl who pretended to be a witch, it contains definite hints that the author believed that witchcraft still existed and that she knew somewhat more about magic and witchcraft than she was admitting.

One book that stands out is *The Folklore of Herbs*, published in 1946.[2] According to her obituary in the *Christchurch Times* for 12th July 1963:

Miss Oldmeadow had many friends among gypsies, in whom she took a great interest and when she wrote a book about herbs - another subject in which she took a great interest - they were able to supply her with some of the material for the book.[3]

Gipsies had been part of the New Forest, probably for hundreds of years. They are, of course, by tradition nomadic, but the settlement of Thorney Hill, between Highcliffe and Burley, has for many years been the traditional site where the gipsies settled. Sybil Leek claimed to have lived with the gipsies in the New Forest for several months, and there is an interesting saying which goes: "Where there are gipsies you will find witches also". I think the meaning of this is that both were persecuted people and they used to help each other when they could. It is also, of course, true that both gipsies and witches had a lot of knowledge, particularly about herbs, that they could use to heal and help people in various ways.

Doreen Valiente seems to confirm this connection when she writes of a traditional witch coven that she had encountered:

...[they] regarded certain places as being of more significance than others in an occult sense. I was told that gypsies shared this knowledge and used certain woods and heaths as traditional encampments for this reason.[4]

The Folklore of Herbs includes a chapter on "Witches: Black and White", where the author writes of witches as healers: "*After ordering you a soothing herbal medicine, and reminding you of the comforting white paternoster* [clearly, from the context, not the Christian kind], *she would take you into her garden - witches always had herb gardens - pick you a large bunch of St. John's wort and tell you to place it in your window or over your door.*"[5]

In the same chapter the author writes, revealingly : "*The white witch of today still holds queer beliefs ...*"[6], which certainly seems to imply that she knew some witches, even if she was not one herself. And in a later chapter she suggests planting a garden with solar herbs, and including a sun dial "*to represent the Deity of the garden*".[7]

Whilst not demonstrating unequivocally Katherine Oldmeadow's involvement in witchcraft, the above quotations and comments leave some very definite hints, to say the least.[8] It is certainly interesting that a very close friend of Dorothy's should be so interested in herbs as to write a book about them, to be helped to do so by the gipsies, and to refer positively to present-day witches, particularly when we know that the collections in Gardner's museum from the witches that he knew consisted largely of implements for the harvesting and preparation of herbs.

Dorothy gives a little bit of information about Arthur Lawrie in her diary, where there are entries to celebrate his birthdays on 28th March 1942 and 1943. We learn from these entries that he was an accomplished actor and producer, also a playwright, whose plays included one called *Before the Moon Rose*. He was also an able croquet player. Dorothy writes:

> Then he could also tell your fate, if it were dark or bright,
> He only has to hold your hand, for he has second sight.
> [28 March 1942]

Whilst evidence to link the Oldmeadows and the Lawries with the Craft is as yet fairly sparse, the fact that Katherine was very friendly with the gipsies, who helped her with a book she was writing on the folklore of herbs, the fact that Arthur Lawrie had "second sight" and that Ann Eliza died in 1951, all strike me as being interesting and worthy of closer study.

It is in the nature of things that we shall probably never know the identity of most of the 'New Forest people' to whom Gardner refers. The Craft was a secret one and they were not going to advertise their presence. It is possible that some of Dorothy's staff or members of the Mill House Players, or other local people in various trades who had dealings with Dorothy might have been members of the Craft. I mention one possible individual in Chapter 17 who came to prominence in an unexpected and dramatic way, but generally one would not expect this to be the case.

I have, however, seen an intriguing annotation in Doreen Valiente's copy of *Gerald Gardner: Witch* mentioning, as one of the 'New Forest people', a "Mother Sabine".[9] I do not know how Doreen came upon this information, possibly from the occult writer, Bill Gray or possibly direct from Gardner. Although there is little to go on, apart from the name, I am trying to find out what I can about her. Doreen also refers to her as "Old Mother Sabine".

The only other contemporary reference to the existence of the coven is given by Francis King, occult writer and author of numerous books, who has an interesting chapter in his book *Ritual Magic in England* entitled "The Contemporary Witch-Cult". In it, he writes of his introduction, in 1953, to Louis Umfraville Wilkinson, who, according to King, had been the son of the proprietor-headmaster of a preparatory school in Sussex. He had been sent down from Oxford for blasphemy and had then transferred to Cambridge, where he was friends with the Powys brothers. He had subsequently written several novels under the name of Louis Marlow. He knew Aleister Crowley, had read the Last Ritual at Crowley's funeral service in 1947, and was his joint literary executor. Wilkinson told King that:

... in the late 'thirties or early 'forties, he had himself become friendly with members of a witch-coven operating in the New Forest. The social composition of this group ... was a peculiar amalgam of middle-class intellectuals with the local peasantry, and, while the foundation of the group might have dated from after

the 1921 publication of Margaret Murray's Witch Cult in Western Europe, *he was himself reasonably confident that there had been a fusion of an authentic surviving folk-tradition with a more intellectual middle-class occultism.* [10]

Wilkinson never mentioned in his writings that he had met any of the members of the coven, but it seems quite possible that this could have happened and the information given as indicated. An additional reason why we should take Wilkinson's word seriously has come to light only recently and which raises the intriguing possibility that Wilkinson's report is to be believed because he was actually there.

Prior to a visit to America in 1992 Patricia Crowther had been scrying into an obsidian sphere. When she had finished, she says that:

...I sensed Gerald Gardner's presence very strongly, and then, clairaudiently, heard his voice. He seemed quite agitated: 'Pat! I say Pat! You must tell them in America that Louis Wilkinson was a member of the New Forest coven at the time I was initiated into it.' He went on to say that Wilkinson had refuted this for several reasons, and that it was quite all right to mislead people in those days (the late 1930s), because the Craft and those within it had to be protected. The witches were afraid some sort of persecution would be revived if it came to the ears of the Establishment. [11]

Whilst there is no objective way of assessing this information, Patricia Crowther goes on to say:

In my own experience, spirit messages have regularly proved to be accurate, and so I see no reason to doubt Gerald's sudden and unexpected intrusion upon my thoughts. All the more so, since he was talking about someone I had never known, and whose name was the last thing on my mind at that particular moment. As I mulled over Gerald's words, it seemed to me that what he had said was the truth of the matter, i.e. that Wilkinson had indeed been an initiate of that coven. Otherwise, why would Gerald have contacted me, and been so anxious for me to inform the witches in the States about it? [12]

Mention must also be made here of the writings of W.E. Liddell ('Lugh')[13]. He claims that George Pickingill, a 'cunning man' from Canewdon in Essex, founded nine covens in various parts of the country in the 19th Century and that these departed from the Craft as traditionally practised in England, in (amongst other things) revering the feminine above the masculine.

There is little independent corroboration for any of his writings, but what he has to say about the New Forest coven actually sounds quite plausible:

The Hampshire coven founded by George Pickingill stopped convening during the First World War, but a remnant of elderly members tried to resurrect it in the 1920s. This attempt met with mixed success. Some Hereditary witches and several solitary practitioners joined this revamped coven. During the 1930s there was an influx of middle-class intellectuals.[14]

Gardner's parent coven contrived an ad hoc theology derived from Dr Margaret Murray's ideas. However, Pickingill's borrowings from grimoires were retained, as was his method of describing the circle.[15]

There was a marked paucity of Craft material because the pre-existing coven did not observe Sabbats and did not have a full moon ritual. A number of 'Hereditary' companies convene to mark the phases of the moon. Most rituals are still performed at the new moon.[16]

It is interesting that this latter seems to correspond with what I have found from an examination of Dorothy's diaries. However, the question of the validity of Liddell's evidence must, at this stage, remain open until independent evidence comes forward to back it up.

We still don't know anywhere near enough to answer definitively the question as to whether there was a New Forest coven into which Gardner was initiated. But we do certainly have some clues as to possible meeting-places.

Witches do not require special temples or other buildings in which to meet, so could, within reason, meet anywhere. Being secretive, however, particularly in the late 1930s and during the war, they would clearly want to meet where they would not be disturbed.

Meeting indoors, of course, would be the easiest, and I have already stated that I do not believe that Gardner's initiation was the only time that Mill House was used.

Indeed, the garden of Mill House was so secluded, particularly in summer, that it seems an obvious place to choose, particularly on a level area in amongst the trees close to the stream, and I have already suggested that the adaptation of Crowley's poem *"By the Cam"* that Gardner quotes in *Witchcraft Today*[17] is a description of a ritual on the opposite side of the stream as viewed from Mill House.

Then there are persistent rumours that the witches met on the seashore at Highcliffe to perform their ritual against threatened invasion in 1940 that we shall be looking at in the next few chapters. My guess is that this could well have happened (although Sheila Herringshaw[18] writes that the coast was very well guarded), perhaps as a preliminary to the great ritual which Gardner describes which, from his description, clearly takes place in a forest environment.

Michael Hodges[19] draws attention to a feature on the cliff edge just to the east of Chewton Bunny. It is called "Lob's Hole" and is clearly marked on the 1872 6-inch Ordnance Survey map as being approx. 300 yards east of the point where the Walkford Brook flows into the sea. According to Hodges it has now been quite eroded, but the name "Lob" suggests an ancient god-name, like "Lud", which may ultimately be derived from "Lugh", the Celtic sun-god. How Lob's Hole got its name, we don't know, but it does perhaps suggest a meeting place where the old gods were worshipped at some time in the past when it might have been a depression in the ground a little way inland, before it was claimed by erosion.

Two other outdoor locations also spring to mind.

In Gardner's novel, *High Magic's Aid*, the heroine, Morven, says:

"I have heard that the people of the Witch Cult band together at St. Catherine's Hill, and that is but a league beyond thy mother's farm."[20]; and

"... so say that you will ride with me to St. Catherine's Hill (as they call it now, though better is it known as Kerewidens Hill) and I will risk the night there."[21]

St. Catherine's Hill is a prominent feature on the outskirts of Christchurch, settled from Bronze Age times onwards and covered with ancient earthworks of various kinds, including two forts, the site of St. Catherine's Chapel and the remains of four 'Watchtowers'.

Gardner seems to be hinting that it was a witch meeting-place and, indeed, would be convenient for those living in Christchurch, being the nearest wild and uncultivated land to them as well as having a link back to pre-Christian times. Gardner is clearly suggesting a derivation of Catherine from the Celtic Cerridwen. Whether this is objectively true or not, he is clearly drawing attention to the place, with the implication that it has some witchcraft connection.

The other site is the Naked Man. I first heard of it when I was camping near Lyndhurst in 1961. It is the remains of an old tree, long decayed, and there is now not much more than a stump. Wilks says:

The Naked Man is a stark and withering oak trunk near Wilverley Post, Lyndhurst, in the New Forest, standing alone amid sparse bracken and typical open forest tract. It is fenced, resembles a man with two arms, and from one aspect is popularly supposed to depict a man engaged in an act of nature. Some say the relic earned its name from the gruesome fate of a highwayman who was allowed to hang from the tree until the rooks had picked him to the bone. More cryptically, it is also known as the Tree of Good and Evil Knowledge.[22]

Bracelin says:

There is a story among New Forest folk that around a certain tree in the forest, called the Naked Man, witches used to dance. Few believe that the legend is true - yet witches dance there yet! "The Tree was blown down just after the War. But I hear they still use the site."[23]

Bracelin is obviously quoting Gardner, so the implication of this is that even as late as the 1950s, witches were using the Naked Man as a meeting place. There is also a very definite picture caption in Doreen Valiente's *The Rebirth of Witchcraft*[24] which calls it unambiguously "the meeting-place of the New Forest witches", not only confirming that they meet there but that by the use of the word "the" suggesting that it was the only place, which I doubt.

50. The Naked Man

The tree-stump and its surroundings have a marvellous atmosphere, particularly at dusk and in many ways one can imagine the witches meeting there or at least in the vicinity, but, up until at least the 1950s, there was a fairly main road running within about 50 yards of it and although it is now just an unmetalled track, it is still in a prominent location. However, in the 1930s and during the war there was far less traffic than there is nowadays, so it may be that we should take it as being a traditional meeting-place. However, I have recently discovered that Gardner told Doreen Valiente something about the traditional ritual sites in the New Forest. He told her that the Naked Man was used as a meeting-place, but that its role was that of the 'coven-tree' - an assembly point where the witches would gather before going on to the true ritual site.

Gardner told her that the witches met there but that they then crossed two streams to get to the ritual site. The only route within reasonable walking distance which crossed two streams would be to the north-east, ending up near Ferny Knap Inclosure. However, Doreen Valiente has speculated that they may have gone on from the Naked Man by car, crossing the Ober Water and the Black Water. This would bring them into the vicinity of the Knightwood Oak and Mark Ash Wood, the other places which Gardner indicated to Doreen Valiente were traditional ritual sites. Knightwood Oak is a prominent and ancient tree, and Mark Ash Wood is one of the few places in the New Forest which has a legend of witchcraft associated with it.

Despite the evidence in this chapter, I do not feel that I have so far successfully demonstrated that the "old coven" referred to by Bracelin actually existed. There is a lot more evidence that needs to be accumulated (and, I have no doubt, in due course will be), but for the moment the question of the existence or otherwise of the New Forest coven must remain open.

We do know, however, of one series of rituals in which the New Forest coven participated. If ever the name of 'coven' were to be bestowed on any working group, it can hardly be argued that the group who performed those rituals was unworthy of it. Indeed, even if they got together for no other purpose, they will be remembered for those rituals alone. The story of those rituals, to stop the invasion of England in 1940, and what they cost those involved, is told in the next three chapters.

Chapter 15
The Threat of Invasion

Gardner mentions only one magical working carried out by the group of witches which he joined in the New Forest area, but it was a momentous one. What he claims is that the witches, not just the group into which Gardner was initiated, but others as well, got together and carried out a ritual in an attempt to stop the German invasion which was then thought to be imminent. He also claims that a certain number, because of what they did in the ritual, died a short time afterwards.

Some have questioned whether any such ritual was ever carried out, such as Lois Bourne, who suggests that it could have been "... a rather splendid myth, faithfully repeated and passed on until it becomes the lore of the craft, jealously protected and believed."[1] Yet others, such as Cecil Williamson[2], have accused Gardner of purveying a distorted version of something which was supposed to have happened elsewhere! And others point to a lack of concrete evidence.

I propose to turn this argument on its head and state that it would actually be most surprising if such a ritual (and others like it) had not in fact taken place. And, if there was a local tradition concerning the use of witchcraft to repel invasions, this was just the area where one would expect to find it.

Magical Techniques
It is generally agreed that magic works by using the will to cause certain changes to take place, either in the physical world or in the deeper planes of the mental, emotional or spiritual realms. The key is to work with the natural flows of the universe so that only a relatively small input can cause potentially great changes.

When considering how to stop an invasion, or something of that nature, witches have attempted to do a combination of two things - one having a physical effect and one a mental effect.

Weather magic is a very common physical technique - affecting the weather to help achieve a particular outcome. Rain-making is a very common use of magic in societies which rely very heavily on agriculture. And, conversely, we have already seen the 79 rain-free days which accompanied the building of the Rosicrucian Garden Theatre. This was an example of conscious and deliberate weather magic, and I would be most surprised if Ernie Mason had not had a hand in it.

Of course, to stop an invasion, particularly in the days of sail and primitive navigation techniques, wind, rain and fog were called for. Witches were often accused of being able to 'whistle up a wind' and they are known to have sold knotted cords to sailors, the knots to be undone when a wind was wanted. The North Berwick witches were accused, at their trial in 1590, of raising a storm to drown King James VI of Scotland.

Weather magic was (and is) a popular technique because it deals with things which are fluid - air and water droplets - things more easily amenable to the direction of the will than solid rock, for example. As those who live in Britain may particularly appreciate, the weather is often both changeable and unpredictable. It consists of basic, though immensely powerful, elemental forces, particularly those of air and water, which are active and usually in constant movement. This makes the weather particularly amenable to the working of magic and, traditionally, this was one of the particular skills possessed by the witch. So it is perhaps significant, particularly in the days of sail, where navies were very much affected by the vagaries of the wind, that weather magic would have been an obvious choice for those wanting to prevent an invasion.

Also fluid is the human mind, and mind magic is the other major technique which is used to influence events. Here, the mind of an individual or group of individuals is worked upon to change what they are thinking - either to change their opinion about something they wanted to do, to cause confusion or to sap their confidence in their ability to carry out some action.

If we look particularly at the two examples given by Gardner - the Spanish Armada and the Napoleonic invasion scare - we can see how the interplay between these two forms of magic would indeed appear to have had a major influence on the outcome of those events.

The Spanish Armada 1588

The Spanish Armada has been called "...*one of the greatest, most significant and decisive defeats in the annals of war at sea*"[3], and the popular myth about it is that the invasion fleet was dispersed and wrecked by heavy storms.

The Armada consisted of a fleet of about 130 ships. It was first sighted on Friday 29th July 1588, off Lands End and the Lizard, and news quickly reached Drake at Plymouth, by all accounts when he was playing bowls on Plymouth Hoe. He probably immediately sent a message for the English fleet to be ready to sail by the next tide and, being able to do no more until then, carried on with his game of bowls.

The English fleet sailed, engaged the Armada off Plymouth on the 31st, off Portland Bill on 2nd August and off the Isle of Wight on the following two days. The Spaniards were hoping to capture the Isle of Wight as a base for further assaults, but the wind, currents and pressure from the English ships prevented this. By 6th August, the Armada was off Calais, where it was dispersed by English fireships.

A change of the wind enabled the Armada to flee northwards. They were then subject to severe storms as they attempted to navigate around the coast of Scotland and Ireland and fewer than half the ships which had set out made their way home.

The Witches' Response

The power of the mind must not be underestimated, and those of the Old Religion who were alerted to the potential threat could doubtless see the course of events in their scrying bowls and pools.

The chain of beacons, prepared in readiness, was probably lit the same day, confirming the message and particularly alerting those further up the Channel who were to follow the course of the Armada, rarely out of sight of the English shore. As Macaulay wrote:

For swift to east and swift to west the ghastly warflame spread,
High on St. Michael's Mount it shone: it shone on Beachy Head.
Far on the deep the Spaniard saw, along each southern shire,
Cape beyond cape, in endless range, those twinkling points of fire.[4]

If there were indeed witches in the New Forest/Solent area, then they would certainly have been aware of the imminent invasion by 30th July at the latest.

The proximity to Lammas is striking and it would seem likely that any magical working would have taken place on that date. Gardner has this to say:

At the time of the Spanish Armada the invading force was off the coast before the cult really heard about it. They knew it was useless trying to get at King Philip; he was out of touch with and could not change the Armada's course, and they had not the slightest idea who was in command. The only thing they could do was to send out a general idea: "Go on," "Go on," "Go on," "You cannot land," "You cannot land," and hope it would take effect. If they could have raised a storm, they would have done so, but they did not know how, though naturally they would pray to their gods to bring disaster to the fleet and this would probably include storms.[5]

Despite Gardner's insistence that the witches of his time did not know how to affect the weather (which I do not believe for one minute), it seems clear that those towards the end of the 16th Century could, and did!

Perhaps there was a psychological element to it as well, making the Spaniards think the weather was worse than it was. Thomas states:

...it is worth recording that the Spaniards on the whole were less experienced than the English in encountering gales at sea, and it is noticeable that they seem to have recorded worse storms and sea conditions than did their adversaries. This storm, for example, ... has been described in a Spanish log as having "the sea so high that all the mariners said they had never seen the like in July". Yet it rates no mention at all in the English reports except for the casual remark by John Hawkins that "a little flaw took them".[6]

Two further attempts at invasion were made by the Spanish. The first of these was in November 1596, one of the stormiest months of the year, when the fleet was wrecked shortly after it left Spanish water. The following year, the fleet got as far as Cornwall and was within sight of Falmouth when a northerly gale sprung up out of nowhere. With these examples, one might strongly suspect magical workings influencing, in the first case, decision-making about the time of the invasion, and, in the second case, the raising of a sudden storm. In fact, we can look even further back, to the Hundred Years' War and the invasion threat of 1386-87:

The French readied themselves to invade England, assembling a fleet of ships in the Scheldt estuary. On standby were 100,000 men and nearly 1,000 barrels of wine. But a combination of bad weather and dithering scuppered their plans and the French went home.[7]

Bad weather and dithering - just the sort of thing we might expect to happen if those two methods of magic had been adopted.

Sir Francis Drake

The defeat of the Armada is inevitably linked with the name of Sir Francis Drake, explorer and Vice Admiral. There has been a persistent legend that Drake was actually an adherent of the Old Religion. Patricia Crowther says:

Sir Francis Drake was considered by some to have been a member of the witch cult in Devon. A well-known headland in Plymouth is called Devil's Point, which the locals say was a witches' meeting-place...[8]

Other legends take this further, as Peter Underwood recounts:

So successful was Drake with his victory over the Armada and other achievements against overwhelming and seemingly impossible odds that the belief grew - both during his lifetime and after his death - that he must have allied himself with the devil and had perhaps sold his soul in return for the invincible powers of seamanship and warfare that he undoubtedly possessed.

In particular it was widely believed that the pact was made at the place now known as Devil's Point in exchange for the storm that drove the Spanish fleet northwards to its doom. Devil's Point is reported to be haunted to this day by the ghosts of magicians and witches who took part in the satanic ceremony; many people have reported hearing and seeing strange figures muttering their mysterious incantations.[9]

This may well have been a distorted memory of Drake's membership of a witchcraft tradition that held meetings, perhaps into living memory, at Devil's Point.

Drake's Drum

Certainly Drake has joined King Arthur and Robin Hood in the exclusive band of those who have promised to return in times of need. When Drake was dying, in 1596, it is said that he requested that his drum was to be taken to his home at Buckland Abbey, in Devon, and that if it was beaten when the country was in serious danger, he would awaken from his sleep and use his magical powers to save it once again, as dramatised in the famous poem by Sir Henry Newbolt.[10] Katherine Kurtz, in her novel, *Lammas Night*[11], makes use of this legend.

The drum has been beaten in modern times, as Theo Brown recounts:

There have been several reports of people hearing the Drum during the First world War. The Drum is heard playing itself: no one thumps it to summon Drake. In 1915 a Mrs. Amphlett was working in a hospital at Honiton and she recalled many years later, in 1965, that a friend of hers had a gardener who said one morning that he had heard Drake's Drum beating quite plainly.[12]

Dorothy Clutterbuck, in her diary for 1943, recounts a story told to her during the Great War by Mr. Crispin, a Devon man, about how he heard the sound of the drumming on the Moor:

> *I was told a tale that's true*
> *And by a Devon man*
> *No Imagination's story*
> *This is how it ran*
> *Across the Moor they heard it*
> *From Princetown to Dartmeet*
> *From Okehampton to Plymouth*
> *Where lay a waiting fleet*
> *'Twas in those burning, lowering days*
> *August 1914*
> *When Europe's lights were dying out*
> *Dying where they had been*
> *Across the Moor they heard it*
> *The Beating of Drake's Drum*
> *A muffled sound of dread and fear*
> *And they knew*
> *That war would come*
> *In the dead of night they heard it*
> *And they heard it in the day*
> *They knew that Drake was drumming*
> *And, that he was on his way!*

The Napoleonic Invasion Scare

The Napoleonic invasion scare took place in 1803-4, but had been building up for some years since war broke out in February 1793. Bonaparte proceeded with the construction of some 2000 invasion craft and military camps in the coastal area, accommodating upwards of 150,000 soldiers. He is quoted as having said of the Channel that "it is a ditch which will be leaped whenever one has the boldness to try."

Diversions, however, meant that it was to be another two years before a serious attempt was made to invade. The grand plan was to group the French and Spanish fleets in the West Indies and then sail for Boulogne. Unfortunately for Bonaparte, things didn't work out that way. A combination of a lack of communications and poor weather resulted in the non-appearance of the fleet. Having arrived at Boulogne on 3rd August 1805, Bonaparte had by 25th August turned his attention to the east, and by 28th August the army was in full march towards Germany and would then attract the military attention of Russia and Austria.[13]

This seems to accord with Gardner's account of the oral tradition which the witches claimed to have about the threatened Napoleonic invasion, and it is most interesting to note that the same thing happened as took place following the 1940 threat - that the potential invasion was recognised to be too difficult and attention was refocused on the east.

Ross Nichols, the Druid, whom Gardner knew well, mentions certain details which I have never seen written anywhere else, so he may well have got them directly from Gardner. He writes:

... in the Napoleonic wars the witches of Sussex (even now a famous witch area) organized a consistently-blowing, south-west wind that prevented Napoleon's pontoons ranged at Boulogne from carrying over the 'Army of England'.[14]

Gardner says:

The witches told me that their great-grandfathers had tried to project the same idea into Boney's mind.[15]

Older members of the coven, those who came from a generation when magic enjoyed a matter-of-fact acceptance in some households, could remember family talk of a similar rite against "Boney" at the time of the threatened Napoleonic invasion.[16]

It is quite likely, if the witches of the time had carried out some ritual to deter the invasion that they would have told their grandchildren about it some time in the middle of the 19th Century. And it is quite possible that the oldest members of the group which Gardner joined could be those same grandchildren. In any case, the events were sufficiently recent to have been handed down orally to not more than three generations. The ancestors of the Mason family, for example, lived in Southampton and Portsmouth in the early 19th Century, just the area where 'invasion fever' was likely to be strongest.

Chapter 16
"Operation Cone of Power"

War had been declared on 3rd September 1939, but it was only on 10th May 1940 when German troops invaded Holland and Belgium and Winston Churchill became Prime Minister, that a sense of urgency started to come into focus. Very quickly the German troops over-ran those two smaller countries and they surrendered on 28th May. British troops were forced back on the small French coastal town of Dunkirk, but, with the help of a flotilla of assorted vessels, over 300,000 British and French troops were safely evacuated. By 14th June, German troops had reached Paris and, on 22nd June, the French government surrendered.

Planning the Ritual
Invasion was felt to be imminent. For all most people knew, disaster threatened. They had to do something.

But what could they do about it? They were beyond the age where they could have joined the armed forces and been accepted for active combat. Gardner was 56 in 1940. Edith Woodford Grimes was 52, Ernie Mason was 54, Susie Mason was 57 and Dorothy Clutterbuck had turned 60.

Admittedly, some, like Gardner, could join the Home Guard but most of them almost certainly would have felt that they should use the skills which they already possessed to deter the invasion - and those skills were magical ones. Particularly as they had been brought up with the tradition that witches in the past had worked to prevent the success of similar invasions, they would naturally turn towards using a method similar to that which had been handed down to them.

The crucial moment was probably when some of the witches (presumably the Masons) revealed that their families had lived in the area for many years and that they had a tradition that when there had been invasion threats in the past, from the Spanish Armada in 1588 and from Napoleon in 1805, they had successfully carried out magical workings to stop them.

I think it was likely to have been Gardner who first had the idea: what could be done once could be done again! If so, then he obviously convinced them, as it was decided to perform a ritual or rituals to help stop the threatened invasion. Bracelin says:

Old Dorothy called up "covens right and left; although by Witch Law they should not be known to each other". And this was the start of "Operation Cone of Power", when the witches, as they claim, sent up a force against Hitler's mind.[1]

Allen Andrews adds the following:

... an extraordinary summons was sent out to members of the Southern Coven of British Witches. It brought seventeen men and women to a clearing in the New Forest.[2]

When?

Those who have written about the ritual give varying dates for its performance. Bracelin[3] says simply "after Belgium, Holland and France fell", i.e. after 22nd June. Patricia Crowther[4] says "Lammas eve"; Doreen Valiente[5] says "Lammas", and Andrews[6] says unambiguously "the night of 1st August". Only King[7], quoting Wilkinson, says "May", but he does add "when Hitler's invasion was felt to be imminent." As it was really only in mid to late June that "invasion fever" began to take hold, I think that King, reporting at least second-hand, and possibly third-hand, quite simply got it wrong. Doreen Valiente attempts to resolve this difference by saying the following:

... Wilkinson described the ritual which this coven had performed in the New Forest in order to deter Hitler's threatened invasion in 1940, although the date he gives is May 1940 and the date I was

given was Lammas 1940. However, I was told that, in fact, there was a series of rituals, which may account for the discrepancy. Gerald is quoted in his biography as saying that the ritual was repeated four times, so we may guess that it started on or just after May Eve, was repeated at the full moons of June and July and again at Lammas (1 August)[8].

Their concern for invasion is likely to have been greater than elsewhere because of their 'front line' i.e. coastal location. It might also have come into the mind of the public somewhat earlier, let us say by the time of Dunkirk (4 June). Patricia Crowther says the following:

Gerald told me that, when working magic, the timing of a rite was very important, and that the Four Tides of the year should be taken into consideration. An ideal time lay between the summer solstice and the autumn equinox, when nature has reached her greatest potential and the etheric emanations are strongest. A time when they could most profitably be tapped. This, he said, was why the witches in the New Forest had chosen Lammas to work against Hitler's proposed invasion of Britain. It was also the reason why the ritual was performed in the forest, on Lammas Eve 1940, when the Moon was in the last days of her waning. The ideal time for getting rid of something! The date, time of year, the phase of the Moon and the site were as conducive as they were ever likely to be for such a fateful ritual. A ritual that became known as 'Operation Cone of Power'![9]

I am sure that Patricia Crowther is right regarding the particular time of year for working such a ritual. However, things were urgent, and magical workings cannot always wait for the ideal time. As Churchill says:

As the month of June ground itself out, the sense of potential invasion at any moment grew upon us all.[10]

After Dunkirk, and still more when three weeks later the French Government capitulated, the questions whether Hitler would, or secondly could, invade and conquer our Island rose, as we have seen, in all British minds.[11]

And those living on the coast would be more likely to be thinking of such possibilities earlier and taking them more seriously than the rest of the population. Now, Highcliffe and the New Forest area generally, are potentially very vulnerable to invasion, being right on the south coast, close to the undoubted military targets of Southampton and Portsmouth: an undoubted "front line" location. Ian Stevenson, the Highcliffe local historian, recalls that his family always had their bags packed ready for retreat at a moment's notice.[12] This was not so true, generally, for those living in other parts of the country.

Time was pressing - history was in the making. Every day through the month of June brought changing circumstances, from the evacuation of Dunkirk, completed on 4th June to the fall of France on 22nd. So by Midsummer at the latest it was certainly clear that something would have to be done.

In these circumstances, I think it highly unlikely that the witches would have waited over a month before carrying out a ritual to try and stop the invasion. For all they knew, the invasion could have happened and be all over before Lammas. They would, in my opinion, have organised a ritual, probably just in their own group, soon after the fall of France on 22nd, and buoyed up by Churchill's speech on 18th:

What General Weygand called the "Battle of France" is over. I expect that the battle of Britain is about to begin. Upon this battle depends the survival of Christian civilisation. Upon it depends our own British life and the long continuity of our institutions and our Empire. The whole fury and might of the enemy must very soon be turned on us. Hitler knows that he will have to break us in this island or lose the war.

If we can stand up to him, all Europe may be free, and the life of the world may move forward into broad, sunlit uplands; but if we fail, then the whole world, including the United States, and all that we have known and cared for, will sink into the abyss of a new dark age made more sinister, and perhaps more protracted, by the lights of a perverted science.

Let us therefore brace ourselves to our duty and so bear ourselves that if the British Empire and its Commonwealth lasts for a thousand years men will still say, "This was their finest hour."[13]

The effect of this speech cannot be overestimated. It set the atmosphere for determined action, and it is my guess that it was this moment, more than any other, which decided the witches to carry out the type of ritual which, by tradition, had been so successful against Napoleon and the Spanish Armada.

With the sense of urgency felt by all at the time, it need only have taken a day or two to organise. We do not know the extent to which the group celebrated the seasonal festivals or met at the Full Moon, but they would certainly be aware of the symbolism of the cycles of the year and the month. The Summer Solstice was on Friday 21st June and the Full Moon had been two days before, on the night of Wednesday 19th June. So both solar and lunar cycles were in a waning phase by Saturday 22nd June, and it is my guess that some ritual would have been performed on that date.

However, it became clear that something special was needed. The older members of the coven would have told of the traditions of preventing the Spanish Armada and the Napoleonic invasions from succeeding, and plans would have been drawn up for something that would need quite a bit of preparation, involving "calling up covens to left and right", deciding on a suitable location and details of the ritual. Discussion would need to take place.

As July progressed without sight of the invasion, it became clear that Lammas would be the obvious time to perform a ritual of a more elaborate nature. Astrologically, it was a highly significant time because it was within a week of an exact Jupiter-Saturn conjunction, something which only happens once every 20 years and which is a balance point in the mundane cycle when things can be both started and finished. That it occurred very close to a sensitive point on Hitler's own chart (his Venus-Mars conjunction) could only help any efforts which were being directed towards his decision-making abilities and preferences for action.

Where?

As well as the reasons set out by Patricia Crowther, there is an additional reason why the ritual should have taken place in the New Forest at Lammas, particularly when, as we shall see, the theme of sacrifice comes into the picture. There is one place, and one place only in the New Forest, that combines the themes of Lammas and sacrifice, and that is the Rufus Stone, which marks the spot where, according to such writers as Margaret Murray, William Rufus was shot and became a divine victim - a pagan sacrifice - at Lammas in the year 1100. Indeed, the ritual would have taken place on the 840th anniversary of those events, or ten Uranus cycles.

We are not concerned here as to whether Murray was right in her theories, or even whether the Rufus Stone marks the actual spot where Rufus fell. Certainly in 1940 there was no doubt about the location in the popular mind, and the more well-read of the witches, including Gardner, would certainly have known of

51. Possible site of the 1940 Rituals near the Rufus Stone.

Murray's theories, even if they had no tradition of their own through which the story was passed down.

On one of my research trips, I visited the Rufus Stone, parking my car in the car park on the opposite side of the road and went to have a look at the stone. I then felt a strong urge to walk in the opposite direction, over a slight rise. The woodland scene I then saw was striking. It felt very similar to the picture I had built up in my mind of the location of the 1940 ritual - an open wooded area with tall trees and little undergrowth.

It had a very powerful feel to it which I cannot put into words, and I got the very vivid impression that, quite by "accident", I had stumbled on the actual location.

There are also a few clues which suggest this.

Justine Glass, in her 1965 book, *Witchcraft, The Sixth Sense and Us*[14] refers to the Rufus Stone as a current witches' meeting-place. Now, the stone itself is close to, and fully visible, from the road, so would not itself make a good ritual site. However, the site I am suggesting for the 1940 ritual is over a low ridge, close to the road but not visible from it. It seems then that on this evidence it was used for quite a long time after 1940 and perhaps for generations before as well. Also, the nearest village to the Rufus Stone is Brook, which is mentioned by Sybil Leek as being the location of one of the four New Forest covens.

Gardner says "*We were taken at night to a place in the Forest ...*".[15] He had been initiated almost a year previously and would therefore presumably have attended several rituals of the group. His statement implies that the place was not his usual meeting place, or one of their usual meeting places. It may well therefore have been chosen by one of the other covens in the Forest. Also, the use of the word "we" suggests that he was not the only one in that situation, i.e. being taken somewhere unfamiliar.

How many?

Gardner says that Old Dorothy called up "*covens right and left; although by Witch Law they should not be known to each other*".[16] Andrews mentions seventeen[17], which seems a reasonable and feasible number - the sort that could be got together quickly, bearing in mind wartime travel restrictions, and the vigilance of the Home Guard, particularly in a vulnerable coastal area where the threat of imminent invasion might be most strongly felt.

They could probably get into three cars, possibly organised by Old Dorothy as she did in previous years for the Mill House Players. Locals would have walked, bicycled or even, following tradition, ridden. Nevertheless, they were clearly at risk of being stopped. The Local Defence Volunteers had been formed on 17th May 1940, their name being changed at Churchill's insistence by mid-July to the Home Guard, and Mackenzie quotes the example of one man who had been stopped 20 times on a journey of eight miles.[18] Therefore, anyone travelling at night, particularly during this first burst of enthusiastic attention to duty, and in an area near the coast, might be expected to be stopped by the Home Guard. They would certainly have to have had good excuses prepared.

In my opinion, claims that a substantially larger number of people attended the gathering really have to be discounted on the grounds that there were travel restrictions and great difficulties about assembling people from all parts of the country without being noticed. A large gathering would probably not have been as effective magically in any case.

It is, however, possible that a larger number could, in small and isolated groups, be equally working towards the same end, even gravitating towards the same date, although probably not as organised as Katherine Kurtz suggests in *Lammas Night*. It would be most surprising if there were not, though it is really impossible, particularly at this distance in time, to even give an estimate of the number involved in this way. Some examples that I have been able to find out something about are given in the next chapter.

What was to be done?

The ritual was to be both special and serious. Gardner sets the tone:

...that was done which may not be done except in great emergency.[19]

By this, he suggests something which was known about, and which had been done before (perhaps in the oral tradition dating back to Napoleonic and Spanish Armada times) but could only be used in an emergency of that magnitude. It was clearly felt that the present state of what they felt was imminent invasion met that criterion amply. He gives a further hint:

... mighty forces were used, of which I may not speak. Now to do this means using one's life-force; and many of us died a few days after we did this.[20]

Gardner is obviously not intending to go into detail, and it is clear that he has been forbidden to do so, either by specific individuals or by some Craft Law, as well as by the obvious and natural concern to keep the details of such rituals secret. However, we have a possible clue in what Gardner wrote about magicians in the Far East and how they operated. He says:

How do they do it? By starving themselves or weakening the bodily functions in some way ... They do it by taking away a part of their life - dying in part, if you like - in order to obtain this power.[21]

This sounds very similar to what Gardner was hinting at, so could fasting before the ritual, perhaps for a considerable period, have been an element in the 1940 workings?

Whatever it was it was certainly something which by his own admission:

- used mighty forces
- used the life-force of the individual; and
- resulted in the deaths of several individuals a few days later

King, quoting Louis Wilkinson, provides a different explanation of what this might be. He also calls this action by a powerful name - that of sacrifice:

The witches felt that it was essential that he [i.e. Hitler] *should be deterred from invasion plans by a powerful ritual, the central point of which was to be the death of a (volunteer) sacrificial victim. The oldest and frailest member volunteered for sacrifice and left off his protective grease so that he might die of the effects of exposure.* [22]

This account has the ring of truth about it. Summer nights can be very cold, even at the end of July/beginning of August, let alone May. This is particularly true of those who are old and frail, especially if, as Wilkinson implies, they were skyclad. Wilkinson told King that:

The New Forest coven ... used an ointment, but it was simply a heavy grease, largely consisting of bears' fat, rather similar to that used by channel-swimmers and having a similar purpose, for it was simply designed to protect their naked bodies from cold at open-air gatherings.[23]

Now the use of the term 'bears' fat' should not, I feel, be taken literally. It was probably just goose grease or something of that nature. I am reminded of the red wine known as 'Bull's Blood'. This acquired its name in the 16th Century when the Turks, who were attacking the castle of Eger in Hungary, could see the defenders drinking something red and concluded that it was the blood of bulls, which gave them their strength. I think the mention of 'bears' fat' was a little in-joke amongst the witches and nothing more.

As we shall see, there was only a small functional fire rather than the more usual large (and warm) bonfire.

And, contrary to what one might think, bodily activity can actually lower core body temperature and induce hypothermia because the blood is thereby sent to the extremities of the body and therefore thinned.[24]

However, June 1940 was the second warmest June of the century in England and Wales; July was one of the wettest of the century; and August one of the driest. As Bob Prichard writes:

There had already been a good deal of warm and sunny weather in May, and it was the momentum from this that led to the heat in June; the hottest weather was in the first 10 days ... It was a sunny month, and most places only had small amounts of rain, but the second half of the month was generally less settled and cooler than the first; there was a very cool day on the 23rd, when the temperature only reached 13 [degrees C] at Boscombe Down in Wiltshire.

Then came the copious rains of July ... The weather became rather more settled towards the end of the month...[25]

This does not seem on the surface to be a particularly cold period, and there is no mention in Prichard's report, which was about the weather in the summer of 1940, of "the coldest May (or any other month's) night for several years", which one would think would be worth a mention. However, the New Forest is considered by meteorologists to be "a notorious cold spot."[26]

All we can say is that, even in the summer, it seems at least possible that someone who was frail or not otherwise in the best of health could contract hypothermia if they were performing a vigorous ritual in the middle of a clearing in the forest at night with no clothes on. It might certainly exacerbate certain conditions which the individual might be prone to and which might well come to the fore with fatal consequences a week or two later.

Indeed, we have confirmation of this from Gardner himself: "*My asthma, which I had never had since I first went out East, came back badly.*"[27] Following this, Gardner remained an asthma sufferer for the rest of his life.

Gardner had returned from the East in 1936, but it was more than four years later that the asthma returned, and it is known to be something that can be brought on by extreme cold. John Illman confirms this when he says that:

Cold air can also trigger asthma, by chilling the respiratory passages. In his book, All About Asthma and Allergy, *Dr Harry Morrow Brown warns that cold air alone can cause constriction of the bronchial tubes. A short walk on a frosty morning may be enough to trigger an attack.*[28]

Asthma is, incidentally, also known as "the occultist's disease". Several have noticed a correlation, one of the most well-known sufferers being Aleister Crowley. I am also reminded of one of the central characters in Dion Fortune's novel, *The Sea Priestess*, Wilfrid Maxwell, who was an asthma sufferer.[29] His asthma, brought on after asserting himself with his family for the first time, seemed to result in an attunement with the moon and opened up a series of dreams which originated in a previous lifetime.

The Cone of Power

Gardner says:

We were taken at night to a place in the Forest, where the Great Circle was erected...[30]

The circle was marked out on the ground in a clear space between the trees. Doreen Valiente says that Gardner told her that "on this occasion a very large circle was marked out with brushwood".[31] This was presumably done beforehand and would indicate that the ritual took place in an area where brushwood, i.e. twigs and small branches, was easy enough to find. One can perhaps imagine those witches local to the area setting this up by gathering brushwood into a large pile a day or two before, and then on the evening of the ritual, laying it out immediately outside the circle which would be cast in the normal fashion.

With regard to the size of the circle, Gardner says:

The only time I have seen a larger [than 9 foot] *circle used was when we tried to work on Hitler's mind, and that was a totally different operation, 'Sending Forth', performed in an entirely* different way, needing as many people as we could get together and plenty of room to work in.[32]

The brush wood could then be returned to its pile before dawn to be ready for the repeat of the ritual in the near future.

Valiente gives the following details about the illumination:

A fire or candle was within [the circle], *in the direction where the object of the rite was supposed to be.... The candle referred to would have been in a lantern ... and the fire, not too large because of wartime blackout restrictions, was lit in what was roughly the direction the invasion was thought likely to come from, presumably the south-east.*[33]

Andrews adds that: "*Their ceremonial firebrands were expertly kept dim, yet alive, by such of the company as were air-raid wardens...*"[34] This last comment about air-raid wardens almost certainly referred to Gardner himself. It was a recognition that, in wartime, any light could draw unwanted attention.

This statement is, however, interesting in that no other candle or light is mentioned, certainly not at the four quarters, plus two altar candles as would be usual today. It seems as if they only had what was absolutely necessary, but the statement is ambiguous as to whether the candle and the fire were alternatives or if both had to be present: the latter seems likely, as details about both are given. It is also clear that the candle and fire are directly related to the object of the rite and not mere decorations.

There is also a mention of 'ceremonial firebrands', presumably some sort of stick held by each of the participants, which were lit at one end but perhaps impregnated with something which kept them from going out but which didn't give too much flame. The implication of the statement is that this was a substance with which the air-raid wardens were familiar. It certainly sounds the sort of thing that Ernie Mason would have known about.

Valiente also records that people were "stationed to whip up the dancers". This reminded her of a reference to:

... a Scottish witch meeting which took place in August 1678, when a leading male witch, one Gideon Penman, '... was in the rear in all their dances, and beat up all those that were slow'. This is mentioned in The Geography of Witchcraft *by Montague Summers.*[35]

This was obviously during the part of the rite when everyone (presumably excluding the 'whips') danced round in a circle to raise the cone of power. *"The Cone of Power. This was the old way."*[36]

Gardner was told by the witches that power resides in their bodies and that this can be released by various techniques including chanting and dancing. By working together within the magic circle, they can raise what they call a "cone of power", which can then be directed towards a particular objective. It is this that they were intending to raise through the ritual.

Andrews says that:

... the coven proceeded to conduct rites intended to raise the first colossal "cone of power" they had ever produced - and direct it against Hitler. And the great Cone of Power was raised and slowly directed in the general direction of Hitler.[37]

This seems to indicate that they (i.e. those particular individuals) had raised a cone of power before, but never anything on this scale, although they knew, from tradition, that it could be done.

There were at least three aspects to this - the dancing itself and the energy generated; the chanting; and the state of mind of the participants. Valiente writes, from notes made as Gardner was talking:

Then all danced round until they felt they had raised enough power. If the rite was to banish, they started deosil and finished widdershins, so many rounds of each.[38]

She also makes an interesting comment when she says: "I suppose, if the raising of the Cone of Power had not been to banish something, all the dancing would have been deosil. Also, the rite would have been considerably less stressful."[39]

The raising of the Cone of Power was only the first stage in the proceedings, however. The next stage was actually to send it with its message to its destination. So what was the message and what was the destination? Valiente gives the following details of what they were trying to achieve:

... when the witches raised the Cone of Power against Hitler's invasion, they sought to reach the minds of the German High Command and persuade them that the invasion could not succeed, or alternatively to muddle and stultify their thinking so that the plans for the invasion fell through. Generally, old Gerald said, there was someone somewhere whose actions would vitally affect whatever it was that the witch ceremony was trying to bring about. This person's mind would be acted upon, without their knowledge, so that they would behave in one way rather than another, and thus the desired result would happen.[40]

It is clear that this was mind magic - trying to get to those who were in a position to make decisions, and ultimately Hitler himself, to put into their minds that they could not succeed with the invasion. The way in which they did this was quite distinctive. Valiente, quoting Gardner, says "Then they formed a line with linked hands and rushed towards the fire shouting the thing they wanted."[41] This is a variation of holding hands in a circle, dancing in towards the centre and then out as far as one can without letting go of the hand of the person next to you, which is an old witch dance and is still a feature of many country dances.

We can see now the real purpose of the fire being on the edge of the circle in the direction in which the Cone of Power was to be sent. As it was on the edge, people wouldn't be able to dance round it. So, as Gardner describes, they formed a line, then rushing towards the fire shouting, and then back again, so that the efforts were focused in the right direction. As Andrews says: *"The climax of a long ritual came with the members, in a state of tense excitement, projecting their defiance in shouts of rhythmic unison ..."*[42]

So, what were they shouting? Gardner records two concise commands: "You cannot cross the Sea. You cannot cross the Sea. YOU CANNOT COME. YOU CANNOT COME."[43] Valiente gives a slightly different version, and one that would probably be easier to chant: "Can't cross the sea! Can't cross the sea! Not able to come! Not able to come!" As she says: "The words had to be simple and capable of falling into a chanted rhythm that expressed the purpose of the rite."[44] Gardner told Patricia Crowther that the two phrases were "You cannot cross the sea" and "Not able to come".[45]

It is said that they directed the thought at Hitler's brain.

Valiente, quoting Gardner, says that "They kept it up till they were exhausted or until someone fell in a faint, when they were said to have taken the spell to its destination."[46]

Gardner says "we repeated the ritual four times".[47] Now, it is possible that this merely means that the cone of power was raised several times on the same night, but this is highly unlikely as it would be too exhausting physically and mentally for those involved. Indeed, the Cone of Power would only be successful if those raising it 'gave their all', which they would be unlikely to do if they knew they would have to repeat it immediately. Indeed, Gardner told Patricia Crowther, and mentions in *Witchcraft Today*, that they repeated the ritual several times after the initial one at Lammas. Also, Gardner goes on to quote the elders as saying "We must not kill too many of our people."[48] Now, it is highly unlikely, as well as difficult to explain to the authorities, that they were actually dying in the ritual itself. These comments were almost certainly made some days following the last ritual.

Chapter 17
Their Finest Hour

It has been said[1] that the Goddess does not demand sacrifice. But I think we have to look at the circumstances of the time and how the witches viewed things.

First of all, there was a genuine and very real threat of invasion. It is perhaps an obvious point but one that can be subtly overlooked, and that is that they didn't know how things were going to work out. For all they knew, Britain would be invaded, and in the very near future. In other words, there was a crisis, and if their working involved sacrifice, then that was no more than what thousands of their compatriots were facing every day.

It is also important to recognise that what the group was doing was to raise a very large cone of power and to direct it towards its objectives. The more energy that could be put into it the better, and I think this is why Gardner spoke about "using one's life-force"[2]. I take this to mean the energy which sustains one's life and that if too much is taken one will die or be severely affected.

This was not deliberate sacrifice. It was carrying out an operation that was known to be risky. Sacrifice is thus merely a possible by-product of this course of action, certainly not the intention. It is similar to the RAF pilots who knowingly put themselves in danger in order to fulfil their objectives. They did not want to die or be injured and it was certainly not a requirement for the success of their mission. But they were prepared to die, and, if they did so, 'sacrifice' would be an appropriate word to use. So, I think, it was with the witches.

Gardner was often prone to exaggeration, but there was usually a core of truth in what he was saying - he rarely made things up completely. So, let us see what he actually has to say about this:

...mighty forces were used, of which I may not speak. Now to do this means using one's life-force; and many of us died a few days after we did this. My asthma, which I had never had since I first went out East, came back badly.[3]

Doreen Valiente writes:

I was told that a number of the older and frailer people who took part died shortly afterwards, and it was believed that the cold and the exertion had contributed to their deaths. They were regarded as having died for the cult and for the success of the ritual and were honoured accordingly.[4]

And Gardner told Bracelin:

We repeated the ritual four times; and the Elders said: 'We feel we have stopped him. We must not kill too many of our people. Keep them until we need them'[5]

In addition, King says: "... *not only the volunteer but two other members of the coven died from pneumonia within the next fortnight.*"[6]

So, how many died? "many of us"; "three"; or "a number"? This can only be speculation, but in my researches I have come upon two individuals who may well have fulfilled that role of willing sacrifice. There could have been others.

In suggesting names for two who might have died as a result of the Lammas 1940 ritual, I appreciate that I am putting forward something which can never be proved conclusively. I freely admit that I may be totally wrong. Nevertheless, I feel it only right to put forward the names of Walter Forder and Charles Loader - the editor of the local paper and the local blacksmith - as strong possibilities and to invite further research and informed discussion to try to confirm or discount my suggestions.

Walter Forder

Walter John Forder was born on 3rd November 1881 to Alice Maud Forder (formerly Duncan) and Walter Jabez Forder (an upholsterer and cabinet maker) of All Saints Terrace, 65 Caistor Road, Great Yarmouth in Norfolk.

In the report of a talk which he gave, it was explained that:

... in his profession of journalism he had early in life acquired the urge for prospecting and inquiring, and as a youth his first engagement had been with a provincial journal owned by the late Edwin Lawson Burgess. This journal displayed for its service to the citizens of Norwich a militant spirit of inquiry, and where necessary, attack and frequently exposure. This journal had inspired the publication of "The Slate", a national journal, upon which Mr. Forder was later employed, and "The Slate" proved to be the publication upon which Horatio Bottomley eventually framed his famous "John Bull" periodical.[7]

Walter Forder moved to Highcliffe in 1932 as an employee of the *Christchurch Times*. Shortly afterwards, the ownership of the business changed hands and he was appointed Managing Editor. He made his mark on the paper very quickly, particularly in his weekly column. As Brian Mead says in his obituary:

During his Editorship he was well-known for the character and vitality of his writings. Possessed of a fluent style and a flair for discovering the spectacular, he contributed to local journalism a certain scintillation which will long be remembered. A sense of humour and apt phrasing witnessed to his undoubted ability in a particular style of journalistic work.[8]

What comes over in Forder's writings is someone who was not afraid to puncture pomposity, wherever it occurred, particularly in the local council, but essentially someone who was human and approachable. He was certainly someone who was interested in the unusual, particularly in the spiritual or religious line. This is shown in two talks which he gave to the Christchurch Post-War Brotherhood, in January 1938 and August 1939.

"A GODDESS ARRIVES"

FINE NEW NOVEL BY HIGHCLIFFE WRITER

A STRANGE story, yet throughout, refreshingly strange, scholarly and bearing with it the imprint of a fine imagination, "A Goddess Arrives" carries with it locally an added interest, since its author is a Highcliffe resident.

MAIDEN LANE TO ANCIENT CYPRUS.

To select a theme built upon re-incarnation and to swing the story back and forth between Maiden Lane, London, that dingy little thoroughfare so steeped in Victorian theatrical history and ancient Cyprus of 1450, was surely some undertaking. But to evolve a thrilling novel out of the theme, playing with history and fact, with all the skill of a Rider Haggard, makes it little short of a masterpiece.

THE TROJAN WARS.

From the Trojan Wars with finely conceived imaginings as to how their cumbersome engines of attack were made, to a sordid triangular drama in a gloomy flat in London of to-day, and back again from a picture of a man lying still as death in catalepsy to the thrilling recounting of how, in ancient Cyprus, Venus, Aphrodite, a goddess arrives, is no mean accomplishment, when it is done, as Mr. G. B. Gardner effects it—just like scenes on a revolving stage: it fits and flows.

"The marriage in the Temple of Juske"—one of the chapters—is absolutely of the quality of Haggard.

I suppose this impresses because the central character is a wonderful woman. Haggard uses "She" and Mr. Gardner Venus Aphrodite.

Magnificently bound, in get up and format and pictorial jacket, faultless, "A Goddess Arrives" is told leisurely (and yet with every line vibrating with interest and thrill) in no less than 382 pages.

It's a grand yarn, and on many occasions a most scholarly and informative narrative, and throughout is a romance that grips. Mr. G. B. Gardner may take the unction to his soul that he has accomplished something of which he must be justly proud. W.F.

"*A Goddess Arrives.*" By G. B. GARDNER (Arthur H. Stockwell Ltd., London, 7/6).

HIGHCLIFFE CONSERVATIVES

ELECTION OF OFFICERS

A committee meeting was held at the Globe Hotel on Monday, for the election of officers for the Highcliffe Branch of the New Forest and Christchurch Conservative Association, and was well represented. President, Mrs. R. Fordham.

Col. F. Adams, D.S.O., was elected chairman in the place of the retiring chairman (Mr. C. P. Kirton), Mrs. Rowland Smith vice-chairman in the place of Mrs. W. T. Cooksey retiring. Mr. C. P. Kirton, hon. treasurer, and Mrs. R. Turner, hon. secretary,

52. Review of "A Goddess Arrives" by Walter Forder in the "Christchurch Times" 27th January 1940

The first talk was entitled "*I Met the Last Wizard*". This was about Cunning Murrell, the Norfolk village wise-man, and gave "an admirable wealth of fact and detail". The title cannot refer to Murrell himself, as he died in 1860, but Forder may have met his son, Mayday Murrell, the Ploughboy Poet, whom he also mentioned in his talk.

The following year, Forder gave a talk entitled "*Strange Religions - I've Explored Them All*". He spoke of the 'Prayer Shop' of Regent Street, where "a retired stockbroker literally dealt commercially in "prayer" - meting it out with the aid of a complete office staff and prayerful assistants, in return for fees which were printed upon a tariff."; the automatic writing of the Vale Owen scripts; and his discovery of a 'Sanctuary' in the heart of the Sussex Downs where "sinners may slip in beside saints".

This sounds very like a community at Storrington at the foot of the South Downs in Sussex. Ronald Hutton writes that it was:

... established by a rich Londoner, Vera Pragnell, in 1923 and called 'The Sanctuary'. Pragnell herself was a mystical Christian socialist, inspired by Edward Carpenter, but tolerant enough to permit (though not to encourage) naturism, 'free love' and paganism. [9]

Forder said that he "*had found in all the movements detailed a substratum of uplift and a certain aspiration, however garnished or foolish the deckings may have been. The fact that these movements received support and sincere sponsors all indicated that mankind sought for hidden spiritual Laws ...*"[10]

In 1937, Walter Forder first started reporting the activities of the Crotona Fellowship, and, indeed, my writing of Chapters 4, 5 and 6 was made much easier because of the frequent articles and news items about the Fellowship and its activities which appeared in the *Christchurch Times*. On reading these, it soon becomes apparent that Forder took a more than professional interest in the Rosicrucians. He gave support to them in the paper whenever he could, publicising their philosophy and aspirations and, finally, lamenting the lack of interest which the citizens of Christchurch seemed to take in their theatrical performances and other activities.

He was, in return, invited to give a speech at the ceremony to mark the laying of the foundation stone of the new theatre in March 1938. The wreaths at his funeral included one from "The Brethren of the Rosy Cross".

Little over a week after his talk on "Strange Religions", Walter Forder's wife, Alys Sara, died. She was only 42, and had, in her earlier years, been a concert performer and an entertainer in the Great War. He chose to write an obituary for her in the *Christchurch Times* for 2nd September 1939 - the day before war was declared - which ended "To bid her farewell is to signalise the honour of having been highly privileged to care for and be loved by so splendid a woman."[11]

Forder had not been well himself and, in February 1940, he resigned from the directorship of the *Christchurch Times* company. He does, however, give a very good review of Gardner's book *A Goddess Arrives* (which had been published in December 1939) in the *Christchurch Times* issue of 27th January 1940.

Walter Forder died on 11th August 1940, from heart failure and coronary thrombosis. In his obituary in the following week's issue of the *Christchurch Times*, Brian Mead, his successor, wrote:

For many months, Mr. Forder has been struggling to overcome a complexity of ailments and, with great exertion of will power, had, until quite recently, hoped and endeavoured to recover his health and strength.[12]

We can perhaps put together some sort of picture of Walter Forder's state of mind in early 1940. His wife had died and war had been declared the same week, and he was not in the best of health. He had probably met Gardner at meetings at the Ashrama but, after reading, and obviously being impressed by, *A Goddess Arrives*, it is my guess that these two got to know each other quite well. It was Forder who had written the humorous piece about Gardner's nude sunbathing in June 1939 and it seems clear that they only got to know each other after then. They were certainly near neighbours, for Forder lived at Chewton House, still known locally as 'Dr. Blood's House' after a former medic who lived there. This was in Highcliffe at the corner of Lymington Road and Chewton Common Road, only five minutes' walk from Gardner's house at Southridge.

By this time (January 1940) Gardner claims to have been initiated for several months and I think it likely that the two men talked of many things. Forder was probably also known to Edith Woodford Grimes and the Mason family, through the Rosicrucians, and to Dorothy through his role as Editor of the local paper: he had attended Rupert Fordham's funeral on behalf of the Directors of the *Christchurch Times*. Indeed, Forder was unique in being the only person we know who was definitely acquainted with both Gardner and his witch friends and with Dorothy.

Whether Walter Forder was offered formal initiation into the Craft, I do not know, but I believe that he was sufficiently trusted for the idea of a ritual to stop the invasion to be put to him, probably by Gardner. I believe that he would have responded enthusiastically. With the death of his wife, his own ill-health and the threat of invasion, he would have wanted to help in any way he could, and if that meant willing self-sacrifice, then that was no more than countless others were facing every day.

I believe that Walter Forder was a participant in the Lammas ritual, that he gave everything he had to it, and was much weakened as a result. I am not a medical expert but it seems likely that performing such a ritual where, as Gardner says, one's life-force is used, could well result in increasing the vulnerability in one's weakest spot - in Walter Forder's case, his heart, making a heart attack that much more likely.

It is a fact that Walter Forder died at the comparatively young age of 58. It is my view that he knowingly hastened his end to save this country from invasion.

Charles Loader

Charles Loader died at Milford Hospital on 13th August 1940 at the age of 76. His cause of death is given as a strangulated hernia.

He was a well-known blacksmith and farrier (his Death Certificate calls him a "Blacksmith Master"), and had, for the past 40 years, shoed for all the farms in the vicinity of Bashley and New Milton, the next villages to Highcliffe, including Major Murray's and Lady Gatty's horses at Ossemsley and Mrs. Ubsdell's at Great Ballard.

He shoed his last horse about a fortnight before he died.[13]

The link here, of course, is more tenuous and I can demonstrate no connection to the other participants of the Lammas ritual. And yet the blacksmith is a very magical figure. As Marion Davies says:

He who lives in a world of smoke and fire, who transforms the shapeless ore into a tool of necessity, a weapon of war or thing of beauty. He is a magician indeed. ... Most ancient cultures have their smith divinities. These deities are very often concerned with healing and the blacksmith was an accepted healer in the community.[14]

There are also traditions in many parts of the country about the Society of the Horseman's Word - those who could communicate with horses and enable them to do things that others could not. Blacksmiths were often members, for, as Marion Davies says:

... knowledge of the Horseman's Word ... affords immediate control over any horse of irascible temperament or in a state of agitation.[15]

Evan John Jones makes the point that: "*By tradition, before any of the four major rituals of Candlemas, May Eve, Lammas and Hallowe'en, there should be a period of fasting for the twenty-four hours preceding the rite. In the case of any serious magical working the same rule should be observed.*" For a ritual as momentous as working against invasion, it is quite possible that a longer period of fasting, as Gardner suggests above in a different context, might have been observed. Jones makes the interesting comment, however, that:

In the case of an office worker, no harm should come from a total abstinence, but a blacksmith or foundry worker who missed out on salt intake would soon find themselves feeling very ill.[16]

It seems a remarkable coincidence that the local blacksmith for 40 years should be taken ill within a day of the Lammas ritual, dying a fortnight later. It fits very well, but I can in no way prove it.

Independent Evidence

So, do we have any independent evidence, from people other than Gardner? And to be eyewitnesses they would have had to be part of the circle, for a ritual as momentous as this would have had no onlookers.

Louis Wilkinson has already been mentioned in Chapter 14 as claiming to have met members of the New Forest coven, and it was suggested that he may even have been a member. He certainly gave an account to Francis King of the 1940 ritual:

... On at least one occasion the Hampshire witches indulged in human sacrifice - but done in such a way that there could not possibly be any legal unpleasantness. ... The witches felt that it was essential that he [Hitler] *should be deterred from invasion plans by a powerful ritual, the central point of which was to be the death of a (volunteer) sacrificial victim. The oldest and frailest member volunteered for sacrifice and left off his protective grease so that he might die of the effects of exposure. Unfortunately enough, it was the coldest May night for many years, and not only the volunteer but two other members of the coven died from pneumonia within the next fortnight.*[17]

This account is interesting, not only because of the independent evidence which it gives of what Gardner is claiming but because it actually specifies the way in which the sacrifice was made - by leaving off a protective cover of grease, and opening that individual, literally, to "catching their death of cold".

The Vegan

Another independent account is provided by Laurence Main, well-known vegan and author of books on earth mysteries themes. He told me about a witch whom he met at a Vegan Society A.G.M. in 1980 or 1982. They were introduced by Jack Sanderson, who was then President of the Vegan Society. Laurence writes:

Jack knew him and knew me well enough to introduce him to me and say he was one of the survivors of the 1940 New Forest ritual. ... The witch must have been nearly, if not, 80 years of age (at least) and was curiously both frail and sturdy (he had an inner strength). What I most noticed was that his strength had been sapped, however. It seemed so obvious that here was a man of great strength who had given it all, or nearly all. Jack Sanderson told me he had nearly died in the New Forest ritual and that others had. This witch had never fully recovered from it. I'm sure he was a long-term vegan, one of the pioneers before the name was invented.[18]

Whilst it has been impossible so far to identify this individual, he may well also have been associated with either the Rosicrucians, the Theosophists or the naturist movement, since vegetarianism and veganism were strong themes in each.

"Lammas Night"

In 1983, a book called *Lammas Night* by novelist Katherine Kurtz was published. It was a work of fiction, but it is said that in doing research for the book, the author had made contact with a woman who had been present at the Lammas ritual that Gardner had attended. She is said to have remarked that whilst the "calling on groups to right and left" was necessary, it did have consequences. Before the ritual, the various groups hadn't known each other (or at most knew that other groups existed but had no contact). In contrast, after the ritual there was more contact, discussions and the interchange of ideas. She felt that this had been a negative thing in that their simple but traditional methods were threatened.[19]

In an Afterword to the book, the author states that: "*At least one New Forest coven did go down to the sea and raise a cone of power for that purpose at least three times that summer"*[20]. The mention of the sea is, of course, a new factor which had not been raised before. Gardner certainly says: "We were taken at night to a place in the Forest", but the above information suggests that perhaps other rituals may have taken place on the seashore, either near Chewton Bunny or some remote spot beyond Lymington where the New Forest comes right down to the coastline.

We must, however, take account of the situation as recorded by Sheila Herringshaw:

Maps found at German Headquarters after the war revealed that the beaches around Christchurch Bay had been chosen as a landing place for a German invasion. The Highcliffe beach was totally inaccessible to the public. The cliffs were protected by mile upon mile of barbed wire and patrolled by members of the Home Guard. Concrete gun emplacements were mounted on the cliffs to deter any who dared to approach the shore.[21]

Other Rituals

That other groups, both of witches, ritual magicians and psychics generally, did what they could on a magical level to stop the invasion is hardly surprising. Individuals from all walks of life would do what they felt was necessary, in the most effective way they could. For those trained in magical, psychic or mind-control techniques of various kinds this would be centred around working some sort of magic (which some might call prayer) to stop the invasion. It is clear that many individuals and groups from many different traditions - occultists, spiritualists, Rosicrucians, members of various religious bodies, etc. - would all be doing something in their own way. Almost certainly the co-ordinated approach which forms the basis of the *Lammas Night* story never happened, but many would doubtless have chosen Lammas as a suitable date to carry out their preferred working.

Paddy Slade, for example, tells of a working by witches in Kent[22]. She says that the witches gathered at a point where the coastline sticks out towards France, which sounds rather like Dungeness. They then proceeded to scatter "Go away powder" into the sea, presumably on an ebbing tide, accompanied by the usual chants. This powder was apparently made to a traditional recipe.

The Druid, Ross Nichols, who knew Gardner personally, tells of a gathering on the Sussex Downs in which Gardner is supposed to have taken part, "to project into the minds of Hitler and Goering the idea that invaders could not come over"[23]. Now, this may be just a mistake on Nichols' part on hearing Gardner's account of the New Forest ritual, but it is possible that Gardner had told him about a previously unrecorded event.

The author and journalist, Doug Pickford, tells of a working that took place at the "Devil's Hole", Alderley Edge, in Cheshire, a place that has long been associated with traditional witchcraft:

It is here that during the second world war when Hitler's evil looked almost certain to defeat the good British that some half a dozen people who had been students together at Manchester University visited The Edge and tried to awaken the sleeping warriors with powerful prayer, some Christian some Pagan.[24]

The occult writer, Dion Fortune, sent out weekly letters to her students during the early part of the war. Each of them meditated on the contents of the letter at a set time each Sunday, thus providing a strong magical link. The purpose included maintaining and strengthening the group soul of the nation by the evocation of symbolism, such as that of the rose cross. The letters have recently been reprinted in the book *The Magical Battle of Britain*[25].

A rather different sort of ritual is reported to have taken place in Ashdown Forest, Sussex in 1941. This is described by Cecil Williamson, who has accused Gardner of putting out a distorted version of this ritual, altering virtually all the details, including venue, time and purpose[26].

This ritual, which is also recorded by Amado Crowley[27], who claims he is Aleister Crowley's son and that he was present at it, was supposedly carried out under the personal supervision of Aleister Crowley and was attended by 40 Canadian soldiers (who controlled the Forest) and 50 assorted "fortune tellers and the like". The climax of the ritual involved setting fire to a dummy of Hitler and then releasing it on a wire leading from the top of a church tower on an estate in the middle of a wood.

It seems as if this ritual had an effect in that shortly afterwards, Hitler's deputy, Rudolf Hess, flew to Scotland in an apparent attempt at peacemaking.

I don't want to get involved in an examination as to whether this event took place, although Ronald Hutton can find no reference to it in Crowley's diaries.[28] Rather, I would point out that as the design, purpose, location, date and personnel are all so different from what Gardner was describing, it is quite clear to me that these are two totally separate events.

Although I have not been able to track down the origins of the story, I have been told that the witches also performed a ritual to assist with the D-Day landings in 1944. It was apparently carried out "in the West Country" (i.e. perhaps in the New Forest area) to allow the D-Day invasion to take place. There had been a delay due to the weather conditions and they cast a spell for good weather. In fact, there was a break in the weather just long enough for the invasion to take place[29].

I have no further information about this, except to point out that the preparations for the D-Day landings were centred on the Solent area, i.e. adjacent to the New Forest. Also, as these preparations were obviously undertaken in great secrecy, it rather suggests that the witches were specifically asked to carry out the ritual.

I have no confirmation, but there was supposed to have been a strange spell of calm weather that held for nine days during late May and early June 1940, and it has been suggested that the witches were involved in a magical working to keep the English Channel relatively placid during the rescue and evacuation of British and French troops from Dunkirk. Dorothy Clutterbuck refers to this indirectly in her diary when she writes: "The Sea turned to a lake ..." [7 May 1943]

The Effect of the Rituals

One important question to ask is "Did all these rituals actually have any effect?" We know, of course, that no invasion took place nor was even started, but did the New Forest ritual actually have the desired effect on the minds of Hitler and the German High Command? What do we now know about Operation Sealion (the planned invasion of Britain)? Evidence has recently come to light which gives a lot more information on Hitler's thinking during that crucial period from May to September 1940[30].

The German Admiralty began a study of the invasion of Britain soon after war broke out in September 1939. However, it was only when the Germans controlled all the French, Belgian and Dutch coasts that the head of the German navy, Admiral Raeder, spoke to Hitler (on 21 May and 20 June 1940) to make sure that any invasion would be adequately planned. Hitler was sceptical from the start, saying that "*he fully appreciated the exceptional difficulties of such an undertaking.*"[31]

It was not until 2nd July that a directive was issued for planning the invasion: "*The Fuehrer has decided that under certain conditions - the most important of which is achieving air superiority - a landing in England may take place.*"[32] Another directive was issued on 16th July: "*Since England in spite of her militarily hopeless position shows no sign of coming to terms, I have decided to prepare a landing operation against England, and if necessary to carry it out ... The preparations for the entire operation must be completed by mid-August.*"[33] On 21st July, Hitler stated that: "*The execution of "Sea Lion" ... must be regarded as the most effective means of bringing about a rapid conclusion of the war.*"[34]

It is now clear that Hitler was always ambivalent about Operation Sealion and balked at the idea of having to put it into practice. To start with, he believed that, following the fall of France, Britain would sue for peace and, as late as 19th July 1940, after the Channel Islands had been invaded and daylight raids had started, Hitler broadcast a 'Peace Offer'. However, it soon became clear to him that this would not be accepted.

In mid-July, a decision was made to put off consideration of the invasion until the following Full Moon (17th August), and towards the end of July, Hitler is reported to have said to one of his Field Marshals: "*I do not intend to carry out Sealion. There is no bridge across the sea. On land I'm a hero: on water I'm a coward.*"[35]

It is clear that, in Churchill's words: "*... at the end of July Hitler accepted September 15 as the earliest D-Day, reserving his decision for action until the results of the projected intensified air battle could be known.*"[36]

On 30th July, the German Naval Staff reported that, even if air superiority were to be gained, the Royal Navy could not be defeated. They concluded that an invasion was out of the question in 1940.

At this time, Hitler was considering what has been called "the most momentous military decision of his life" - should he press ahead with the invasion or should he turn his attention to the east - to Russia?

On 31st July, Hitler presided over a conference of the Commanders of the Army and the Navy:

During the meeting, Raeder ... said that an invasion fleet of sorts would be ready by the middle of September but he urged Hitler to postpone the operation to the following year. Hitler replied that he first wanted to see how the Luftwaffe was doing before making a decision. Raeder then left the meeting and Hitler told the leaders of the army that he was sceptical about the practicalities of an invasion, given the strength of the British Navy.[37]

Hitler then proceeded to outline an alternative strategy which involved crushing Russia first. Patricia Crowther tells an interesting story which might refer to this meeting:

At one of my lectures, a young man mentioned that he had read in a book about the war that Hitler dozed off during a meeting of some sort - something previously unheard of. When he woke up he suddenly announced that he was aborting Operation Sealion for the time being and informed his astonished officers of his decision to invade Russia, instead. The German war machine was immediately deployed towards this other objective, and Britain heaved a sigh of relief. But I wonder if this was the way the magic [was] manifested. Could Hitler's forty winks have been the Magical Sleep through which the intent of the witches became implanted in his mind?[38]

And Michael Howard states: "*At the meeting it is said that the sky turned a peculiar colour and dark clouds gathered. One woman present told Hitler it was an omen.*"[39]

Recent research has shown that: "*... between July and the middle of September 1940 ... the Germans had removed at least half of their divisions in the west to the east of the Reich to become part of the preparations for an attack on the Soviet Union in the following year.*"[40]

Despite this, it is important to remember that Hitler refused to cancel the preparations for "Operation Sea-Lion" and a date was set for the middle of September. "*At the beginning of September, the invasion barges were even moved to French and Belgian launch ports, clearly visible to British aerial reconnaissance.*"[41]

Hitler directed an intensified air war against England on 5th August[42]. However, five days later, the Naval Staff's War Diary refers to: "*... the inactivity of the Luftwaffe, which is at present prevented from operating by the bad weather ...*"[43]

On 13th August, known as 'Adlertag' (Eagle Day), the German air offensive started. Whilst there had been attacks in the South Coast area since the end of June, this was now a major onslaught aimed at destroying the RAF. The Luftwaffe concentrated on bombing airfields in the south of England, hoping to obtain mastery of the air in four days.

In this, they failed and, on 20th August, just a week later, Churchill gave another of his famous speeches: "*Never in the field of human conflict was so much owed by so many to so few.*" Indeed, in the first two weeks, German losses were twice those of the British. However, British losses were also heavy but, just at a time when the RAF might have been defeated, by making the airfields unfit to fly from, German tactics were changed, as Churchill records:

It was therefore with a sense of relief that Fighter Command felt the German attack turn on to London on September 7, and concluded that the enemy had changed his plan. Goering should certainly have persevered against the airfields, on whose organisation and combination the whole fighting power of our Air Force at this moment depended. By departing from the classical principles of war, as well as from the hitherto dictates of humanity, he made a foolish mistake.[44]

Indeed, it is clear that Goering, Head of the Luftwaffe, was not interested in 'Sea-Lion' because he did not believe it would happen. By 10th September, the Naval Staff were concerned that the activity of the Luftwaffe was not supportive of the invasion operation and therefore wrote that "the execution of the landing cannot yet be considered."[45]

However, the British population were still expecting an invasion, as Churchill's broadcast speech of 11th September 1940 makes clear:

We cannot tell when they will try to come; we cannot be sure that in fact they will try at all; but no one should blind himself to the fact that a heavy full-scale invasion of this Island is being prepared ...[46]

At the end of August, the invasion date was put back to 21st September. Churchill states: "*On September 10 the Naval Staff again reported their various difficulties from the weather, which is always tiresome, and from British counter-bombing.*"[47]

They also stated that air superiority over the Channel had not been achieved. On 11th September, Hitler postponed the invasion for a further three days, and on 14th, Admiral Raeder advised him that the risks involved in carrying out 'Sea Lion' were too great, that if it was undertaken and failed, it would be a great boost to British morale, but that it should not be cancelled, as it would still be a valuable psychological weapon against the British[48]. Preparations for 'Sea Lion' should be continued, even if they were just "to confuse the enemy" and "as a political bluff".

Following a particularly severe air battle on 15th September, German losses were so great that the air raids had to be scaled down: the Battle of Britain had been won. On 17th September, the postponement of the invasion became indefinite, with the onset of the habitual bad weather in the second half of September[49], and the specific forecast of a period of turbulent weather[50]. Churchill goes on to record the consequences:

On September 17, as we now know, the Fuehrer decided to postpone "Sea Lion" indefinitely. It was not till October 12 that the invasion was formally called off till the following spring. In July 1941 it was postponed again by Hitler till the spring of 1942, "by which time the Russian campaign will be completed". This was a vain but an important imagining. On February 13, 1942, Admiral Raeder had his final interview on "Sea Lion" and got Hitler to agree to a complete "stand-down". Thus perished operation "Sea Lion". And September 15 may stand as the date of its demise.[51]

We can thus see that Hitler's early scepticism about 'Operation Sea-Lion' was fuelled by the advice of his High Command, each of whom was even more aware of the difficulties surrounding such an enterprise. During the six weeks following Lammas, the date for the invasion was set back several times, mainly due to the failure of the Luftwaffe to gain air superiority and, following their defeat in the Battle of Britain, the invasion was postponed indefinitely.

It seems as if Hitler's mind was already in a state to be influenced by the time of the Lammas rituals, and that his uncertainties, and enthusiasms in other directions, together with the British success in the air, unwise decisions by the German High Command on the deployment of resources and, significantly, periods of bad weather, all contributed to the postponement decision on 17th September.

It can justifiably be considered that the Lammas rituals achieved their objectives and that those who died did not do so in vain.

I will end with two quotations:from Patricia Crowther and Gerald Gardner:

... Whether you believe in the efficacy of this ritual or not, the facts are that the invasion plans were put off, and Hitler turned his attention to Russia![52]

... I am not saying that they stopped Hitler. All I say is that I saw a very interesting ceremony performed with the intention of putting a certain idea into his mind ... and this was repeated several times afterwards; and though all the invasion barges were ready, the fact was that Hitler never even tried to come.[53]

Chapter 18
Learning the Ways of the Witches

To step back a little in time, what happened to Gardner after he met the witches and how did this affect what he wrote about them, their beliefs and practices?

After his initiation and the events surrounding the ritual to stop the invasion in 1940, Gardner was kept busy with his war work as an ARP (Air Raid Precautions) Warden and as an armourer for the Home Guard.

It is clear from Bracelin's account that Gardner got to know the witches quite well before he was initiated. He obviously liked them as people and his statement that he would, even then, have gone through "hell and high water" for any of them, rings true and shows the genuine link that had been created and that this was necessary before initiation could take place.

Initiation would not have been a common ritual in a well-established hereditary group such as that to which Gardner's witch friends seemed to belong. It was probably very much of a "one-off", with the traditional and the new intermingling. Gardner admits to being in something of an emotional state when he was being initiated, and it is easy to imagine that he would find it difficult to recall exactly what had taken place. He would have remembered something - the odd striking phrase perhaps but mostly what happened to him from his own point of view - actions and feelings.

Gardner's first thoughts on realising that he was being initiated into witchcraft are revealed by Bracelin: "*His first feeling about this was: 'How wonderful; to think that these things still survive', his interest as a folklorist stirred.*"[1] Knowing Gardner's personality as we do, we can be sure that, following his initiation, he was full of questions he wanted to ask the witches. What about their history? Did they work spells? What were their gods and goddesses? What other beliefs did they have? I can almost picture Gardner, eager for answers, and I can also picture the witches, parrying the questions as they came thick and fast. For traditionally, the main way of teaching was not to reply to questions, but to impart ideas and ways of looking at things over quite a period of time.

As Bracelin records, Gardner's previous opinions about witches would have to change:

Until then his opinion of witchcraft had been based upon the idea that witches killed for the purpose of gaining or raising power, and he had thought the persecutions of them fully justified. [2]

It was, perhaps, somewhat ironic that his first book to mention witches and witchcraft, *A Goddess Arrives*, was about to be published just at the time he had met some real witches who, from what they told him, had beliefs and practices which demonstrated that some of what he had written in that book was erroneous. And yet, it *was* a work of fiction and probably did represent the situation as it existed in Cyprus in 1450 BCE.

Of course, the teaching would normally have taken place within the family, over a period of some years. Clearly with Gardner it would have to be different, but I can imagine his frustration at not being told everything immediately.

It is a common practice nowadays for someone of the opposite sex to be chosen to teach the new initiate on an individual basis and to act as their magical partner. It is clear to me that in Gardner's case this was 'Dafo' - Edith Woodford-Grimes.

I have come to this conclusion because we know, unambiguously, from the writings of Doreen Valiente and Cecil Williamson that she was a witch. We know that she was a close friend of Gardner's during the right period: Gardner gave away her daughter,

Rosanne, at her wedding; they worked closely on projects to do with the local branch of the Historical Association; and Edith Woodford-Grimes was one of the shareholders of Ancient British Crafts Ltd. set up by Gardner in 1947. Gardner also referred to her in discussions with Doreen Valiente [3] and others, as being the witch from the old New Forest coven that he had kept in contact with.

The story is told by someone who knew Gardner well of how he actually met Edith Woodford-Grimes 'by chance' in London when they were both part of a team of volunteers filling sandbags to protect Westminster Abbey and the Houses of Parliament from bomb blast. They got chatting, discovered they were both naturists, she being a member of the New Forest Club. They got on well and before long Gardner was making frequent weekend visits to the club. There is no reliable way of assessing the veracity of such a story. Gardner certainly seems to have volunteered for such activities, as Bracelin records an occasion when Gardner had joined the A.R.P. and trained as a warden:

When the scare was bad ... shelter trenches were being dug in Hyde Park. So I bought a pair of rubber boots and went there. I found the diggers were being paid, and they did not want me, because volunteers doing the work for nothing might upset their employment; but a couple of halfcrowns settled that, and I was free to dig as much as I liked.[4]

In fact, it is likely that sandbag filling mainly took place at the spots from whence the sand was obtained, Hampstead Heath being a prime venue[5]. This was relatively near the Lotus League premises in Finchley and, if Edith Woodford-Grimes was in London, it would be far more likely that they both met at a naturist club such as the Lotus League, for naturism was a fairly rare thing in those days, and two naturists would be unlikely to meet by chance.

But was Edith in London in the immediate pre-war period? It could be. It is quite possible that she left her husband some time before she moved into 'Theano' in late 1937 or 1938, and that she spent that time in London. But would she have done that while she had a 16-year old daughter? Possibly. Rosanne's husband, Cecil, lived in Orpington, a London suburb, immediately before they were married, so it could be.

We must leave it for the moment, just an intriguing possibility. Further research needs to be done. But certainly Gareth Medway claims that:

... from later statements by Gardner it seems that at the naturist club he met a local school music teacher, generally known as 'Dafo', who introduced him to the Rosicrucian Theatre.[6]

This, of course, would go contrary to Gardner's own account, which was that he discovered the theatre by chance on one of his "long cycle rambles"[7].

We are in the realms of speculation, but I think that Gardner became very close to Edith during this period. Patricia Crowther has recently confirmed to me, from someone who knew them both well, that Edith was the one who actually initiated Gardner and was definitely present at the series of rituals to stop the invasion. And I think Edith is the one referred to by Ralph Merrifield, sometime Deputy Director of the Museum of London:

...in 1954, I received a visit at the Guildhall from [Gardner], and took the opportunity of asking where he had learnt his witchcraft. His reply was "I fell in love with a witch when we were fire-watching together during the war".[8]

Fire-watching was an activity carried out at night, usually by pairs of volunteers, for individual buildings or areas, to make sure that, if an air raid took place, they could spot where an incendiary bomb had landed and take what action they could, mostly with primitive stirrup pumps and buckets of water, to put out any fire before it started to spread, or to alert others if they couldn't tackle it themselves, though the fire-fighting authorities would be likely to be fully stretched.

I can imagine conversations during the long hours of fire-watching (possibly at Rushford Warren) where Edith was able to tell

Gardner much of what she had learned in the previous 20 or more years from the Mason family. It would, of course, have been dark, and Gardner would not have been able to write anything down at the time. When later he came to write down what he remembered, he would have forgotten much and perhaps misinterpreted some of the rest, and he may well have lost what notes he did make.

In August 1940, Edith Woodford-Grimes' daughter, Rosanne, got married. She was 19. *The Christchurch Times* of 24th August 1940 reported the ceremony.

LOCAL WEDDINGS

THOMPSON—GRIMES

The wedding took place at the Priory Church, Christchurch, on Saturday, between Cecil A. Thompson, only son of Mr. and Mrs. W. H. Thompson, of Orpington, Kent, and Rosanne Woodford Grimes, only daughter of Mrs. E. Woodford Grimes, of "Theano," Dennistoun Avenue, Christchurch; the Rev. H. M. Brownlow officiating.

The bride, who was given away by Dr. G. B. Gardner, a close friend, wore an afternoon dress of a soft brown shade with hat to match, and wore a spray of pink carnations. Her bridesmaid, Miss Joyce Morgan, wore a dress of autumn tint to tone with the bride's dress, and also wore a spray of pink carnations. The best man was Mr. J. Sarah.

Mr. L. Cardew-Buckley presided at the organ, the one hymn sung being "Lead us, Heavenly Father, lead us."

The reception was held at the Nelson Hotel, Mudeford, where between 50 and 60 guests assembled.

The honeymoon is being spent in Somerset, the bride travelling in a brown frock with an off-white serge wrap. Their future home will be at "Theano," Dennistoun Avenue.

53. Report of the wedding of Rosanne Woodford-Grimes and Cecil Thompson in The Christchurch Times 24 August 1940

It is clear that Edith Woodford-Grimes' marriage must have broken down completely, as her husband was not even present to give his daughter away at the wedding, as was the custom. Gardner, who was chosen to give her away, is described as 'a close friend', and I think he must clearly have been a close friend of both Edith and Rosanne, which implies, I would suggest, quite a long period of friendship on Gardner's part, initially with Edith and then, after he began to visit her house regularly, with Rosanne.

I think a clue to Gardner's relationship with Edith is provided by a passage which he wrote in *A Goddess Arrives*:

Dayonis and he were constantly together and her quick observation and essentially practical mind saw deficiencies and made suggestions which were of real value to him. Their friendship and understanding of each other grew rapidly and he found her a charming, intelligent companion, one who would enter into his schemes and his moods in a way which he had never experienced with a woman before.[9]

Indeed, as Rosanne used to perform regularly in the plays put on by the Crotona Fellowship, it is quite possible that at some stage she had also been initiated into the Craft. She would, I imagine, have been well known to the Mason family, having lived in the same street in Southampton during her childhood. Certainly in many hereditary traditions, children are initiated at quite a young age.

When Rosanne and her husband, Cecil, returned from their honeymoon in Somerset, Edith had moved out of 'Theano' leaving them in sole possession. She had moved into a much larger property, Avenue Cottage, 22 Avenue Road, Walkford. This was, in fact, not far from Highcliffe and within half a mile of Gardner's house, Southridge.

Avenue Cottage (and it is a much larger house than its name would suggest) was built in 1929-30 for George and Mary Piercy. This was three or four years after Avenue Road had been laid out and piecemeal development was taking place along it. So the house was only 10 years old when Edith bought it. Initially it would appear that she lived there on her own, although later she had a lodger.

I am sure that Gardner would have spent quite a lot of time with Edith at Avenue Cottage. His instruction in the ways of the witches probably continued off-and-on over the war years, and I think it likely that together they devised and performed rituals both there and out in the woods and heaths of the nearby New Forest as well. There was a multitude of suitable isolated woodland glades to choose from, as there are for groups of witches and pagans today. We shall probably never know, although I have seen reference to an "Autumn leaf-fall" ritual which was performed under a beech tree.

And what did Gardner's wife, Donna, make of all this? She is always represented as being a really nice person, but someone who didn't particularly want to get involved in his witchcraft activities. Indeed, there is a hint of this in a passage in *Witchcraft Today*. After writing about married or other couples, he says:

54. Avenue Cottage, Avenue Road, Walkford, Edith Woodford-Grimes' home from 1940 until her death in 1975

There are ... some unattached people, or some whose respective spouses are for some reason or another not members of the cult. I have heard fierce purists declare that no married man or woman should belong to, or attend, any club or society to which their respective partners did not also belong; but such strict views are not part of witchcraft.[10]

When Daniel Mannix went to Castletown to interview Gardner in about 1959, he met Donna. In a subsequent article, he says about her: "*... she refuses to enter the museum or have anything to do with witchcraft. "You see, my father was a parson and I've been brought up to consider such things wicked", she told me cheerfully.*"[11] Yet there are suggestions that Donna was more involved than has been hitherto thought. We shall have to wait for the results of others' research to take this line further.

I have no way of knowing how Edith taught Gerald what she knew (or, more likely, some of what she knew) about witchcraft. She certainly knew a lot and could well have been initiated (possibly by George Miles Mason) over 20 years previously.

However, I do have the experience of making contact with, and being initiated into, a surviving witchcraft tradition myself. This is not the place to give any details about this (and, in any case, I have given my word not to do so) except to comment on the feel of the whole thing, because it will shed some light on what I believe was Gardner's experience.

Things are rarely imparted in a straightforward way. I was very keen to find out as much as possible from the group which initiated me, and primarily from one person, but things were not that straightforward! Things might be ambiguous - a piece of information might be taken in different ways, and one might only learn which was right some time later. It was certainly not an organised course of instruction. Indeed, in many ways, it might not be recognised at the time as being instruction. It's just looking back on it that makes it clear that I was being taught, but in a very subtle way.

I had to ask questions, but I didn't necessarily receive straightforward answers. Answers to direct questions were often evaded because, I think, there were certain things one had to find out for oneself in one's own way and in one's own time. This is very similar to the Zen way of teaching where a 'koan' is set and only when the pupil has worked out what it meant can they pass on. I think part of the reason is that, for members of the traditional and hereditary Craft, witchcraft is no mere 'hobby': it is integrated into their life. It may have been a part of their life for as long as they can remember. It is therefore not something to get excited about - you do certain things at certain times in certain places, because it is the right thing to do. In my case, the teachings were fragmentary and much had been forgotten. To quote William Blake: "*The wisest of the Ancients considered what is not too explicit as the fittest for instruction, because it rouses the faculties to act.*"

Now, I am admittedly speculating, but I think that this is the way in which Gardner may have been taught. There is a lot which he admits he did not remember of what the witches told him. Writing in *Witchcraft Today*, published in 1954, he says: "*Fifteen years ago* [i.e. about 1939] *I heard many of the old tunes. Unfortunately I know nothing about music and I did not note them down.*"

Nick Howson, a friend of mine who has been initiated into another old tradition has told me something like: "*You think you are going to be able to remember the words of the rituals, especially when you've heard them a few times, but afterwards you can't.*"

It's also inappropriate to write things down at the time, or to ask afterwards (because of the "feeling" generated by the ritual). I think Gardner never got to the stage of learning them by heart, and the reason, I suspect, was partly that things were never done the same way twice, but mostly that they didn't meet that often. Whereas ideas he could write down afterwards, though often perhaps getting them distorted. And also actions, which would tend to be remembered more easily than words.

The contribution of Edith Woodford-Grimes to the future course of modern witchcraft was probably far greater than has hitherto been realised. She was close to Gardner throughout the war, and it seems to me highly likely that, not only did she teach Gardner what she knew of the Craft, she also helped him to devise rituals which would form the basis for his future books of magic.

Edith was an educated woman with a background in music, literature and philosophy. She was familiar with Co-masonic rituals and the inner teachings of Rosicrucianism. She was a good writer as well as a competent actress and public speaker with a particular interest in elocution. With such a background of skills and knowledge, I would consider it surprising if she had not helped Gardner to write specific rituals and to accumulate material which could be incorporated into them.

Gardner did eventually learn much of the knowledge and wisdom that the witches possessed, and, because of the sort of person he was, his delight at the witches' survival was quickly followed by another urge - to 'tell the world'. But one of the first things he found following his initiation was that there was great concern for secrecy among the witches:

He felt that all this should be generally known, and that if he could make his new knowledge available to all, objections to the cult would die down. But his request to be allowed to write about it all was turned down. No one was ever to know anything.[12]

In early 1960, following Donna's death, Lois Bourne was staying with Gardner on the Isle of Man, and was helping him sort out some of his papers. She remembers that:

... whilst doing so, I came across correspondence from a lady called Mrs. Woodford Grimes. She wrote in a very stern manner, castigating him for his blatant publicity tendencies, warning him about the deplorable people he became involved with, and casting aspersions on the motives of his converts. I recall that he was a little embarrassed by the letter but dismissive of it and said "She is old and has become crabby!"

Lois Bourne went on to write:

I gained the impression that the New Forest coven had been a very select group of people, and that Mrs. Woodford Grimes had intended that it should remain so. It had never been her intention that the teachings and the secrets should be available to people outside her group, and consequently she was displeased that Gerald should act independently by disseminating knowledge without her approval.[13]

She later says:

... Mrs. Woodford Grimes was a music teacher by profession and had no desire to become publicly known as a witch, so she withdrew from active craftwork when Gerald started recruiting new witches after the publication of High Magic's Aid *and* Witchcraft Today.[14]

As Gardner said (and I feel it is likely that he was referring to Edith Woodford Grimes):

... I wanted to tell of my discovery. But I was met with a determined refusal. 'The Age of Persecution is not over', they told me; 'give anyone half a chance and the fires will blaze up again'. When I said to one of them [the first one he knew, according to a similar passage in *Witchcraft Today,* and therefore clearly not Dorothy Clutterbuck, as some have suggested], *'Why do you keep all these things so secret still? There's no persecution nowadays!' I was told, 'Oh, isn't there? If people knew what I was, every time a child in the village was ill, or somebody's chickens died, I should get the blame for it. Witchcraft doesn't pay for broken windows.'*[15]

The witches' concern was two-fold. Firstly, there was a genuine fear of persecution. The word 'witchcraft' conjured up such images in most people's minds that a lot of negative reactions would descend upon them all. It is a sad reflection on our modern society that many witches, over 60 years later, might well say the very same thing.

A second reason for secrecy was a concern that certain very powerful magical techniques could be dangerous if they got into the wrong hands:

... witches have a firmly-rooted belief in their own powers, and the danger of these being misused if uninitiated people learn their methods. Also, they reverence their gods, and do not wish their names to be known, or bandied about and mocked.[16]

This concern with secrecy is still a common, and understandable, attitude amongst many traditional and hereditary members of the Craft. They have been carrying on their practices for many years and want to continue to do so. Publicity, even if it did not result in persecution, would be a disturbance, with people asking questions. As they succinctly told Gardner: "*We only want to be left alone.*"[17] He also writes:

They are happy practising their lovely old rites. They do not want converts: converts mean talk: talk means bother and semi-persecution. All they desire is peace[18]

If I were permitted to disclose all their rituals, I think it would be easy to prove that witches are not diabolists; but the oaths are solemn and the witches are my friends. I would not hurt their feelings. They have secrets which to them are sacred. They have good reason for this secrecy.[19]

Much of the time, as for many during the war, would be spent waiting for something to happen. Gardner was not the sort to fritter time away, and I think it likely that he would have spent this time reading avidly on a wide range of topics. This, I think would be the time when he would be building up his library. It is clear that Gardner did not abandon his presence in London and, despite wartime posters asking "Is Your Journey Really Necessary?", he was likely to have been a frequent traveller between Highcliffe and London to obtain fresh literary supplies. Folklore and mythology, religion, ritual and ceremonial magic, druidry, freemasonry, spiritualism and the history of witchcraft would be just some of the subjects on the agenda, so to speak, and all of this would later prove very useful to him in writing his non-fiction books, *Witchcraft Today* and *The Meaning of Witchcraft*.

Gardner must also have had time to think about what he had been told and what he had seen with his own eyes. It was probably at this time that his instinct as a writer came to the fore. He had had two books published, albeit paid for by himself, and he knew that he had the ability and the desire to write a book about what his friends, the witches, and particularly Edith, had told him, but would he get permission from them?

I think that Edith became cautious as Gardner expressed his concern about 'the witch cult', as he called it, dying out. I am sure there were long discussions culminating in the agreement for him to write *High Magic's Aid,* but I am equally sure that Patricia Crowther was right when she wrote:

There is no doubt that his revolutionary enthusiasm in the area of publishing denied him knowledge of the inner rites of the Craft. The door was now firmly closed in That direction.[20]

Indeed, it is possible that this is one of the reasons why Gardner borrowed and invented so much for the rituals in his Book of Shadows - he felt that he had to compensate for what he had not been told, or what he could not reveal.

Mike Howard writes: "*It has also been said that Gardner's decision to 'go public', even in fictional form, upset the Elders of his parent coven and he left them*"[21].

And Justine Glass says: "... *after a relatively short time he and his coven parted company. The reason seems to have been his urge to publicise Craft matters.*"[22]

I am not clear exactly when, but some time in late 1944 or early 1945, Gardner moved back to London, taking a flat at 47 Ridgmount Gardens, in order to be near the centre of activities.

The ten years from 1944 to 1954 were an important period in Gardner's life, in the development of his ideas and in the development of what is now known as 'Wicca' or 'Gardnerian Witchcraft' from what the witches had originally told and shown him. It was a period which would lead Gardner into contact with many different movements and organisations and he would meet several people who would influence his life considerably.

Druidry and Ross Nichols, who became head of the Order of Bards, Ovates and Druids (OBOD); J.S.M. Ward and the Abbey Folk Park; Aleister Crowley and the Ordo Templi Orientis (O.T.O.); becoming a Council member of the Folk Lore Society; his renewed interest in naturism and the subsequent acquisition of an area of woodland for his 'witch's cottage' adjacent to a naturist club in Hertfordshire; a chance meeting with Cecil Williamson which eventually led him to the Directorship of the Museum of Magic and Witchcraft on the Isle of Man; one fiction and two non-fiction books on the subject - all of these are important in the story of how 'Wicca' developed into what it is today.

But all this is another story and best told in the space which it deserves - another book, which I hope will appear as a companion to the current volume in the near future.

Chapter 19
Witch Beliefs and Practices

Our story has so far been told as a bit of an adventure, with our hero, Gerald Gardner, going through life seeking and exploring and ending up, perhaps without quite knowing why, as an initiated member of an old witch tradition.

But we are now at a crossroads. We know, with hindsight, what sprang from Gardner's contacts with the old witches - the whole of modern Wicca, which has grown as a religion in the 35 years since Gardner's death in a way that he could only have dreamed about. In doing so, of course it has also changed, particularly in its great flowering in the USA, which only took off after Gardner's death, and its beliefs and practices are generally agreed to be rather different from what Gardner was originally taught.

There is a poignant passage in Gardner's first non-fiction book about the Craft, *Witchcraft Today*, published in 1954, which seems to answer the criticisms of those who have accused Gardner of wanting to start a new religion:

... I think we must say goodbye to the witch. The cult is doomed, I am afraid, partly because of modern conditions, housing shortage, the smallness of modern families, and chiefly by education. The modern child is not interested. He knows witches are all bunk - and there is the great fear. ... The other reason is that science has displaced her; good weather reports, good health services, outdoor games, bathing, nudism, the cinema and television have largely replaced what the witch had to give. Free thought or spiritualism, according to your inclinations, have taken away the fear of Hell that she prevented, though nothing yet has replaced her greatest gifts: peace, joy and content.[1]

This was from the heart, and it was a sentiment that Gardner repeated more than once in his writings. Perhaps it was just a periodic depression, however, as elsewhere in the book he appears more confident in the future. Certainly, he need not have feared, for Gardnerian witchcraft, as a now well-established religious movement, has developed considerably since Gardner's time, and there are many books which give both a good overview and more detailed information. One might, for example, quote *The Witches' Way*[2] and *Eight Sabbats for Witches*[3] by Janet and Stewart Farrar; *Lid Off the Cauldron*[4] by Patricia Crowther; *Witchcraft for Tomorrow*[5] by Doreen Valiente and several others. It is not my intention in this chapter to repeat or even summarise what these authors have already done far more adequately than I could.

Nor is it my intention to look at the sources from which the present-day Gardnerian rituals are derived. This has been done already by several researchers, including Aidan Kelly[6].

My purpose is more limited, but also more difficult. It is to examine something of the character, beliefs, rituals and practices of the old witches that Gardner met by seeing what he actually said and wrote about them, both in his published books and in other documents. I make no attempt at a comprehensive study here - just enough to give a feeling for what the witches were like and what they did and believed. Here, I am using my intuition, which I freely admit might be at fault, but which I hope will be able to detect the right "atmosphere" or "aroma" surrounding the genuine material.

Sources of Information

What I have tried to do in this chapter is to select those sections of Gardner's writings which I think represent those things which he was originally told. How have I attempted this?

To answer, it is important to realise that in his published books Gardner had something of a problem. He put it succinctly in his book *The Meaning of Witchcraft*, published in 1959. Referring to his previous book, *Witchcraft Today*, he comments:

In writing this latter book, I soon found myself between Scylla and Charybdis. If I said too much, I ran the risk of offending people whom I had come to regard highly as friends. If I said too little, the publishers would not be interested. In this situation I did the best I could.[7]

I have repeatedly emphasised that it is important to see what was actually said rather than what people imagine was said, and to go back to the most original source of information possible. For the present purposes, what I am interested in is what Gardner actually said about the beliefs and practices of the witches that he claimed to have made contact with, firstly in his published works and secondly in comments and letters to his friends and acquaintances.

It seems as if Gardner took seriously his oath of secrecy with regard to much of the material which he learnt from the witches and therefore he needed to supplement what he was allowed to write with other material on the history of witchcraft and mythology. This does not in any way detract from the two non-fiction books he wrote about witchcraft, *Witchcraft Today* and *The Meaning of Witchcraft*: indeed, the extra material enabled him to show how what he was told fitted into a wider context. These books are probably nine-tenths Gardner's own philosophising and reviewing historical, mythological and literary material relating to witchcraft, which is undoubtedly interesting, but, scattered in amongst this, were snippets of information that the witches had told him about their beliefs and practices.

In this sort of thing, one has to trust one's feelings and intuition, and I think that it is possible to get a feeling of what the witches Gardner met were like and, holding this in mind, to read *Witchcraft Today*, *The Meaning of Witchcraft* and Gardner's other writings, to determine what statements are likely to have come from the original witches by what they feel like. In other words, they would resonate with the qualities which the witches seemed to possess, such as modesty and unpretentiousness, first-hand knowledge of techniques which work, and so on.

What I did in preparation for such an exercise was to take *Witchcraft Today* and *The Meaning of Witchcraft* and extract from them the passages where Gardner is actually writing about what the witches told him or what they actually do. In other words, I excluded all Gardner's philosophising, his accounts of witchcraft in history, literature and mythology and his interpretation of that material. This reduced the two books down to less than one tenth of their original length.

I next used my intuition. Where Gardner was writing on his own behalf, or using his logical mind to decide what the witches might have done or said, I have excluded the passage. Where, on the other hand, I felt as if he was reporting something which the witches told him, I have included it. I freely admit the subjective nature of this exercise, but feel that it yields valuable results.

Feelings

Theirs was a religion of experience: they were practical in everything they did, not relying on books. It is clear that feelings and emotions were an important part of their experience of life in general and of performing their rites in particular.

The feeling of taking part in the rites is clearly important to the witches that Gardner met. Indeed, there are three passages, which subsequently appear in *Witchcraft Today*, which are included in his 1949 novel, *High Magic's Aid,* as if being told by the characters in the story. This does not necessarily imply any deception on his part: it could reasonably be argued that he had accumulated material and statements on what the witches believed and experienced which he incorporated into *High Magic's Aid*, but that when he could write more openly about it all, in *Witchcraft Today*, he made use of the same material, and was able to give it in a more straightforward way and in a factual context. I suspect he took the passages from a notebook into which he put various things as they mentioned them to him. In any case, they are obviously important passages to him.

The passages as they appear in *Witchcraft Today* are as follows:

We worship the divine spirit of Creation, which is the Life-spring of the world, and without which the world would perish ... To us it is the most sacred and holy mystery, ... proof that God is within us whose command is: 'Go forth and multiply'. Such rites are done in a holy and reverent way.[8]

Another [witch] said: 'We ever pick out those who have a little inherent power and teach them, and they practise one with the other and they develop these powers.[9]

"It is a strange mystical experience. You feel a different person, as if much dross were sloughed off. There is some strange mystery of worship, delicate as a dream. It is as if I were in a trance during the rites; I can scarcely remember what happened; something seems to brush against my soul and I ever think of it with excitement - the old secrets of joy and terror quicken my blood."[10]

I think what probably happened was this. Gardner had jotted down in a notebook what are some very evocative pieces from what the witches told him. Years later, he puts them into his archaicised form of English and into the mouth of Morven in *High Magic's Aid*. After having written *Witchcraft Today*, he remembered these passages and, because they were genuine things that the witches told him, he adds them to the text. It is perhaps significant that they are all in the same section of the last chapter of *Witchcraft Today* - Chapter 13 - "Recapitulation", almost as if, after Gardner had written the book, he realised that he still had quite a lot of material that the witches had told him which he hadn't included (perhaps he found that long lost notebook!) and so he tried to put it all into one extra chapter. Certainly there is a much higher proportion of 'relevant' material in this chapter than in any of the others.

On experiencing the rites for himself, Gardner says:

I found, too, what it was that made so many of our ancestors dare imprisonment, torture and death rather than give up the worship of the Old Gods and the love of the old ways.[11]

There is an implication that you have to be a certain type of person to be a witch:

Witches have for hundreds of years held their meetings in private; they are people who want release from this world into the world of fantasy. To certain kinds of person the relief gained has been of enormous benefit and these occasional nights of release are something to live for.[12]

Witchcraft was, and is, not a cult for everybody. Unless you have an attraction towards the occult, a sense of wonder, a feeling that you can slip for a few minutes out of this world into the other world of faery, it is of no use to you. By it you can obtain peace, the soothing of jangled nerves and many other benefits, just from the companionship, but to obtain the more fundamental effects you must attempt to develop any occult power you may have.[13]

The Character of the Witches

What comes over in Gardner's writings is that the witches were strong in their belief that their magic worked and that it was important to keep their methods secret. Yet in other ways they were surprisingly modest and humble, freely admitting when they didn't know something. They seemed to be quite happy not to be noticed at all, just getting on with their everyday lives. As one of them said:

"... I am the sort of person who likes to go about affairs of interest in as unobtrusive a way as possible so that many people who meet me do not really notice me, which is the way I prefer."

This is, of course, one of the magical techniques of invisibility.

One of the reasons why they wanted Gardner to write Witchcraft Today was so that he could dispel some myths about them and present them as they were - ordinary people:

"Write and tell people we are not perverts. We are decent people, we only want to be left alone"[14]

... neither their present beliefs, rituals nor practices are harmful.[15]

They are the people who call themselves the Wica, the 'wise people', who practise the age-old rites and who have, along with much superstition and herbal knowledge, preserved an occult teaching and working processes which they themselves think to be magic or witchcraft.[16]

These Wica generally work for good purposes and help those in trouble to the best of their ability.[17]

Nevertheless, they were obviously friendly enough to Gardner, enjoyed his company and talked with him about many things, including reincarnation, and invited him to their homes. I think it a very good indication of their character that, even before Gardner was initiated or knew they were witches, he said that "... *I would have gone through hell and high water even then for any of them*"[18]. And, as late as 1952, he was still being protective of them:

"Now, I simply cant and wont let my friends, the people who trusted me, be bothered & badgered about ..."[19]

Consistent through all Gardner's statements about the witches is the obvious respect which he has for them. The above statement is, for me, so obviously genuine and from the heart, and it sums up his attitude to them.

The witches were modest in that they were quite willing to admit when they didn't know certain things, primarily about the history of their tradition, even where Gardner is obviously trying to prompt them. Take the following quotation from *Witchcraft Today*:

It is certain that long ago there was some sort of central authority, exercised by a common leader, whom the Church called the Devil, but they know nothing of this nowadays and would not know how to recognise him if he turned up.[20]

Gardner is here taking a lead from Margaret Murray, but the witches' answer is interesting. They refused to go along with

Gardner here, which is one of the many indications that they were not basing their beliefs and practices on Murray's works. It also shows how Gardner mixed a lot of Murray's ideas in with what the witches told him. It was almost as if he had definite ideas of how witchcraft was in the past, and if the witches failed to confirm them, then it was they who were, if not exactly at fault, then certainly possessing gaps in their collective memory.

Gardner mentions several cases where the witches' knowledge is fragmentary at best and, in some cases, either on the limits of memory or completely lacking:

My great trouble in discovering what their beliefs were is that they have forgotten practically all about their god; all I can get is from the rites and prayers addressed to him.[21]

The witches do not know the origin of their cult.[22]

To them the cult has existed unchanged from the beginning of time, though there is also a vague notion that the old people came from the East ...[23]

These statements sound very much as if they are referring to a real tradition: if Gardner was making it all up, he would surely have done better than this!

The witches that Gardner met were somewhat weak in theology, if one might put it like that. For example, he says:

Exactly what the present-day witch believes I find it hard to say. ... The cult god is thought of as the god of the next world, or of death and resurrection, or of reincarnation, the comforter, the consoler. After life, you go gladly to his realms for rest and refreshment, becoming young and strong, waiting for the time to be reborn on earth again, and you pray to him to send back the spirits of your beloved dead to rejoice with you at your festivals.[24]

Indeed, I suspect that Gardner's problem (as well as them not telling him everything) was that the concept of 'beliefs' may not have been that meaningful to them. Being of a practical nature, they were more concerned about relationships in society and in the 'other world', for they were certainly fully aware that we have many lifetimes. According to Gardner they talked of:

... a sort of happy hunting ground, where ordinary folk go and forgather with like-minded people; it may be pleasant or unpleasant according to your nature. According to your merits you may be reincarnated in time, and take your chance where and among whom this takes place; but the god has a special paradise for his worshippers, who have conditioned their bodies and natures on earth, who enjoy special advantages and are prepared more swiftly for reincarnation which is done by the power of the goddess in such circumstances as to ensure that you will be reborn into your own tribe again. This is taken nowadays to mean into witch circles. It would seem to involve an unending series of reincarnations; but I am told that in time you may become one of the mighty ones, who are also called the mighty dead. I can learn nothing about them, but they seem to be like demigods - or one might call them saints.[25]

They seemed to hold to the principle that you could do what you liked as long as that didn't interfere with anyone else. Gardner called it the morality of the legendary Good King Pausol and it has now been formalised (with an input from the works of Aleister Crowley) as the Wiccan Rede:

Eight words the Wiccan Rede fulfill
An it harm none, do what you will.

Gardner adds:

... they believe a certain law to be important, 'You must not use magic for anything which will cause harm to anyone, and if, to prevent a greater wrong being done, you must discommode someone, you must do it only in a way which will abate the harm.'[26]

Rites and Rituals

According to the dictionary, a rite is the actual event whereas ritual relates to the things which are done within it. Nowadays it is more common to speak about a ritual for the whole thing, but Gardner always referred to rites. He gives no detailed order of proceedings or quote what was said in them. Whilst this could be for reasons of secrecy, I think the main reason is that there weren't many. What there were were symbolic and practical actions - things that were done because they had always been done and it was right to do them or because they were needed for some special reason. As Gardner says:

... their own rites ... were made for a definite purpose and ... produced definite results ...[27]

If one goes by Gardner's descriptions, the rites were both simple and, to a large extent, spontaneous:

Rites are performed for certain purposes. These take time, but when they are finished the assembly have a little meal, then dance and enjoy themselves.[28]

I have attended many of these cult rites ... There may be a fertility dance, but the other rites are simple, and with a purpose ... sometimes there is a short ceremony when cakes and wine are blessed and eaten. (They tell me that in the old days mead or ale was often used.) ... The ceremony is simply intended as a short repast, though it is definitely religious.[29]

The dances that follow are more like children's games than modern dances - they might be called boisterous and noisy, with much laughter. In fact, they are more or less children's games performed by grown-ups, and like children's games they have a story, or are done for a certain definite purpose other than mere enjoyment.[30]

Among primitive people dancing was the usual religious expression. In witch tradition it was the necessary preliminary to the climax of the sabbat, the producing of power; it may have had other objects, to bring joy and to express beauty.[31]

These dances are intoxicating, and this intoxication is the condition for producing what they call magic.

... they tell me that in the old days sometimes, when the High Priest was not present, a skull and cross-bones was used to represent the god, death and resurrection (or reincarnation). Nowadays the High Priestess stands in a position representing the skull and crossbones, or death, and moves to another position, a pentacle, representing resurrection, during the rites.[32]

To this day, the witches preserve these traditions: the flame upon the altar, and the ritual knife with which the magic circle is drawn.[33]

Whilst the older rites were joyful occasions and tended to be different each time, they seem to have had an opening and closing structure - invoking and thanking the Gods. Within this structure, in the heart of the rite, there was room for spontaneous words and actions. Gardner also reports:

... they believe that helpful spirits, human or otherwise, come of their own accord to assist in their rites, and that those present who have developed "the Sight" (i.e. clairvoyance) may see such spirits.[34]

In this connection, writing to Gerald Yorke in 1952, Gardner mentions a ritual of invocation which he did not include in the book:

"... there are two, things they do, As soon as the Circle is cast & purified, they go round, what I call, evoking the Mighty Ones. To attend, to guard the Circle & witness the rites, These are meny they are supposed to stand outside, & watch, seeing all is correct. Candidates for initiation are peraded round, introduced to them, & they are supposed to be satisfied all is in order, Also at certain rites, The, God, or Goddess Is invoked to decend & come into the Body of the Priestess or Priest, but first these are purified, & perade round so the mighty ones outside see all is in order, this we speak of as invoking. At ordinary meetings, the God & Goddess are not so invoked, the Priestess & Priest are simply their representitives, & are not the Gods themselves, I think I did not refer to this rite, if I did, I dont think theyll pass it."[35]

This is really now a fairly standard procedure, but it is clear that at the time Gardner felt that the witches would not want him to include it in the book, one of the implications being that it was something they were in the habit of doing, and something which worked.

Raising Power

Gardner is very specific in *Witchcraft Today*, where he says:

...they do not wish it to be known how they raise power.[36]

We are talking here about raising not physical power but some more subtle energy, that which Wilhelm Reich called 'orgone' and which has been known by many names throughout history. The witches used it to perform magic, and I think there were two main reasons for their reticence. Firstly, their morality was to heal and not to harm, and they did not want their techniques falling into the wrong hands. The second reason is that some of the power-raising techniques involved something which the outside world considered particularly depraved, for some reason. They involved sex.

What the witches seemed to be telling Gardner, and this certainly accords with what Wilhelm Reich was discovering across the Atlantic at about the same period, is put by Gardner as follows:

Witches are taught and believe that the power resides within their bodies which they can release in various ways, the simplest being dancing round in a circle, singing or shouting, to induce a frenzy; this power they believe exudes from their bodies, clothes impeding its release.[37]

Reich found that orgone energy was present everywhere, in the atmosphere, but particularly in all living things; it flows from a weaker to a stronger system; it flows in waves and has a pulsating motion; it can be seen flowing from west to east in the atmosphere; it can be observed in darkness and it has the potential to operate as a motor force. It seems to be the same energy that people see in the human aura and in the vortices in the human body known as 'chakras'. Reich also found that it was possible to concentrate this energy into what he called an 'orgone energy accumulator' and that sexual activity was one of the ways in which this energy could be raised.[38]

The witches' use of sex as one way of raising power was natural and straightforward and without any of the inhibitions which we as a society have towards what is a natural process. Such inhibitions would have been even stronger 60 years ago. In his published works, in order to keep faith with the witches, who were his friends, Gardner only hints at it, as in the following quotation:

... it is no use trying to develop these powers unless you have time and a suitable partner, and it is no place to take your maiden aunt, even if she is romantic; for witches, being realists, have few inhibitions and if they want to produce certain effects they do so in the most simple way.[39]

Within the Circle

The witches' circle seemed to have two main functions, both practical and spiritual. The witches gave Gardner an insight into the religious or spiritual principle behind the casting of a circle, which was rather different from what he had previously suspected. He says:

I am also permitted to tell for the first time in print the true reason why the important thing in all their ceremonies is 'Casting the Circle'. They are taught that the circle is 'between the worlds', that is, between this world and the next, the dominion of the gods.[40]

When drawn, this circle is carefully purified, as also are all who celebrate the rites. Witches attach great importance to this, for within the circle is the gods' domain.[41]

Its practical function was to keep the power that is raised contained within a small area so that it can be focused into what the witches call a Cone of Power, as was raised in the ritual to stop the invasion.

This circle is drawn with the idea of "containing" the "power" which is raised within it, of bringing it to a focus, so to speak, so that some end may be accomplished by raising it. This focusing of force is called "The Cone of Power".[42]

The witches told Gardner that they worked naked because only in that way could they obtain power.[43]

They believe the power is within themselves and exudes from their bodies. It would be dissipated were it not for the circle cast ... to keep the power in ...[44]

It is a tradition that fire in some form, generally a candle, must be present on the altar, which is placed in the middle of the circle, and candles are also placed about the circle itself.[45]

That this power could be used for other purposes is made clear by Gardner as follows:

They say that witches by constant practice can train their wills to blend this nerve force, or whatever it is, and that their united wills can project this as a beam of force, or that they can use it in other ways to gain clairvoyance, or even to release the astral body. These practices include increasing and quickening the blood supply, or in other cases slowing it down, as well as the use of will-power ...[46]

The witches did not always confirm Gardner's previous ideas about things. As we have seen in *A Goddess Arrives*, Gardner portrays the heroine as a witch who seems to take both animal and human sacrifice as a normal part of a magical working. Now clearly this is a story but Gardner himself said that until he had talked with witches he thought that they had indeed taken part in such practices and that the persecution of them had been justified. But he quickly found out that this was not the case:

The people I know are taught never to use blood or to make sacrifices ...[47]

The first witches I met denied ever using blood in any way and I think they were speaking the truth...[48]

Witch Powers and Magic

Psychic ability (which we all possess, however buried beneath the trappings of society) and the ability to work magic are like two sides of the same coin, and the witches who taught Gardner were proficient at both. But they were both techniques which needed to be worked at, as Gardner points out:

Being initiated into the witch cult does not give a witch supernatural powers as I reckon them, but instructions are given, in rather veiled terms, in processes which develop various clairvoyant and other powers, in those who naturally possess them slightly. If they have none they can create none. Some of these powers are akin to magnetism, mesmerism and suggestion, and depend on the possibility of forming a sort of human battery, as it were, of combined human wills working together to influence persons or events at a distance. They have instructions in how to learn to do this by practice. It would take many people a long time, if I understand the directions aright. ... to a witch it is all MAGIC, and magic is the art of getting results. To do this certain processes are necessary and the rites are such that these processes may be used. In other words, they condition you. This is the secret of the cult.[49]

Various applications for magical techniques are given by Gardner. He obviously seems to have asked first about cursing and he was told it was not easy:

... a witch told me long ago, 'Before you can do any harm to your enemy by means of a wax image you must be in a genuine and spontaneous rage, as you would need to be before you knocked him down physically.' ... It was agreed that he might be dealt with, but only in a way which would cause him no harm. So I was able to see exactly what was done. Of course I may not tell what this is, but I can say I consider it to be a very ancient practice, a way of directing a curse ... I was talking to a couple who had been present when the "Poppet" was made, and both said, "We saw it done, but still don't know how to do it," and that's exactly my position; I feel there is something which escaped me, and 'she who did it' won't tell me.[50]

Gardner says: "*Witches have many formulae for making all sorts of charms, though few use them nowadays ...*"[51], an indication, I suspect, of a certain reluctance to use them unless they were absolutely sure it was appropriate.

Gardner seems to be quoting from some book or written instructions when he says:

... a charm to make a young couple love each other ends with: "Try to ensure that the pair are thrown together alone, in exciting and if possible dangerous circumstances (or let them think they are dangerous). Soon they will begin to rely on each other; then let them know that a love charm has been made. If they be of the cult, make them perform the rites together and the charm will soon act."[52]

I suspect, by the use of the words 'be' and 'cult' in the last sentence, that Gardner has had a hand in the wording, but he could well have been paraphrasing older writings.

Other magical techniques are just hinted at, either because Gardner had been told to keep the details secret, or because he did not know them himself:

... the witches have formulae for producing [a] *form of autointoxication, of escape into the world of faery. It cannot be induced, however, if people are unsympathetic ...*[53]

... the witches have a rite which involves kissing and then beating an object, with the intention of charging it with power.[54]

... some curious things can be done with the right sort of wand ...[55]

Indeed, it is quite clear, on reading through what Gardner wrote about the witches that they did not tell him everything and that it may well be, as Patricia Crowther surmises, that he was never entrusted with what she calls "the Inner Rites".

Incense, Herbs and Poisons

One example could well be the knowledge of herbal preparations, including magical incenses and plants which had psychoactive properties and poisons. The witches were practical people, but I get the distinct impression that they were not revealing everything they knew.

Gardner says that they used incense [56] but gives few details. He does, however, say:

I am told that in the olden days witches had knowledge of a herb called Kat which, when mixed with incense, would release the inner eye, the subconscious, but unless another herb, Sumach, was mixed with it, it could not be used for long as it would produce hallucinations. If you used both correctly, it was possible to leave the body. Unfortunately they do not know what these herbs were; but both are said to grow in England. It is said that if a man breathes incense with Kat in it, then woman becomes more beautiful, so it is possible that it contained wild hemp.[57]

This seems to be similar to a substance which Gardner said they called 'Soma' or 'Sume'. Replying to Gerald Yorke, he wrote :

"This was not a drink. They had somthing which mixed with the Incense. Burning this they said it opened the inner eye, but you could only use very little, & for a short time only, or it produced Halucanations, But if you mixed some other herb with it it kept off the bad effects, you could use the first stronger, & keep on using it, & could obtain wonderful results, & both of these were things that grew in England, but they dont know what there were, anyhow Ive left the name out."[58]

With regard to aromatic oils, he says:

They have a very powerful scented oil, which nowadays they speak of as anointing oil. This is only used by the ladies, who dab it on their shoulders, behind their ears, etc., much as ordinary perfume. When they are heated with dancing, this gives off very strong fumes, and most certainly produces a very curious effect. What it is made of is kept a great secret; they had to do without it during the war and for some time afterwards, but supplies are coming forward again.[59]

This suggests that it could well have been imported and that it was probably Edith Woodford-Grimes who was using this oil, as it is likely that she was the only one that Gardner kept in touch with after the war.

Gardner does, however, describe another oil, the ingredients for which would have been readily available:

I have never known witches annoint themselves all over, but I have been shown a recipe for an anointing oil. This consisted of vervain, or mint crushed and steeped in olive oil or lard, left overnight, then squeezed through a cloth to remove the leaves. Fresh leaves were then added and the squeezing repeated three or four times until it was strongly scented and ready for use.[60]

Gardner suggests an almost total lack of knowledge about poisons:

... the present-day ones have no real knowledge of them [poisons]. *They know vaguely that hellebore is deadly, as they know weed-killer is, but they do not know the correct dose of either, and they do not know where to get hellebore.*[61]

In fact, such a statement suggests to me that they may have been deliberately hiding something, as hellebore grows fairly readily in many wooded areas, but if, as seems to be the case, they didn't actually use poisons then they wouldn't need to know about them.

Louis Wilkinson told Francis King that:

They also used an hallucinogen, but this was fly-agaric, a common British fungi, which they took orally in extremely small doses. Fly-agaric and similar fungi have been used all over the world from time immemorial.[62]

It is clear from their artifacts which were later exhibited at the Museum of Magic and Witchcraft that the witches whom Gardner initially met (or some of them at any rate) took a keen interest in the gathering, cultivation and preparation of herbs for magical and healing purposes. It is therefore not unreasonable to suppose that they did also possess a working knowledge of incenses and psychoactive plants, if not of poisons.

I have not attempted to cover fully everything that Gardner mentions about the witches' beliefs and practices, but enough, I hope, to give a picture of their approach to things - that combination of the mystical and the practical, with no pretensions of any sort. Their witchcraft was unobtrusive because it was fully integrated into their daily lives.

I think that what happened was that, by about 1953, enough time had elapsed for Gardner to feel free to write a factual book about their beliefs and practices. It seems to me that *Witchcraft Today*, published in 1954, and *The Meaning of Witchcraft*, published in 1959, succeed admirably in portraying the character of those witches and how they approached their Craft.

The existence of a secret book, the contents of which are copied afresh by each newly-initiated witch, is now fairly universal amongst many branches of the Craft, particularly those which are derived, directly or indirectly, from Gardner. Such a book is usually referred to as a Book of Shadows and contains theology, philosophy, seasonal and other rituals, spells, ways of raising power, and numerous other matters.

I do not intend to comment in detail on the various published and unpublished versions of the nominally secret Book of Shadows. However, I will venture my opinion that parts of the Books of Shadows which I have seen have a very similar 'feel' to what I have set out in this chapter, whereas other parts are much more structured and seem to me to have a different and distinctive origin. However, the present book is not the place to debate that.

Fred Lamond gives an idea of Gardner's attitude to the Book of Shadows:

Gerald was always at pains to tell us: "The 'Book of Shadows' is not a Bible or Koran, but a personal 'cookbook' of spells that the individual witch has found to work. I (Gerald) am giving you my book to copy to get you started: it contains the spells and rituals that worked for me. As you gain in experience, add the successful spells that you have made up, and discard those that didn't work for you!" [63]

Such books were never intended to be published and it is clear from Gardner's statement that they were intended to be altered and added to as time went on and to be 'personalised' by the individual witch. I suspect that, insofar as the old witches had such books, they always were.

Chapter 20
"In Another Part of the Forest ..."

In the course of research for this book, I have noted various subjects or individuals who might have a bearing on the story. Whilst I have not yet been able to integrate them into the whole picture, they should certainly be mentioned. So I have, perhaps rather unceremoniously, lumped some of them together here. They are undoubtedly candidates for further research.

Whatever the truth of the tradition of witchcraft that Gardner claimed to have been initiated into, it did not exist in complete isolation. We have seen, for example, that the Mason family, as well as their witchcraft connection, were involved in theosophy, anthroposophy and Co-Masonry, and, of course, it was through their membership of the Rosicrucian Crotona Fellowship that they first met Gardner. It is certainly my impression that there was far less "narrow sectarianism" in esoteric and occult circles than there sometimes is nowadays and people tended to join and get involved with anything that was going on.

And there were certainly things going on in other parts of the New Forest, and elsewhere. Whilst I have not been able to demonstrate any definite links with Gardner, they deserve a chapter to themselves if only to show that the events in Somerford and Highcliffe were not happening in isolation.

The Order of Woodcraft Chivalry

The Order of Woodcraft Chivalry[1] had been founded in 1916 by Ernest Westlake, a geologist, of Fordingbridge, on the edge of the New Forest, together with his son, Aubrey. They were becoming disillusioned with the Boy Scout movement, with which they had been involved, for several reasons, including the militaristic side of Scouting. In contrast, they had been inspired by the writings of Ernest Thompson Seton (1860-1946), a Canadian naturalist, who taught a form of 'woodcraft' based on native American practices. This caught on, and by 1910 there were over 200,000 members.

There was certainly a mystical and overtly Pagan side to Seton's Woodcraft. Adults were admitted into what were called Red Lodges, which had three degrees of initiation. They worshipped a Red God within a ritually cast circle, which had four lamps to mark the quarters.

In 1919, the Westlakes had purchased an area of woodland adjacent to the River Avon at Sandy Balls, Godshill, near Fordingbridge. This really became the centre of activity for the Order of Woodcraft Chivalry for most of its existence.

There are some remarkable similarities between the format for meetings of the Order of Woodcraft Chivalry, apparently based on what was known of Native American spiritual practices, and those later to become common in Wiccan circles, as well as occurring in the same sequence, as Aidan Kelly[2] points out:

- consecrating a circle;
- invoking the spirits of the four directions;
- invoking the Great Spirit;
- dancing around the circle, with drumming;
- sharing a small feast;
- thanking and dismissing the spirits;
- opening up the circle

There are certainly parallels, but it is a fairly universal pattern and does not necessarily imply a direct causal connection.

There were, as with any organisation, particularly one which attracts individualists who are not prepared to follow the 'party line', differences of emphasis and interest. One strand which became woven into the Order of Woodcraft Chivalry was an interest in 'Gymnosophy', the Greek term for naturism, or nudism. This was seen by many to be a part of the Order of Woodcraft Chivalry philosophy, not just of 'back to nature' but the controversial philosophy of recapitulation - the need to relive human evolution through various stages.

Another strand was what, effectively, we might call Paganism, although this was usually referred to as Dionysianism. One of the chief protagonists of this was Harry ('Dion') Byngham. He was the first Editor of the Order's magazine *Pine Cone* in 1923 and his first Editorial gave some of the flavour of Dionysianism:

Life springs out of the star-tissued womb of Nature as the virile son of the all-Mother ... Now Life, this young virile Becoming force, was imaged by those inimitable godmakers the early Greeks as Dionysos, a wild-souled and supple-bodied youth who carried a wand or thyrsos as the symbol of his will, love and power ... the central experience aimed at and attained in the Dionysiac ... religion and ritual was ecstasy.[8]

This proved controversial with the more conservative elements of the Order, but it is undoubtedly true that Dionysianism, with its emphasis on a horned god and a moon goddess, was effectively pagan. This was, however, only a strand within the Order and, with the departure of Bingham and some others, it really ceased to exist after 1934.

This is all (genuinely) very interesting, but, apart from the esoteric viewpoint that one movement can affect another regardless of any physical contact, there really is very little to connect the Order of Woodcraft Chivalry with what Gardner was doing at the time.

That Gardner had any connection with the Order of Woodcraft Chivalry is limited to a statement by Professor Ronald Hutton in his essay *"The Roots of Modern Paganism"* where he states: *"Even a relatively swift examination of his* [Gardner's] *social world between his arrival in England in 1936 and his first 'Wiccan' publication in 1949, reveals that he was ... a member of one of the divisions of the Order of Woodcraft Chivalry."*[4] A footnote reads: *"... Bran Labworth testifies to his connection with the Woodcraft*

Chivalry". Hutton also states that *"...by the 1950s, if not before, Gardner was apparently friendly with members of the Woodcraft Chivalry."* He says that the same informant *"...claims to have seen him beside the sacred fire in the centre of the folkmoot circle at Sandy Balls one evening, chatting to the people there."*[5]

And that is all.

At what stage Gardner made contact with the Order of Woodcraft Chivalry is not known. One might reasonably imagine that it was during his time at Highcliffe (i.e. 1938-1945), but as Ronald Hutton points out, this is really much too late to have experienced the Dionysian and naturist strands within the Order. However, there may have been an intermediary - somewhere that Gardner may have met members of the Order because of their shared interests in Gymnosophy. One place immediately springs to mind - The New Forest Club. The Club may well have attracted former member of the Order who were disillusioned with how things were going. The original site of the Club, at West Moors, was less than 10 miles from Sandy Balls. It is interesting that it opened on 1st May 1934. I do not know whether that date was chosen deliberately, but the fact that it was a Tuesday, not perhaps a normal day to start an enterprise, suggests that the underlying symbol of May Day was a strong influence, as it was to the Order.

It is intriguing to speculate that Gardner may have come into contact with the Order of Woodcraft Chivalry or individual members of it at a date early enough for it to have been an influence on the subsequent development of Wicca. That is a very different matter from claiming, as some have done, that the group that Gardner came into contact with was actually an Order of Woodcraft Chivalry group.

It is quite clear to me that it was not, for several reasons. First of all, none of the people that I feel reasonably confident formed part of the group that Gardner came into contact with (i.e. the Mason family) are mentioned in connection with the Order of Woodcraft Chivalry in, for example, Edgell's book. Nor, indeed, have I found in my investigations into the Mason family any interest in the Order of Woodcraft Chivalry. Nor is there any overlap of personnel between the Order and any of the other organisations that I have investigated such as the Crotona Fellowship.

Secondly, as Ronald Hutton points out, the timing is wrong. The earliest that Gardner might have made contact with the Order of Woodcraft Chivalry is the summer of 1936, when he returned to England. By this time, the pagan and ritual elements of the Order had changed out of all recognition. If contact was made, it was with individuals only, as I have suggested above.

It is undoubtedly true that the Order of Woodcraft Chivalry, in its beliefs and practices, had something in common with what Gardner was later to write about in connection with witchcraft. At most, this would have been merely another influence on Gardner, which is far more likely than postulating a direct link between the Order and the traditional witches that Gardner met, or that what Gardner thought was traditional witchcraft was actually a form of Woodcraft Chivalry.

Sybil Leek and the Horsa Coven

Sybil Leek[6] was born in Staffordshire into a family whose involvement in witchcraft she claimed dated back more than 800 years. She came to the New Forest in the 1950s (so much too late to be an influence on Gardner directly), where she ran antique shops, originally in Ringwood and latterly in Burley. She was a High Priestess of a coven which met on the outskirts of Burley, only six miles from Highcliffe. It was known as the Horsa coven, the Anglo-Saxon word for horse. This, or another coven of which she was High Priestess, was also known as the Three Acres Coven. She told Deric James: *"There are four covens operating in the New Forest area; at Lymington, Lyndhurst and Brook. Witches have met in the New Forest for hundreds of years and we are just carrying on the tradition."*[7] She also said:

The New Forest covens were interested in the social affairs and general welfare of the communities in which they lived. Although there are four covens living in different sections of the New Forest area, we observe the age-old rule of not interfering with each other's activities. Today, with easy transportation, members of the other covens call on each other socially ... The New Forest covens always have their full complement of thirteen people in each group: equal numbers of male and female plus the High Priestess. ... We all had our specialities in one particular aspect of witchcraft. I had a flair for healing. A man in Lymington was the best and most efficacious person I know for making charms and potions ... Shortly after I became High Priestess of the Horsa Coven, the Witchcraft Laws were repealed ...[8]

We of the Horsa Coven have a long history - both as a group and individually ... the heartbeat of witchcraft must always reside in the old established covens, such as Horsa - the sign of the Horse in the New Forest of England.[9]

Details of the Horsa and other covens given in Sybil Leek's writings are (probably deliberately) rather vague and therefore difficult to assess. I am told that the rituals were based largely on Crowley's writings.

Whilst the covens in various parts of the New Forest which she mentions could be genuinely old, the matter must at this stage be left open.

Dolores North

Gardner was bad at spelling. It may have been something to do with having taught himself, and some have speculated that he was dyslexic. Anyhow, the manuscript of *High Magic's Aid* that he delivered to publisher, Michael Houghton in late 1948 or early 1949 was so badly typed that Houghton asked a friend of his, Dolores North, to type it out for him. According to Michael Howard[10], she also edited it, using her skills as a journalist and writer. Dolores North wrote under the pseudonym of Madeline Montalban, including a regular series for many years in the monthly magazine *Prediction*.

She had been born Madeline Sylvia Royals on 8th January 1910 in Blackpool. By the 1930s, she was working as a journalist in Fleet Street and claimed to have worked magically with Aleister Crowley. In 1939, she married George E. North in London.

According to Doreen Valiente, Gardner claimed to have met Dolores North for the first time in London during the war, when she was wearing the uniform of an officer in the WRNS:

This, he told me, was simply a cover for what she was really doing. According to him, Lord Louis Mountbatten, who knew her because of her family's connection with his estate, had retained her as his personal clairvoyant and psychic adviser.[11]

The family connection was that her husband, Commander "Bill" North, was Mountbatten's agent at Broadlands, the 'stately home' immediately south of the town of Romsey, in Hampshire, which was the family home of Mountbatten's wife. Presumably Dolores must have spent a certain amount of time there during the war and immediately afterwards, though I understand that she and Bill North divorced at some stage prior to her death in 1982.

Doreen Valiente points out the proximity of Broadlands to the New Forest. I would point out that it is even closer to Toothill, which I mentioned in Chapter 8 as a possibly being the traditional meeting place for the witch tradition to which the Mason family belonged. The hill is only two miles from Broadlands House and, in fact, virtually adjoins the Broadlands Estate. It is intriguing to speculate on any connection and whether Dolores knew any of the witches during the war. Apparently, she and Gardner did not get on well and, in later years, after she had formed her own Order of the Morning Star she got upset if anyone called her a witch. She has been described as "the best ceremonial magician in London", but Mike Howard, who belonged to her Order, thinks it highly unlikely that she was involved with the same group that Gardner worked with.

The Secret Service

There is a whole interweaving between Gardner, the witches, the New Forest and what one might call the Secret Service - wartime activities by such organisations as the Special Operations Executive. I have not really studied this in any detail, but there is an undoubted story to tell which may well shed some light on things.

Cecil Williamson, for example, whose parents at one time lived at Newlands Manor, just four miles east of Highcliffe, was a member of MI6 during the war. He was part of a group which tried (successfully) to convince the Germans that there were 250,000 troops on reserve in Essex and Suffolk and that they were ready to invade. He did this by broadcasting fake radio conversations from a hut in the New Forest near Southampton. He claims to have contacted a witch group in the New Forest not connected with Gardner. Williamson also claims to have met Edith Woodford-Grimes during the war, whilst investigating a haunting at a tower somewhere in the New Forest area.[12]

James Laver, CBE, Hon. RE, FRSA, FRSL (1899-1975), who wrote the Foreword to *Gerald Gardner: Witch*, was for many years Keeper of Prints and Drawings at the Victoria and Albert Museum. In addition he was a fashion expert, novelist, dramatist and broadcaster. He had long been interested in the occult and, during the war, had, to all appearances, been a public lecturer extolling the virtues of the National Savings Campaign.

However, it is rumoured that he ran a 'disinformation and occult department' and had 'collected a team of leading occultists of the day ... to advise on matters that might arise from Hitler's supposed obsession with the occult.'[13] This supposedly included faking some Nostradamus prophecies and dropping them on France. Laver had written a book about Nostradamus in 1942. He knew Gardner well and it is possible that there was, through that link, some participation by the witches in aspects of the war effort.

It is interesting that Laver grew up in Liverpool: his educational benefactor was Lawrence Durning Holt, of the same family as Rupert Fordham's second wife.

And at Beaulieu in the New Forest was the training school for the Special Operations Executive, set up in July 1940, supposedly to send agents into enemy territory.

Dennis Wheatley (1897-1977), the occult novelist, knew Crowley, Montague Summers and Rollo Ahmed, had links with the Special Operations Executive through his step-daughter, Diana, and worked as one of Churchill's staff officers during the war. His wife, Joan, was a member of MI5 and Wheatley had contacts in all the intelligence services.[14] In 1945, Wheatley moved to Grove Place, Lymington, a house previously owned by the sister-in-law of the director of Naval Intelligence during the Great War.

I do not know the extent to which Gardner and his witch friends were involved with any of this activity. And I do not yet know how the New Forest witch traditions that Sybil Leek refers to should be treated. I do, however, feel confident that the effect of the Order of Woodcraft Chivalry was at best marginal.

The 'unwoven strands' in this chapter must remain that way for the present. The threads will still be there to be taken up again in the future, along with others that can as yet barely be discerned but which may well prove fruitful.

Chapter 21
A New Myth?

Preliminary Conclusions

It must be obvious to anyone who has read this far through the book that there are still many unanswered questions. The jig-saw is incomplete: many of the pieces are missing, but at least I hope that there is enough material for future researchers to work on.

I started this book by saying that I wrote it because I wanted to find out more about the origins of a movement - modern witchcraft - of which I was a part: I wanted to explore the historical dimension.

Well, I have succeeded, at least partially. I think I have demonstrated the following:

- Gardner did not invent the whole thing.

- He did meet the people he said he did at the Crotona Fellowship meetings.

- They were Susie Mary Mason, Ernest William Mason and Rosetta Fudge.

- These people were part of a hereditary witch family, based in Southampton, historically having some connection with the Toothill area between Southampton and Romsey. They probably brought Edith Rose Woodford-Grimes ('Dafo') into the Craft when she was living near to them in the 1920s.

- Gardner was initiated by 'Dafo', probably in September 1939

I have also engaged in 'intelligent speculation', which has enabled me to attempt a reconstruction of the 1940 rituals to stop the threatened invasion. I suggest when and where these took place, the names of some of those who were present and I name certain individuals who may have given their lives in sacrifice as a result.

I have failed to find independent evidence of the extent of Dorothy Clutterbuck's involvement in the Craft, but I have been able to present much information about her life, including extracts from her diaries, which I am convinced would repay much closer study.

I am still uncertain as to whether there was a 'New Forest Coven' in the sense in which it has been understood - a group which met regularly to perform seasonal and other rituals. There may have been a looser network of individuals, skilled in magical and healing techniques, some of whom have been mentioned in these pages, who got together as needed, most notably for the invasion ritual.

As something of an aside, I give a fair amount of detail about the Rosicrucian Order Crotona Fellowship.

I have enjoyed this research, meeting those who have been enthusiastic about the project. I hope that I have given sufficient leads to enable further research to be undertaken - there is certainly much to be done!

Myths Old and New?

It may be the moment to have another look at the myth with which I started this book, the one which has become conventional wisdom, the one which runs:

"Retired civil servant, Gerald Gardner, moved to the New Forest in 1939 and was initiated into one of the few surviving witch covens - the New Forest coven - by its High Priestess, Dorothy Clutterbuck."

I think I am now in a position to re-write that. What follows is my own attempt at a myth. It may not be right (indeed, it most likely isn't), but I feel confident that it is probably somewhat closer to reality than the current myth. It goes something like this:

There was a tradition of adherence to the old religion in the countryside to the north of Southampton between the New Forest and Winchester - the land through which Purkis brought his cart with the body of William Rufus to lie and be buried in Winchester Cathedral. It was a land sanctified (metaphorically at least) by the blood of the King of England as the cart passed through it.

And in the middle of this land lay Toothill, a wooded prominence with the remains of Iron Age earthworks surrounding it - a reminder of an earlier time when it was in use as a settlement.

But, at the beginning of the 19th Century, the settlement is below the hill. It is a village where the old religion is strong, and the seasonal festivals are held on the summit of the hill, as they have for as long as anyone can remember.

The Mason family are strongly represented in the village: they are the guardians of the ancient secrets and possess the powers of the Craft to practise healing and to work magic. They were called upon to perform a ritual in 1805 to stop Napoleon's threatened invasion.

Others joined the Craft - among them Sophia Hulton and her daughter Elizabeth. Elizabeth's seventh child, Thomas St. Quintin Clutterbuck, was also initiated into the Craft at a young age.

Urbanisation proceeded. One branch of the Mason family, William, and his wife Mary went to live in the nearby seaport of Southampton. They and their descendants carried on the Craft. The family also became involved in other esoteric activities, including Theosophy, Anthroposophy, Co-Masonry and Rosicrucianism.

It was when William and Mary's grandchildren, Ernie, Susie and Rosetta started to come regularly to meetings of the Crotona Fellowship in Christchurch in 1936 that they came across the name of Dorothy St. Quintin Fordham. They asked about her. Was she formerly known as Dorothy St. Quintin Clutterbuck? Yes, they replied, but she married Rupert Fordham in 1935 and took his name.

They remembered Dorothy and her father coming to visit their own parents in Southampton in the 1890s, knew that she was "of the blood" but had rarely thought of her since. They wrote a letter to her - she replied and said that she remembered them but was obviously a bit cool about meeting them again, so they left it at that.

In June 1939 they heard about Rupert's death and sent a note of sympathy. Perhaps surprisingly, Dorothy replied and invited them to come and meet her at Mill House, on Midsummer Day, as it was more private than Latimers. They had a good talk about what the Masons were doing with the Crotona Fellowship and about the old days. Dorothy asked them about the Craft and they admitted they had not been that active themselves recently but they had a good friend, Edith Rose, who had been brought in some years ago by their father, George.

In the meantime they had got to know a strange character called Gerald Gardner who had started to attend the Crotona Fellowship meetings. He seemed to have had an interesting life out East and had recently retired to Highcliffe. He seemed to know a lot about unusual esoteric subjects, he was writing a book about a witch and, what was more, he had an ancestress who was burned to death as a witch in Scotland.

Gardner seemed to get on particularly well with Edith Rose and her daughter Rosanne. Edith suggested to the Masons that she felt he was "of the blood" and should be brought in. But it was a long time since the last initiation ritual had been held. No-one seemed to know the words though they agreed on the main things that needed to be done.

But where should it be held? Someone suggested Mill House. It was isolated and just the right sort of place. But they felt it unlikely that 'Old Dorothy' would agree. They had started to call her 'Old Dorothy' because she was a bit older than they were, they had known her from a long time ago, and her bearing was such that she naturally seemed to command respect. Dorothy was surprisingly enthusiastic about it all. She offered the use of a ritual sword which had belonged to her father when he was in the Indian Army.

The ritual was held, with Edith Rose performing the initiation. Gardner was overjoyed and immediately started asking questions and querying why it should all be kept secret.

They asked Edith to 'keep him under her wing' as it were, as she got on so well with Gardner. In fact, they really left Gardner and Edith to get on with things together, and never performed another ritual with Gardner apart from the momentous rituals which took place, at the initial suggestion of Gardner, the following summer to stop the threatened invasion.

Edith tried hard to keep Gardner's desire for publicity in check, but with the publication of High Magic's Aid *in 1949 and when he took on the Directorship of the Museum of Magic and Witchcraft, she realised that she would not succeed in that direction. She was accepting but not enthusiastic when Gardner initiated Doreen Valiente at her house in 1953.*

Gardner kept in touch with Edith throughout the 1950s and a friend drove him down from London on several occasions to see her. However, when she began to be contacted by those seeking information, following the publication of Witchcraft Today *in 1954, she responded by denying any involvement in the Craft and even denied ever having met Gardner. She died in 1975.*

Thus the myth comes to an end and the recorded history of Wicca starts to be written.

Any movement, however full of life and determination to live in the present, needs the fourth dimension of time and I hope that I have helped to explore the existence of what I have called Wiccan Roots.

In doing this I have, as I said in the Introduction, tried to write the sort of book that I would want to read myself: I feel that I have succeeded in this and I hope that others will want to read it as well.

Appendix A
Acknowledgements

This has not been the sort of book where I can sit at my desk and write, with most of the references that I need close at hand on my bookshelves. It has involved going out and meeting other people and asking for help. There is literally no way that I could ever have started this project without them.

And people have, overwhelmingly, been enthusiastic and supportive of what I was trying to achieve. Some stand out as having been especially helpful and supportive.

I may well have never started this project if it had not been for the encouragement and support of **Michael Howard,** editor of the long-running magazine of the 'Old Religion', *The Cauldron*. He has given freely of references and other material. In particular, the series of articles which he wrote which appeared under the title *"Gerald Gardner - The Man, the Myth and the Magick"* gave me a good start.

Ronald Hutton, Professor of History at the University of Bristol, has shared freely of the research which he was carrying out for his book *The Triumph of the Moon*, and put me in touch with some very useful contacts. I am immensely grateful for his time and encouraging and positive attitude.

Patricia Crowther, who is a High Priestess and a Grand Mother of the Craft, has contributed more than most people to the revival of interest in witchcraft. She knew Gerald Gardner well and has assisted me with information and in so many ways, including giving generously of her time in detailed criticism of the text, to help make the book more interesting and accurate. She has also very kindly given me permission to use the portrait of Gardner which was painted by her late husband, Arnold Crowther.

Ian Stevenson, the Highcliffe historian, has willingly provided me with much information about people and events, of which he usually has personal memory. He has also provided me with introductions to those who could help me further. I am grateful for his permission to use several of the photographs in his collection, particularly those of Dorothy.

Helen Bassett has very generously allowed me to study Dorothy's diaries in the depth which they deserve and has made me most welcome on my research trips. I am most grateful.

John Ferguson and **Chris Wallis,** of The Mill House, in Highcliffe, have also been particularly welcoming, not only giving me hospitality but taking time to show me features of the house and garden, allowing me to look at the deeds and associated documents and generally being interested in what I was doing.

Bill Wakefield has been so helpful, not just in providing me with much Rosicrucian material, but in speaking freely of his memories of Ernie Mason and providing a vivid impression of a remarkable man. He found his photograph of Ernie just in time for it to be included in this book, for which I am most grateful.

Gareth Medway's letters have been such a store of valuable information which he has very generously shared with me, often providing a missing piece for the jig-saw which filled me with delight.

Roger Dearnaley, a historian of Gardnerian witchcraft, has provided much information from his own knowledge, has provided leads to new material and has checked through an earlier draft of this book very thoroughly for errors of fact, for which I am immensely grateful.

In doing this research, I have plagued librarians and archivists with a veritable stream of requests and queries. They have, almost without exception, taken up the challenge gladly and have moved my researches on in a way I would never have thought possible.

The staff at Hull Central Library, including **Simon Green** and **Gareth Watkins**, their genealogist, who responded cheerfully to my pleas for help; **Penny Rudkin** at Southampton Central Library, who has supplied information that has often been a major breakthrough in my researches; the staff of the Lansdowne Library in Bournemouth who willingly searched through their map collection for me and who provided facilities to enable me to view back copies of the "*Christchurch Times*"; **Michael Farrar**, British Naturism's archivist, provided details of the clubs which Gardner must have joined; the Warburg Institute for allowing me access to the wealth of information in the Yorke Collection; and so many others that I can do no more than name them - **Susi Balls**, Librarian at Watford; **C.M. Woolgar**, Head of Special Collections at the University of Southampton Library; **Carolyn Maunder**, Librarian at Henley-on-Thames; the very helpful Local History Librarian at Crosby Library; **Miss J. Grayson**, Librarian at the Theosophical Society Headquarters in London; **Richard Price**, Curator of Modern British Collections at the British Library; and the staff of Lymington Library, the Public Record Office at Kew, the Hampshire County Record Office and the Liverpool City Library.

Book dealers and the proprietors of bookshops always seem to be willing to help and to talk. **Caroline Wise** and **Steve Wilson**, of Atlantis Bookshop have provided some very valuable leads, particularly about Gardner; **Ben Fernee** of Caduceus Books has spent valuable time talking to me and has helped, both with contacts and with Gardner's relationship with Crowley and the O.T.O. And **Edward Saunders** of Post-Horn Books, Giggleswick, has shared his knowledge of the Home Guard and directed me accordingly.

I am particularly grateful to **Carey Littlefield** of Christchurch Borough Council's Building Consultancy section and **Mike Allen**, the Council's Publicity and Public Relations Manager, for the time spent dealing with my often obscure queries. Having worked for a local authority myself, I appreciate the time constraints under which they work.

I must say a particular "Thank you!" to the members of the Christchurch Local History Society who have gone out of their way to help me - **Jane Rutter, Peter Tawpey, Olive Samuel, Sue Newman** and **Mike Hodges.**

In fact, without exception, small organisations and societies have helped tremendously, despite running on a very limited number of volunteers: they include **Jeanne Heaslewood**, Grand Secretary of the British Federation of International Co-Freemasonry; **Else Churchill** of the Society of Genealogists.

Graham King of the Museum of Witchcraft at Boscastle, deserves special mention for allowing me access to their archives on the museum's busiest day ever, which was much appreciated.

But above all it is the individuals who have helped me most. They include:

Desmond Bourke, for information on the Crotona Fellowship revival;

Lois Bourne, for assistance with verifying certain stories;

Amanda Class, for providing valuable background information;

Ann Cook, for providing information about Edith Woodford-Grimes and for allowing me to use the photograph of her;

Janet and Stewart Farrar and **Gavin Bone,** for background information;

Clive Harper, for providing me with a copy of *A Goddess Arrives* and for valuable information;

Lizzie Harris, for information about Amy Woodforde-Finden;

Kenneth Heselton, for details about firewatching and wartime attitudes to the threatened invasion, and clues to the inscription on Rupert Fordham's gravestone;

Nick Howson, for insights into the memorising of ritual;

Deric James, for providing information, including photographs, about the Rosicrucians and about Sybil Leek;

Louise Jennings, for providing hospitality and for information about the workings to assist with the D-Day landings;

Chris Lycett, for information about the Co-Masons and for putting me in touch with those who could help me further;

Bryan McCoy, who has helped to make this book attractive by taking, developing and printing photographs, and doing a marvellous job with some very poor originals;

Laurence Main, for telling me about the survivor of the 1940 invasion ritual whom he met at a vegan meeting, and for trying to find out more details about him;

Doug Pickford, for providing details of the workings carried out by Manchester scientists to help stop the invasion in 1940;

Jane Sharman, for insights into how Gardner may have been taught by 'Dafo';

Tony Steele, for providing information about James Laver;

John Tait, for providing Rosicrucian material, which has proved a valuable resource;

Marion Toffolo, for giving freely of her genealogical knowledge and being generally supportive.

I am sure that I will have missed someone! This is no reflection on their contribution, but more on my failing memory and the fact that so many were willing to help. I apologise in advance!

Appendix B
References

Note: The page numbers quoted are those in the original edition of the work, apart from *Witchcraft Today*, which is the Arrow paperback edition of 1966.

Introduction
[1] Bracelin, J.L. *Gerald Gardner: Witch* (Octagon 1960; republished I-H-O 2000)
[2] Gardner, G.B. *A Goddess Arrives* (Arthur Stockwell 1939)
[3] Gardner, G.B. *High Magic's Aid* (Michael Houghton 1949; republished Pentacle 1993; I-H-O 1999)
[4] Gardner, G.B. *Keris and Other Malay Weapons* (Progressive, Singapore 1936; republished EP 1973)
[5] Gardner, G.B. *Witchcraft Today* (Rider 1954; republished various times including Arrow 1966 and I-H-O 1999)
[6] Gardner, G.B. *The Meaning of Witchcraft* (Aquarian 1959; republished various times)

Chapter 1 - Gerald Brosseau Gardner
[1] Hutton, Ronald *The Triumph of the Moon - A History of Modern Pagan Witchcraft* (Oxford University Press 1999) 400
[2] Gardner (1954)
[3] Most of the information in this chapter is taken from Bracelin's *Gerald Gardner: Witch*.
[4] see *History of Joseph Gardner and Sons Limited* 1748-1948 (1948) and *Two Hundred Years in The Timber Trade - The Story of Joseph Gardner and Sons* in *The Liverpolitan* June 1949
[5] Bracelin 19
[6] Bracelin 19
[7] Bracelin 19-20
[8] Bracelin 20
[9] Bracelin 20
[10] Bracelin 19
[11] Bracelin 28
[12] Bracelin 28
[13] Bracelin 29-30
[14] Bracelin 121
[15] Bracelin 122
[16] Bracelin 45
[17] Bracelin 54
[18] Bracelin 87
[19] Bracelin 125
[20] Bracelin 133
[21] I am indebted to Roger Dearnaley for this information.
[22] Bracelin 73
[23] Bracelin 139

Chapter 2 - Naturism and the New Forest
[1] Gardner (1939) 10
[2] Bracelin 151
[3] Bracelin 151

[4] Bracelin 67
[5] Bracelin 151-152
[6] Michael Farrar, Archivist to the Central Council for British Naturism, letter to the author 22 June 1999.
[7] Bracelin 155-156
[8] Crowther, Patricia *One Witch's World* (Hale 1998) 18
[9] Howard, Michael *Gerald Gardner - The Man, the Myth & the Magick - Part Two* in *The Cauldron* 84 (Beltane/Midsummer 1997) 15-21
[10] Gardner, G.B. *Witchcraft* in *Folk-Lore* - Quarterly Transactions of the Folk-Lore Society June 1939.
[11] Howard, op. cit.
[12] Bracelin 159
[13] Bracelin 159
[14] Medway, Gareth J. *The Origins of Wicca* (from a forthcoming book edited by Shelley Rabinovich)
[15] Gareth Medway - letter to the author
[16] The Third Handbook of the New Forest Club (1936)
[17] Christchurch Times 2 November 1935
[18] Medway, Gareth J. *The Origins of Wicca* (from a forthcoming book edited by Shelley Rabinovich)
[19] Christchurch Times 7 September 1940
[20] Murray, Margaret A. *The God of the Witches* (Sampson Low 1931); *The Divine King in England* (Faber 1954)
[21] Williamson, Hugh Ross *The Arrow and the Sword* (Faber 1947)
[22] De Crespigny, Rose C. and Hutchinson, Horace *The New Forest, Its Traditions, Inhabitants and Customs* (Murray 1895) 104
[23] Herringshaw, Sheila D. *A Portrait of Highcliffe* (1981)
[24] Hutton (1999) 209
[25] Herringshaw 68
[26] I am indebted to Christchurch Borough Council's Building Consultancy for this information.
[27] Christchurch Times 24 June 1939
[28] Personal communication from Ian Stevenson to the author

Chapter 3 - "A Goddess Arrives"

[1] Grant, Joan *Winged Pharaoh* (Arthur Barker 1937)
[2] Bracelin 153
[3] Bracelin 154-155
[4] Gardner, G.B. *A Goddess Arrives* (Arthur H. Stockwell 1939)
[5] Gardner (1939) v
[6] Gardner (1939) 33
[7] Gardner (1939) 98
[8] Gardner (1939) 100
[9] Murray, Margaret A. *The Witch Cult in Western Europe* (Oxford University Press 1921)
[10] Gardner (1939) 123-124
[11] Gardner (1939) 161
[12] Gardner (1939) 349
[13] Gardner (1954) 60-61
[14] Gardner (1939) 133
[15] Gardner (1939) 156
[16] Gardner (1939) 136-137
[17] Gardner (1939) 148
[18] Gardner (1939) 212-213
[19] Letter to the author 27 October 1998

Chapter 4 - The Rosicrucians And The Crotona Fellowship

[1] Bracelin 159
[2] McIntosh, Christopher *The Rosicrucians - The History, Mythology and Rituals of an Esoteric Order* (Aquarian 1980; revised edition Weiser 1997)
[3] McIntosh 100
[4] Christchurch Times 3 August 1940

[5] Sullivan, George A. *"Rules"* (Crotona Fellowship 1926) I am indebted to Gareth Medway for this information.
[6] Howard, Michael *Gerald Gardner - The Man, the Myth & the Magick - Part I* in *The Cauldron* 83 (Candlemas/Eostre 1997) 4
[7] McIntosh 133
[8] *Christchurch Times* 13 June 1942
[9] *Dictionary of National Biography* Vol 37 (1894) 34-41
[10] Mathews, Alex. (G.A. Sullivan) *Henry VII* Part II (n.d.)
[11] I am indebted to Roger Dearnaley for this information.
[12] Koestler, Arthur *The Sleepwalkers* (Hutchinson 1959) 27-28

Chapter 5 - Activities At The Ashrama

[1] Christchurch Times 13 November 1937
[2] Christchurch Times 2 April 1938
[3] Christchurch Times 2 April 1938
[4] Christchurch Times 2 April 1938
[5] Christchurch Times 21 August 1937
[6] Christchurch Times 2 April 1938
[7] Christchurch Times 2 April 1938
[8] Christchurch Times 18 September 1937
[9] Christchurch Times 8 January 1938
[10] Christchurch Times 21 August 1937
[11] Christchurch Times 2 April 1938
[12] Christchurch Times 21 August 1937
[13] Christchurch Times 2 April 1938
[14] Christchurch Times 2 April 1938
[15] Christchurch Times 2 April 1938
[16] Christchurch Times 21 August 1937
[17] Bracelin 163
[18] Bracelin 163
[19] Caddy, Peter *In Perfect Timing* (Findhorn 1996) 34-35
[20] Bracelin 163
[21] Caddy 32-33

Chapter 6 - "The First Rosicrucian Theatre in England"

[1] Christchurch Times 4 September 1937
[2] Christchurch Times 18 September 1937
[3] Christchurch Times 19 February 1938
[4] Christchurch Times 19 March 1938
[5] Christchurch Times 23 April 1938
[6] Christchurch Times 29 October 1938
[7] Christchurch Times 13 August 1938
[8] Christchurch Times 10 September 1938
[9] Bracelin 164
[10] Christchurch Times 25 May 1940
[11] Christchurch Times 25 May 1940
[12] Bracelin 164
[13] Christchurch Times 13 June 1942
[14] Bracelin 163
[15] Tillett, Gregory *Gerald Gardner: Some Historical Fragments* in *The Australian Wiccan* 14 (n.d.)
[16] Bracelin 164
[17] Caddy 33
[18] Caddy 71

Chapter 7 - Mabs And The Co-masons

[1] Much of the material for this chapter has been obtained from *Annie Besant - A Biography* by Anne Taylor (Oxford University Press 1992)

[2] Taylor 35
[3] Taylor 36
[4] Taylor 59
[5] Taylor 138
[6] Taylor 252
[7] Geoffrey Serle (ed.) *The Australian Dictionary of Biography 1891-1939 Vol II* (Melbourne University Press 1988) 544-546
[8] *The History of International Co-Freemasonry and Its Structure* (The Consistory Council of the British Federation 1992)
[9] I am grateful to Gareth Medway for providing this information.
[10] Letters to the author from Jeanne Heaslewood, Grand Secretary of the British Federation of International Co-Freemasonry dated 11 November 1998 and 22 December 1998
[11] Bracelin 163
[12] Bracelin 163

Chapter 8 - "The Most Interesting Element ..."

[1] Bracelin 162
[2] Bracelin 163
[3] Bracelin 163
[4] Bracelin 164-165
[5] Gardner (1959) 11
[6] Bracelin 164-165
[7] Penny Rudkin, Southampton City Library letter to the author 11 August 1998
[8] Christchurch Times 7 August 1937
[9] Bracelin 163
[10] Southern Daily Echo 19 August 1948
[11] Andrews, Allen *Witchcraft In Britain* in *Illustrated* 27 September 1952 41
[12] Gardner (1954) 36
[13] Gardner (1959) 14
[14] Gardner (1954) 22
[15] Gardner (1959) 44
[16] Gardner (1954) 51
[17] Gardner (1954) 53
[18] Glass, Justine *Witchcraft, The Sixth Sense and Us* (Neville Spearman 1965) 32
[19] Valiente (1989) 121
[20] 1881 British Census and National Index Family History Resource File CD ROM Library (The Church of Jesus Christ of Latter-Day Saints 1999)
[21] Valiente (1989) 38
[22] King, Francis *Ritual Magic in England* (Neville Spearman 1970) 179
[23] Bracelin 165

Chapter 9 - 'Dafo'

[1] Johns, June *King of the Witches* (Peter Davies 1969) 15
[2] Valiente, Doreen *The Rebirth of Witchcraft* (Hale 1989) 38
[3] Bourne, Lois *Dancing with Witches* (Hale 1998) 58
[4] *An Interview with Cecil Williamson* Part 2 in *Talking Stick* VIII Autumn 1992
[5] Tan Wee Cheng In the Land of Heaven on Earth with a Lap Top [http://weecheng.simplenot.com/sichuan2/leshan.htm]
[6] History of Joseph Gardner and Sons Limited 1748-1948
[7] I am indebted to Roger Dearnaley for this information.
[8] Fuller, Sophie *A Pandora Guide to Women Composers: Britain and the United States* 1629-Present 343-344
[9] Watkins, Allen *Alfred Watkins of Hereford* (Garnstone 1972) 28
[10] Information from the Teachers Registration Council
[11] Christchurch Times 24 August 1940

Chapter 10 - Dorothy St. Quintin Clutterbuck

[1] Talk by Fred Lamond at Pagan Federation National Conference 1998
[2] Bourne 59-60
[3] Hutton (1999) 212
[4] Valiente, Doreen *Appendix A - The Search for Old Dorothy* in Janet and Stewart Farrar *The Witches' Way* (Hale 1984)
[5] Valiente, Doreen *Appendix A - The Search for Old Dorothy* in Janet and Stewart Farrar *The Witches' Way* (Hale 1984)
[6] Mee, Arthur *The King's England - Hertfordshire* (Hodder and Stoughton 1939) 111
[7] Jones, K.R. *The Clutterbuck Family in Hertfordshire* in *Hertfordshire Countryside* Vol 28 No 167 (March 1973) 20
[8] Williams, Henry *History of Watford* 87
[9] Burnett, Frances Hodgson *The Secret Garden* (1911)
[10] Gilbert, Martin *Finest Hour - Winston S. Churchill 1939-1941* (Heinemann 1983) 900-901
[11] Heselton, Philip *Mirrors of Magic* (Capall Bann 1997)
[12] Samuel, Olive J. *Chewton Bunny, Highcliffe - The History of a Romantic Glen* (Olive J. Samuel 1986) 2
[13] Marryat, Captain Frederick *The Children of the New Forest* (1847)
[14] Christchurch Times 24 September 1910
[15] Kitcher, Reg *My Early Years at Hinton Admiral and Highcliffe, Hampshire (1910-1939)* (Olive J. Samuel 1985) 8-9
[16] Herringshaw 39
[17] Sheldrick, Albert *A Different World - Ashwell before 1939* (Cortney n.d.) 16
[18] I am indebted to Ian Stevenson for this information.
[19] Christchurch Times 19 January 1935
[20] Christchurch Times 23 May 1936
[21] Sheldrick 103
[22] Christchurch Times 6 November 1937
[23] Christchurch Times 14 January 1939

Chapter 11 - Dorothy's Diaries

[1] I am indebted to Ian Stevenson for this information
[2] Cooper, Joe *The Case of the Cottingley Fairies* (Hale 1990)
[3] Farrar, Janet and Stewart *Eight Sabbats for Witches* (Hale 1981) 113
[4] Chumbley, Andrew D. *The Golden Chain and the Lonely Road: a typological study of Initiatory Transmissions within the Sabbatic Tradition* in *The Cauldron No. 94* (November 1999) 16

Chapter 12 - Initiation

[1] Bracelin 165
[2] Bracelin 165
[3] Farrar, Janet and Stewart *The Witches' Way* (Hale 1984)
[4] Hutton (1999) 210
[5] Farrar and Farrar (1984)
[6] Gardner (1954)
[7] Gardner (1959)
[8] Jones, Evan John with Valiente, Doreen *Witchcraft - A Tradition Renewed* (Hale 1990) 38-39
[9] Bracelin 165
[10] Gardner (1954) 19
[11] Gardner (1949)
[12] Gardner (1959) 19
[13] Gardner (1954) 78
[14] Gardner (1954) 79
[15] Gardner (1949) 80-81
[16] Bracelin 166

[17] Bracelin 166
[18] Samuel 4

Chapter 13 - Old Dorothy - High Priestess Or Red Herring

[1] Bracelin 166
[2] Bracelin 167
[3] Patricia Crowther - personal communication to the author
[4] Valiente (1984) 283
[5] Christchurch Times 28 January 1939
[6] Hutton (1999) 211
[7] I am indebted to Roger Dearnaley for identifying this.
[8] Gareth Medway letter to the author
[9] Gardner, G.B. *The Museum of Magic and Witchcraft - The Story of the Famous Witches' Mill at Castletown, Isle of Man* (Photochrom n.d.)
[10] Mannix Daniel P. *Witchcraft's Inner Sanctum* in *True* (c. 1960)
[11] Gardner (1959) 82
[12] Hutton (1999) 212
[13] I am indebted to Roger Dearnaley for this observation.

Chapter 14 - The New Forest Coven?

[1] Oldmeadow, Katherine *The Witch of Whitestones* in *Hulton's Girls' Stories* (Allied Newspapers Limited 1926) 143. I am indebted to Ian Stevenson for this reference.
[2] Oldmeadow, Katherine *The Folklore of Herbs* (Cornish Bros. 1946)
[3] Christchurch Times 12 July 1963
[4] Valiente, Doreen *Witchcraft for Tomorrow* (Hale 1978) 129-130
[5] Oldmeadow (1946) 13
[6] Oldmeadow (1946) 15
[7] Oldmeadow (1946) 63
[8] I am indebted to Gareth Medway for providing this information.
[9] I am indebted to John Belham-Payne for allowing me to use this information.
[10] King 177-178
[11] Crowther (1998) 181
[12] Crowther (1998) 182
[13] Liddell, E.W. and Howard, M.A. *The Pickingill Papers* (Capall Bann 1994)
[14] Liddell and Howard 150
[15] Liddell and Howard 151
[16] Liddell and Howard 152
[17] Gardner (1954) 169
[18] Herringshaw 81
[19] Hodges, Michael *Helis, Perhaps the Original Badge of Dorset and His Links with Christchurch* (M.A. Hodges 1998) 4
[20] Gardner (1949) 47
[21] Gardner (1949) 48
[22] Wilks, J.H. *Trees of the British Isles in History and Legend* (Muller 1972) 86
[23] Bracelin 140
[24] Valiente (1989) Illustration between pages 128 and 129

Chapter 15 - The Threat Of Invasion

[1] Lois Bourne - letter to the author April 1999
[2] *An Interview with Cecil Williamson Part Three* in *Talking Stick No. 9* (Winter 1992) 25-26
[3] Thomas, David A. *The Illustrated Armada Handbook* (Harrap 1988) 2
[4] Macaulay, Thomas Babington *The Armada* (1833)
[5] Gardner (1954) 123
[6] Thomas 69
[7] The Guardian 2 March 1999
[8] Crowther (1998) 23
[9] Underwood, Peter *Ghosts of Devon*

(Bossiney 1982) 30
[10] Newbolt, Henry *Drake's Drum* (1897)
[11] Kurtz, Katherine *Lammas Night* (Ballantine 1983)
[12] Brown, Theo *Devon Ghosts* (Jarrold 1982) 88
[13] Barnett, Correlli *Bonaparte* (Wordsworth 1997) 102-104
[14] Nichols, Ross *The Book of Druidry* (Aquarian 1990) 28
[15] Gardner (1954) 123
[16] Andrews, Allen *Witchcraft In Britain* in *Illustrated* 27 September 1952 41

Chapter 16 - "Operation Cone Of Power"

[1] Bracelin 167
[2] Andrews 41
[3] Bracelin 166
[4] Crowther (1998) 21
[5] Valiente (1989) 45
[6] Andrews 41
[7] King 179
[8] Valiente (1989) 45
[9] Crowther (1998) 21-22
[10] Churchill, Winston S. *The Second World War Volume II - Their Finest Hour* (Cassell 1949) 152
[11] Churchill 247
[12] Ian Stevenson - personal communication with the author
[13] Gilbert 570-571
[14] Glass, Justine *Witchcraft, The Sixth Sense and Us* (Neville Spearman 1965)
[15] Bracelin 167
[16] Bracelin 167
[17] Andrews 41
[18] Mackenzie, S.P. *The Home Guard - A Military and Political History* (Oxford University Press 1995) 57
[19] Bracelin 167
[20] Bracelin 167
[21] Bracelin 113-114
[22] King 178-179
[23] King 178
[24] BBC1 Television programme '999' broadcast on 11 May 1999
[25] Prichard, Bob *Weatherwatch* in *The Guardian* 23 April 1997 4
[26] Fish, Michael Radio 4 19 September 1997
[27] Bracelin 167
[28] Illman, John *Madness of the winter myths* in The Guardian 17 November 1998
[29] Fortune, Dion *The Sea Priestess* (1938)
[30] Bracelin 167
[31] Valiente (1989) 46
[32] Gardner (1954) 135-136
[33] Valiente (1989) 45-46
[34] Andrews 41
[35] Valiente (1989) 46
[36] Valiente (1989) 45
[37] Andrews 41
[38] Valiente (1989) 45
[39] Valiente (1989) 46
[40] Valiente (1978) 73
[41] Valiente (1989) 45
[42] Andrews 41
[43] Bracelin 167
[44] Valiente (1989) 46
[45] Patricia Crowther - personal communication with the author
[46] Valiente (1989) 45
[47] Bracelin 167
[48] Bracelin 167

Chapter 17 - Their Finest Hour

[1] 'Robin' *Reminiscences of Gerald Gardner and his Crafte* in *The Cauldron* 87 (Candlemass/Eostre 1998) 26
[2] Bracelin 167
[3] Bracelin 167
[4] Valiente (1989) 46
[5] Bracelin 167

[6] King 179
[7] Christchurch Times 26 August 1939
[8] Christchurch Times 17 August 1940
[9] Hutton (1999) 169
[10] Christchurch Times 26 August 1939
[11] Christchurch Times 2 September 1939
[12] Christchurch Times 17 August 1940
[13] Lymington Times 24 August 1940
[14] Davies, Marion *Lore of the Sacred Horse* (Capall Bann 1995) 105-106
[15] Davies 111
[16] Jones with Valiente 160
[17] King 177-179
[18] Laurence Main - letter to the author 19 January 1999
[19] I am indebted to Pete Jennings for this information.
[20] Kurtz 436
[21] Herringshaw 81
[22] Lennon. Peter *Rite attitude* in *The Guardian* 14 July 1999 3
[23] Nichols 28
[24] Pickford, Doug *Cheshire - Its Magic and Mystery* (Sigma Leisure 1994) 107
[25] Fortune, Dion *The Magical Battle of Britain* (Golden Gates 1993)
[26] *An Interview with Cecil Williamson Part Three* in *Talking Stick No. 9* (Winter 1992) 25-26
[27] Crowley, Amado *The Secrets of Aleister Crowley* (Diamond 1991) 123-125
[28] Hutton (1999) 209
[29] Louise Jennings - personal communication with the author
[30] BBC2 Television programme - Timewatch - Hitler and the Invasion of Britain - 7 April 1998
[31] Churchill 267
[32] Churchill 267
[33] Churchill 267
[34] Churchill 268
[35] Timewatch
[36] Churchill 274
[37] Timewatch
[38] Crowther (1998) 22
[39] Michael Howard - letter to the author 12 May 1998
[40] Timewatch
[41] Timewatch
[42] Churchill 285
[43] Churchill 285
[44] Churchill 292
[45] Churchill 290
[46] Gilbert 778
[47] Churchill 274
[48] Churchill 274
[49] Churchill 269, 297
[50] I am indebted to Patricia Crowther for this information
[51] Churchill 297
[52] Crowther, Patricia *Lid Off The Cauldron* (Muller 1981; republished Capall Bann 1998) 31
[53] Gardner (1954) 123

Chapter 18 - Learning The Ways Of The Witches

[1] Bracelin 165-166
[2] Bracelin 166
[3] Valiente (1989) 37-39
[4] Bracelin 159
[5] McDowall, David and Wolton, Deborah *Hampstead Heath - A Walker's Guide* (David McDowall 1999)
[6] Medway, Gareth J. *The Origins of Wicca* (from a forthcoming book edited by Shelley Rabinovich)
[7] Bracelin 159
[8] Merrifield, Ralph *G.B. Gardner and the 20th Century 'Witches'* in *Folklore Society News* No. 17 (June 1993) 10
[9] Gardner (1939) 174-175

[10] Gardner (1954) 31-32
[11] Mannix
[12] Bracelin 166
[13] Bourne 58
[14] Bourne 59
[15] Gardner (1959) 11
[16] Gardner (1959) 41-42
[17] Gardner (1954) Foreword
[18] Gardner (1954) 32
[19] Gardner (1954) 25
[20] Crowther, Patricia *Foreword* to Gerald Gardner *High Magic's Aid* (Pentacle Enterprises edition 1993) 1
[21] Howard, Michael *Gerald Gardner - The Man, the Myth & the Magick Part Two* in *The Cauldron 84* (Beltane/Midsummer 1997) 19
[22] Glass 131

Chapter 19 - Witch Beliefs And Practices

[1] Gardner (1954) 152
[2] Farrar and Farrar (1984)
[3] Farrar and Farrar (1981)
[4] Crowther (1981)
[5] Valiente (1978)
[6] Kelly, Aidan A. *Crafting the Art of Magic Book 1 - A History of Modern Witchcraft 1939-1964* (Llewellyn 1991)
[7] Gardner (1959) 12
[8] Gardner (1954) 166
[9] Gardner (1954) 166
[10] Gardner (1954) 166-167
[11] Gardner (1959) 11
[12] Gardner (1954) 131
[13] Gardner (1954) 32
[14] Gardner (1954) Foreword
[15] Gardner (1954) Foreword
[16] Gardner (1954) 121
[17] Gardner (1954) 121
[18] Bracelin 165
[19] Letter from Gardner to Gerald Yorke dated 24 October 1952 in Scrapbook EE2 of the Gerald Yorke Collection in the Warburg Institute, London.
[20] Gardner (1954) 137
[21] Gardner (1954) 47
[22] Gardner (1954) 47
[23] Gardner (1954) 25
[24] Gardner (1954) 44
[25] Gardner (1954) 35
[26] Gardner (1959) 127
[27] Gardner (1954) 24
[28] Gardner (1954) 29
[29] Gardner (1954) 24
[30] Gardner (1954) 27
[31] Gardner (1954) 131
[32] Gardner (1954) 28-29
[33] Gardner (1959) 69
[34] Gardner (1959) 18
[35] Letter from Gardner to Gerald Yorke dated 24 October 1952 in Scrapbook EE2 of the Gerald Yorke Collection in the Warburg Institute, London.
[36] Gardner (1954) 27
[37] Gardner (1954) 20
[38] see, for example, David Boadella *Wilhelm Reich - The Evolution of His Work* (Vision 1973)
[39] Gardner (1954) 32
[40] Gardner (1954) 28
[41] Gardner (1954) 28
[42] Gardner (1959) 17
[43] Gardner (1954) 20
[44] Gardner (1954) 52
[45] Gardner (1954) 52
[46] Gardner (1954) 21-22
[47] Gardner (1954) 118
[48] Gardner (1954) 173
[49] Gardner (1954) 31
[50] Gardner (1959) 147-149
[51] Gardner (1954) 175
[52] Gardner (1954) 175
[53] Gardner (1954) 74
[54] Gardner (1954) 91
[55] Gardner (1959) 99
[56] Gardner (1959) 17
[57] Gardner (1954) 131
[58] Letter from Gardner to Gerald Yorke dated 24 October 1952 in

Scrapbook EE2 of the Gerald Yorke Collection in the Warburg Institute, London.
[59] Gardner (1954) 60
[60] Gardner (1954) 60
[61] Gardner (1954) 121
[62] King 178
[63] Lamond, Fred *Magicking the Art of the Craft* in *The Deosil Dance* 34 (Imbolc 1993)

Chapter 20 - "In Another Part Of The Forest ..."

[1] Edgell, Derek *The Order of Woodcraft* Chivalry 1916-1949 as a New Age *Alternative to the Boy Scouts* (Mellen 1992)
[2] Kelly, Aidan A. *Inventing Witchcraft - The Origins and Nature of Gardnerian Neopagan Witchcraft as a New Religion* (Art Magickal 1998)
[3] Edgell 191-192
[4] Hutton, Ronald *The Roots of Modern Paganism* in *Paganism Today* ed. Graham Harvey and Charlotte Hardman (Thorsons 1995) 12
[5] Hutton (1999) 216
[6] Leek, Sybil *Diary of a Witch* (Leslie Frewin 1975)
[7] James, Deric *Profile of Sybil Leek* in *Insight 27* (n.d.) 28
[8] Leek 104-106
[10] Michael Howard, personal communication with the author
[11] Valiente (1989) 50
[12] *An Interview with Cecil Williamson Part Two* in *Talking Stick* VIII (Autumn 1992) 20
[13] Tony Steele - personal communication to the author 8 June 1999
[14] Howard, Michael *Prince of Thriller Writers* in *The Cauldron* 90 (November 1998) 3-8

Appendix C
Further Reading

The main reason for writing this book was that there was nothing published that covered the subject matter in the level of detail that I desired.

Gerald Gardner's books are, of course, vital. *Witchcraft Today* and *The Meaning of Witchcraft* are the ones to start with, and both have recently been re-issued.

His works of fiction, *A Goddess Arrives* and *High Magic's Aid* have recently been re-issued by I-H-O books, who have also re-issued J.L. Bracelin's *Gerald Gardner: Witch*.

Professor Ronald Hutton's *The Triumph of the Moon - A History of Modern Pagan Witchcraft* (Oxford University Press 1999) is excellent and puts the subject matter of the present volume into a wider context.

In the last few years, several books have been written by those who knew Gardner which have added significantly to our knowledge of him and about the revival of the Craft. I would mention particularly Doreen Valiente *The Rebirth of Witchcraft* (Hale 1989), Patricia Crowther *One Witch's World* (Hale 1998) and Lois Bourne *Dancing with Witches* (Hale 1998).

The Witches' Way by Janet and Stewart Farrar (Hale 1984) is still an important and informative book, not least for Doreen Valiente's inspiring appendix on "The Search for Old Dorothy".

Articles by Michael Howard, Cecil Williamson, Gareth Medway and others, all of which are mentioned in the 'References' section, have proved invaluable, though nothing to do with this subject should be read uncritically.

In conclusion, I must mention *The Cauldron*, a quarterly magazine edited by Michael Howard which has been produced since 1976. It often contains articles of relevance to the history of the modern witchcraft revival, and details of subscription rates can be obtained from Mike Howard, Caemorgan Cottage, Caemorgan Road, Cardigan SA43 1QU. He asks that you do not put 'The Cauldron' on the envelope.

Index

A Goddess Arrives, 9, 24, 41-51, 99, 178, 186, 245, 247, 262, 266, 288
Abbey Folk Park, 27, 274
Academia Rosae Crucis, 66-69, 78
'Adlertag', 257
Africa, 14, 52, 117, 120
air-raids, 86, 238
alchemy, 53
Alderley Edge, 253
Amberwood Farm, 153, 180
Amberwood House, 153
Amen-Ra, Lodge, 95
Amphlett, Mrs., 223
Amphlett, Sarah Emily, 146
Ancient and Mystical Order Rosae Crucis, 54
Ancient British Crafts Ltd., 263
Andrew, Martin, 74, 105
Andrews, Allen, 110, 227, 233, 238-240
Antiquaries, Society of, 128, 131
Aphrodite, 42-43, 45
Archer Shee, Martin, 130
Archives, Crotona Fellowship, 71, 107
Armada, Spanish, 134, 175-176, 219-222, 227, 230, 234
Ashdown Forest, 253
Ashrama, 39, 63, 65-67, 74, 76, 78-80, 87-88, 96-98, 100, 247
Ashwell, 141-145
asthma, 13, 236-237, 243
astrology, 26, 53
astronomy, 106
As Ye Sow, 62
'Aunt Agatha', 189, 198-199
Aureolis, 58
Aurora, Lodge, 95

Australia, 93-94
'Autumn leaf-fall' ritual, 267
Avon, River, 34, 296

Bacon, Francis, 53, 61-63, 71, 75, 98
Bailey, Doris, 140
Baker, Hilda, 74, 76
Baker, Ivor, 74, 76
Baker, Peggy, 76
Banning, R.H.F., 79
Barnes, Cyril (Jim), 74-75, 88, 108
Barnes, Elizabeth, 75, 108
Bashley, 249
Bassett, Helen, 156,
Baynes, Donald Stuart, 146
bears' fat, 235
Beaulieu, 302
Beausant, Lodge, 95
Beazley, Arthur Stuart, 130
Bedfordshire, 128, 141, 143-144
Beechwood, 103-106, 108, 110, 116
Belgium, 75, 226-227, 255, 257
Berkshire, 27, 132-133
Besant, Annie, 56, 91-92, 94-96
Besant, Frank, 91-92
Besant-Scott, Mabel, 58, 73-74, 91-96, 99, 100, 188
Biggleswade, 143
Birkenhead, 72
Bishopsgate Institute, 158
Black Water, 215
blacksmiths, 243, 249-250
Blake, William, 269
Blundellsands, 12-13, 19
Bohemian Press, 58
Boldre, 133
Bootle, 12
Borneo, 17-19, 21

Bottomley, Horatio, 244
Bourne, Lois, 116, 126, 217, 270
Bournemouth, 32, 34-35, 63, 74, 85, 119, 122, 140, 152, 158, 192
Bowerwood, 141
Bowland, Forest of, 17
Bracelin, Jack, 8-9, 14-16, 19-20, 24-28, 41-42, 52, 72, 74, 85-86, 88-89, 95-100, 105, 114, 177-180, 186-189, 205-206, 214-215, 227, 243, 261-263
Branksome, 74
British Astronomical Association, 106
British Legion, 150
British Library, 50
British Museum, 21, 131
British Naturism, 25
British Watercolour Society, 159
Broadlands, 301
Brockenhurst, 140
Brodrick-Bullock, Vincent Walter, 89
Brondesbury, 94
Brook, 33, 133-136, 212, 232, 299
Brooke, Charles, 18
Broom, 143-144, 146, 203
Brown, David, 74-75
Brown, Gladys, 75
Brown, Dr. Harry Morrow, 237
Brown, Peter, 76
Brown, Theo, 222
Brownlow, Rev. Henry, 196
Brownsea Island, 137
brushwood, 237
Bryant, W.J., 79
Buckland Abbey, 222
Buddha, 117
Buddhism, 15
'Bull's Blood', 235
Burgess, Edwin Lawson, 244
Burley, 135, 207, 299
Byngham, Harry ('Dion'), 297

Caddy, Peter, 72, 75-76, 89, 107
Cam, River, 212
Cambridge, 93, 141, 209
Canary Islands, 13-14
Canterton, 33

Capper, James, 129
Capper, Marianne, 129
Cardrew House, 25-26
Carpenter, Alison, 158
Carpenter, Edward, 246
Castletown, 268, 320
Cat and Fiddle Inn, 135
Ceylon, 15-16, 18
Chalk, Catherine, 63, 66, 74, 79, 105
Chalk, E.G., 76-77
Chalk, Thomas, 63
Charing Cross Road, 24
Chester, 206
Chewton, 35, 133-137, 140, 169, 187, 212
Chewton Bunny, 187, 212, 252, 259
Chewton Common Road, 248
Chewton Glen, 133-136, 140, 169
Chewton House, 248
Chewton Mill, 133, 135-137, 140, 170, 180-184, 187, 212
China, 70, 117
Christ, 34, 162, 193-194
Christchurch, 29-30, 34-36, 39, 52, 54, 63, 72, 74-76, 78-79, 82-85, 88-89, 94, 96, 99-100, 105, 107-108, 119, 124, 134, 136, 140, 149, 158, 162, 206, 213, 244-246, 252, 306
Christchurch Times, 6, 32, 39, 51, 57, 62, 66, 69, 72, 75, 79-80, 82-85, 88, 124, 148, 153, 192, 207, 244-248, 265
Chumbley, Andrew, 175
Churchill, Winston, 132, 226, 228-229, 233, 256-259, 303
Clutterbuck, Dorothy, 4-5, 7-8, 124-126, 128-133, 137-141, 144-154, 156-165, 168-169, 171-177, 179-180, 184, 188, 195, 199, 204, 206, 208-209, 211, 223, 226-227, 233, 247-248, 254, 271, 305-307
Clutterbuck, Arthur, 132
Clutterbuck, Ellen Anne, 130
Clutterbuck, George Watlington, 130
Clutterbuck, James, 132
Clutterbuck, James Hulton, 130
Clutterbuck, Jane, 129

Clutterbuck, Marianne, 129
Clutterbuck, Robert (Sen.), 128
Clutterbuck, Robert (Jun.), 129
Clutterbuck, Thomas, 128
Clutterbuck, Thomas St. Quintin, 129-133, 136-137
Co-Masonry, 58, 91, 93-96, 99-100, 104-105, 108, 116, 295, 306
Cochrane, Robert, 113
Colombo, 16
'Com', 13-16, 318
Cone of Power, 226-228, 237, 239-242, 251, 287-288, 297
Confessio Fraternitatis, 53
Cornelius Agrippa, 86, 88, 98
Cornwall, 221
Cory, Adela Florence, 120
Cottingley, 106, 169, 319
coven-tree, 215
Cox, Frances, 149
Cox, George William, 144
Cox, Julia Blanche (see Fordham)
Cranemoor Common, 135
Crotona Fellowship, 4, 9, 39, 52, 54, 56-63, 66, 71-72, 75, 83, 86, 89, 96, 100, 105, 107-108, 114, 116, 178, 246, 266, 295, 299, 304-307
Crowley, Aleister, 13, 203, 209, 212, 237, 253-254, 274, 283, 300, 302,
Crowley, Amado, 253
Crowther, Arnold, 8, 26
Crowther, Patricia, 8, 26, 110, 166, 178, 189, 199, 210, 221, 227-228, 231, 241, 256, 260, 264, 273, 276, 290
Curtis the Willing, 149
Cyprus, 40-44, 262

D-Day, 254, 256, 313
Dafo, (see Woodford-Grimes, Edith)
Davies, Leslie, 77
Davies, Marion, 249
De Crespigny, Rose, 34
Deall, Archibald, 77
Dee, Dr., 88
Demon Monk, The, 85-86

Dennistoun Avenue, 124
Deraismes, Mlle., 94
Devil's Hole, 253
Devil's Point, 222
Devil's Seat, 113
Dewey, Billy, 15
dewponds, 132
Dillon, Viscount, 131
Dionysianism, 297
Ditchley, 131-133
Donaldson-Palmer, J., 77
Dorchester, 159
Dorset, 28, 321
Doyle, Arthur Conan, 106
Drake, Francis, 175-176, 219, 221-223
Druidry, 75, 198, 224, 253
Du Cane, Charles Edward Byron, 191-192
Dungenous, 252
Dunkirk, 226, 228-229, 254
Dunn, Harry, 77
Durning Holt, Janet Elizabeth (see Fordham)
Durning Holt, Laurence, 302
Durning Holt, William, 143
Dyaks, 17-18

Ecclesia, 66, 70-71
Edgell, Derek, 298
Eger, 235
Egypt, 21, 41, 43, 54, 61, 70, 86
Elgar, Edward, 6
elocution, 66, 68-69, 115-116, 120, 123-124, 270
Elphinstone Road, 37, 39
Englefield, 132
Essex, 211, 302
Estcourt, Caroline, 37-38
Estcourt, Ethel, 37-38
Everton, 56

Falmouth, 221
Fama Fraternitatis, 52
Farrar, Janet and Stewart, 25, 174, 179-180, 190, 276
Ferguson, John, 154

Ferny Knap, 215
Finchley, 25, 263
Findhorn, 59, 75, 317
Finlay, Edith Ethel (see Morgan)
firebrands, 238
First World War, 56, 119, 211, 223
fly-agaric, 292
Folklore of Herbs, The, 207-208
Folk-Lore Society, 26, 51, 274
Forder, Alys, 247
Forder, Walter, 243-248
Fordham, Caroline, 143
Fordham, Dorothy St. Q. (see Clutterbuck)
Fordham, Edward King, 141-142
Fordham, Herbert, 142
Fordham, Janet Elizabeth, 143-144
Fordham, Julia Blanche, 144, 148, 153
Fordham, Rupert Granville, 153
Fordham, Rupert Oswald, 140-146, 148-149, 152-154, 191, 193-194, 202-203, 248, 302, 306-307
Fordham, Wolverley, 143
Fordingbridge, 295-296
Forrest, Dorothy, 140
Fortune, Dion, 26, 237, 253
France, 22, 35, 94, 227, 229, 252, 255, 302
Freemasonry, 16, 46, 53, 58, 66-68, 71, 76, 79, 85, 94-96, 107, 272
Friar's Rest, 146, 149
Froggy Lane, 135
Frythe, The, 129
Fudge, Rosetta, 100, 104, 108, 110, 114, 199, 304, 306
Fudge, William, 100, 104

Gaddesden, 128
Galloway, C.F.J., 77
Garden Theatre, 65, 78, 80, 83-85, 218
Gardner, Donna, 20-22, 24, 27, 32, 267-268, 270
Gardner, Harold, 16
Gardner, Joseph, 17
Gardner, Robert, 12

Gardnerian witchcraft, 12, 185, 273, 276
Gaza, 21
Germany, 22, 52-53, 56, 217, 224, 226, 240, 252, 255-259
Gilbert, W.S., 139
Gilholey, E., 77
Gill, M.C., 140
Gilpin's Cottage, 133
gipsies, 207-208
Glass, Justine, 112-113, 232, 273
Glen, The, 12-13
Glen House, 155, 206
Gloucestershire, 128
'Go away powder', 252
Goering, 253, 258
Golden Dawn, 53-54
Goring-on-Thames, 133
Gosport, 102
Grant, Joan, 41
Griffin, Edward, 149, 200
Griffiths, Frances, 169
Grimes, Samuel William Woodford, 119
gymnosophy, 297-298

Hall, Ailsie, 73
hallucinogens, 292
Hampshire, 27, 102, 113, 133, 150, 211, 250, 301, 311, 319
Hann, Margaret, 140
Harper, Irene, 140
Harpham, 129-130
Harris, Gavin M., 77
Harrison, Caroline, 118
Harrison, Helen, 140
Harrogate, 95
Harvey, E. Marshall, 74
Harvey-Packer, Kenneth, 158
Hatton, C.O.S., 140
Hatton, S.H.M., 140
Hazel, W., 119, 122
Hecate, 47
Heindel, Max, 54, 57
Hengistbury Head, 30, 34, 152
Henley-on-Thames, 132-133
Henry VII, 61-62, 83, 316

herbs, 4, 49, 81, 168, 207-208, 291, 293
Hereditary Craft, 3-4, 102, 110, 189, 211, 261, 266, 269, 272, 304
Herringshaw, Sheila, 35, 140, 212, 252
Hertfordshire, 128-129, 141, 274
Hess, Rudolf, 254
Highcliffe, 9, 32, 34-35, 37-39, 63, 74, 125, 132-134, 137, 139-140, 145, 148-150, 152, 154, 156, 180, 187, 189, 191, 193-196, 207, 212, 229, 244, 248-249, 252, 266, 272, 295, 298-299, 302, 307
Highland Avenue, 37-38
Hildburgh, W.L., 26
Hinxworth, 128, 144
Hitler, Adolf, 162, 227-230, 235, 237, 239-241, 250, 253-260, 302
Hodges, Mike, 212
Hope, Laurence, (see Cory)
Horsa Coven, 299-300
Horseman's Word, 249
Houghton, Michael, 300
Howard, Michael, 56, 257, 273, 300-301
Hudson, 148-149, 152-153, 200
Hulton, Elizabeth Ann, 129, 306
Hulton, Sophia, 129, 306
Hungary, 235
Hutchinson, Horace, 34
Hutton, Ronald, 1, 11, 35, 126, 180, 194, 203, 246, 254, 297-299
Hyde Park, London, 130, 263
Hypatia, Lodge, 95

Illman, John, 236
incense, 50, 165, 168, 174, 291
invasion, 8, 35, 43-45, 134, 175, 185, 189, 212, 216-221, 223-230, 233-235, 238, 240, 242, 248-250, 252, 254-261, 264, 287, 305-306
Irmgarde, Elza, 77

James, Deric, 299
James, Ruby, 140

James VI of Scotland, 218
Jesselton, 17
Johns, June, 116
Johore, 18, 20-22, 39
Jones, Evan John, 183, 249
Joseph, J.W., 29
Joyce, Evelyn, 140

Kaye, Gerald, 140
Keen, Francesca, 72-73, 268, 292
Keeping, William, 140
Keiller, Alexander, 22
Kelly, Aidan, 276, 296
Kent, 252
Kirtley, Eliza, 197
Kitcher, Reg, 139
Knight, R.K., 140
Knightwood Oak, 215
koans, 269
kris, 18-19
Kurtz, Katherine, 222, 233, 251

Labworth, Bran, 297
Lachish, 22
Lady Well, 118, 121
Lammas, 170, 173-174, 220, 222, 227-231, 233, 241, 243, 248-252, 259
Lamond, Fred, 8, 126, 293
Landport, 102
Lansdowne Library, 158
lantern-slides, 104
Latimers, 145-150, 154, 180, 202, 307
Laver, James, 302
Lawrie, Arthur, 140, 156, 206, 208
Leadbeater, Charles, 95
Lee, Harry, 140
Leek, Sybil, 189, 207, 232, 299-300, 303
Leland, Charles G., 4
Lewis, H. Spencer, 54
Liddell, W.E., 53, 211
Liveda, 85
Liverpool, 12, 18-19, 54, 56-58, 62, 70, 72, 76, 98, 143, 302
Lloyd, Leonard, 29
Lloyd, Walter, 202
Loader, Charles, 243, 249

Lob's Hole, 212
Locris, 73-74, 96
London, 19, 21-22, 25, 27, 32, 35, 44-45, 50, 57-58, 75-76, 89, 92-95, 112, 119, 124, 130-131, 148, 152-154, 158, 258, 263-264, 272-273, 300-301
London Academy of Music, 119, 124
London College of Music, 119, 124
Lotus League, 25, 117, 263
Lud, 212
Luftwaffe, 256-259
Lugh, 211-212
Lymington, 35, 137, 140, 156, 159, 196, 206, 248, 252, 299-300, 303
Lyndhurst, 213, 299
Lyon-Clark, Rene, 74-75

Maat, Lodge, 94
Macaulay, Thomas B., 220
Macfarlane, Laurie, 140
Mackenzie, Hewart, 19
Mackenzie, S.P., 233
Main, Laurence, 251
Malaya, 18-20, 22, 24, 39
Malton, 117-119, 121
Man, Isle of, 196-197, 270, 274
Manchester, 253
Mannix, Daniel, 198, 268
Mark Ash Wood, 215
Marlow, Louis (see Wilkinson, Louis)
Marryat, Florence, 15
Marryat, Frederick, 136
Martin, Georges, 94
Mason, Alf, 106, 108
Mason, Ernest William ('Ernie'), 100-102, 104-110, 114, 199, 218, 225-226, 238, 306-307
Mason, George Miles, 102-105, 112, 199, 268
Mason, Rosetta, 102, 105, 112, 114, 199
Mason, Susie Mary, 100, 102, 105, 108, 110, 114, 199, 226, 304, 306-307

Mason family, 102, 111-114, 116, 178, 189, 199, 205-206, 225, 227, 248, 265-266, 295, 298, 301, 304, 306-307
Master Beyond, The, 82
Mathers, S.L. Macgregor, 53-54
Mathews, Alex. (see Sullivan, G.A.)
Mathews, Charles, 57
Mathews, Charles James, 57
McCombie, Josephine ('Com'), 13
McIntosh, Christopher, 53
Mead, Brian, 244, 247
'Meadow Way', 63, 66, 72-73, 88
Mediterranean, 13, 47
Medway, Gareth, 28, 32, 153, 197-198, 264
Meidling, Nora, 75
Melbourne, 93
Merchant of Venice, The, 82-83
Merrifield, Ralph, 264
Middle East, 21-22, 41, 52, 120
Milford, 140, 249
Mill House (see Chewton Mill)
Mill House Players, 138-141, 148, 191, 209, 233
Mind Undying, 62
Monmouthshire, 102
Montalban, Madeline, (see North, Dolores)
Morgan, Edith Ethel, 108
Morgan, Ellen Anne, 130
Morgan, William Domatt, 130
Mountbatten, Louis, 301
Mudeford, 28-29, 34
Murray, Major, 249
Murray, Margaret, 4, 27, 33, 46, 50, 205, 210-211, 231-232, 281-282
Murrell, 'Cunning', 246
Museum of London, 264
Museum of Magic and Witchcraft, 11, 39, 197-199, 208, 268, 274, 292
Music, 60, 116, 119-120, 124, 138-139, 170, 264, 269-271

Naked Man, The, 213-215

Napoleon Bonaparte, 14, 219, 223-224, 227, 230, 234
Natural Therapeutics, 56, 66, 70
naturism, 24-30, 32, 38, 47, 52, 246, 251, 263-264, 274, 297-298
New Forest, 5, 24, 27-32, 35, 39, 112, 116, 120, 126, 133-136, 159, 180, 188-189, 205-207, 209-211, 213-215, 217, 220, 227-229, 231-232, 235-236, 250-255, 263, 267, 271, 295, 298-303, 305-306
New Forest Club, 27-30, 32, 39, 263, 298
New Forest Coven, 126, 188, 205, 209-211, 214-215, 235, 239, 243, 250-251, 263, 271, 273, 299-300, 305
New Milton, 75, 140, 159, 249
Newbolt, Henry, 222
Newlands Manor, 302
Newman, John Henry, 194
Nichols, Ross, 224, 253, 274
Nicosia Museum, 42
North Berwick, 218
North, 'Bill', 301
North, Dolores, 300-301
Northampton, 92-93
Nottingham, 95

O'Malley, Caroline, 143
O'Malley, William, 143
Ober Water, 215
OBOD, 274
occultism, 17-18, 26-27, 53-54, 56, 70-71, 94, 96, 98-99, 207, 209, 253, 280-281, 295, 302
Odsey, 141
oils, 47, 81, 291-292
Oldmeadow, Ann Eliza, 156, 199, 206, 209
Oldmeadow, Katherine, 156, 199, 206-208
Oldmeadow family, 206, 208
olive oil, 292

Order of the Temple of the Rose Cross, 56, 96
Order of Woodcraft Chivalry, 295-299, 303
Ordnance Survey, 13, 28, 104, 121, 134, 146, 212
Ordo, 66-68
Ordo Templi Orientis (O.T.O.), 274
orgone, 286-287
Orpington, 264
Osborne House, 32
Osborne Road, 100, 103-104, 121, 123-124
Ossemsley, 249
Oxford, 133, 138, 146, 194, 209
Oxfordshire, 131-133, 137, 189

Palestine, 22, 41
palmistry, 26
Pangbourne, 133
Paphos, 43, 45
Pausol, Good King, 283
Payne, Anthony, 6
Pelly, John, 140
Pelly, William, 140
Pendle, 17
Penman, Gideon, 239
Pennines, 17
Petrie, Flinders, 21
Pickford, Doug, 253
Pickingill, George, 211
Piercy, George, 266
Piercy, Mary, 266
Pine Cone, 297
Plymouth, 175, 219, 222-223
poisons, 291-293
Poole, 35, 105, 137
Portland, 219
Portsmouth, 32, 35, 102, 110, 225, 229
Portswood, 100, 103-105, 121, 123, 129
Pragnell, Vera, 246
Prichard, Bob, 236
Princes Park, Liverpool, 58
Pritchard, Frederick Ellis, 58

Purkis, 33, 306
Pythagoras, 57, 60-61, 71, 74, 78, 83, 89, 96-98, 100, 124

Qabalah, 53
'Queen' (see Edith Ethel Morgan)
Queen Elizabeth I, 96, 131, 175-176
Queen Victoria, 32, 130

Raeder, 255-256, 258-259
RAF, 160, 242, 257-258
rain, 82, 173, 218, 236
Reich, Wilhelm, 257, 286-287
Rhetoric, 68
Rickman, Irene, 140
Ridgmount Gardens, 273
Ridout, A.V., 38
Ringwood, 299
Rodmell, Harry Hudson, 103
Romsey, 113, 301, 304
Rose-blood, 175
Rosenkreutz, Christian, 52-53
Rosicrucian Fellowship, 54
Rosicrucian Players, 68-69, 84
Rosicrucians, 9, 39-40, 52-54, 56-58, 60, 69, 71, 74, 78-82, 84-89, 96-97, 100, 104, 107-109, 124, 139, 175, 218, 246, 248, 251-252, 264, 270, 295, 305-306
Royal Astronomical Society, 106
Royals, Madeline Sylvia (see North, Dolores)
Rushford Warren, 28-30, 264
Russell, Jeffrey, 126
Russia, 224, 256-257, 260
Ryde, 15, 102
Ryedale, 119

Sabine, Old Mother, 209
sacrifice, 48-50, 231, 235, 242-243, 250, 288, 305
St. Catherine's Hill, 34, 213
St. Quintin, Arabella Bridget, 129-130
St. Quintin, William Thomas, 129-130

Samuel, Olive, 134, 154, 187
Sanctuary, The, 246
sandbags, 263
Sanderson, Jack, 251
Sandy Balls, 296, 298
Sawkins, Robert, 77
Sawkins, Will, 77
Scotland, 75, 99, 205, 218-219, 254, 307
Scott, Ernest, 92-93
Scouts, 137, 295
Sealion, Operation, 255-259
'Sending Forth', 237
Seton, Ernest Thompson, 296
Shah, Idries, 8-9, 178, 180
Shakespeare, William, 53, 61, 63, 69, 71, 82, 86, 98, 161
Shapiro, Lea, 77
Singapore, 17-18, 21
skyclad, 26, 235
Slade, The, 252
Slatter, Elizabeth, 133, 138, 152, 192
Societas Rosicruciana in Anglia, 53
Solomon Islands, 117
Somerford, 34, 39, 63, 65, 74-76, 78, 83-84, 86-87, 124, 295
Southampton, 32, 35, 71, 89, 99-100, 102-108, 110, 113, 116, 119, 121, 123, 129-130, 189, 225, 229, 266, 302, 304, 306-307
Southampton Astronomical Society, 106
Southern Coven of British Witches, 134, 220, 227
'Southridge', 37-39, 97, 248, 266
Spain, 52, 134, 175, 219-222, 224, 227, 230, 234
spells, 116, 262, 293-294
spiritualism, 14-15, 19-20, 26, 272, 275
Staffordshire, 299
Starkey, J.L., 22, 41
Steiner, Rudolf, 45, 104
Stevenson, Ian, 39, 151, 229
Stockwell, Arthur H., Ltd., 50
Stone, George, 140

Storrington, 246
Stour, River, 34
Streatley, 133
Stronglos, 42
Stuart Wortley, E.J.M., 133
Stuart Wortley, Violet, 154
Stubbs, Luther William Newby, 63, 74
Suffolk, 302
Sullivan, Arthur, 139
Sullivan, Brenda, 72
Sullivan, Catherine, 54
Sullivan, Charles W., 54
Sullivan, George Alexander, 54-58, 60-63, 66, 70-76, 78, 80-83, 85, 88-89, 96-98, 107-108, 124
Sullivan, Jane, 72
Summers, Montague, 239, 302
Sunday Play Producing Society, 69-70
Sussex, 209, 224, 246, 253

tarot, 53
Taylor, Anne, 91-92
Taylor, Philip, 140
Templum, 66, 71
'Theano', 61, 124, 263, 266
Theatre, 52, 54, 57, 60, 63, 65-66, 68-69, 73-76, 78-86, 96-97, 99, 114, 124, 139, 177, 218, 247, 264
Theatrum, 66, 68
Theosophy, 56, 58, 71, 92-93, 95, 100, 104-105, 108, 251, 295, 306
Thompson, Cecil, 124, 264-266
Thorney Hill, 207
Three Acres Coven, 299
Toms, Mary Ann, 102
Toms, Rosetta (see Mason)
Toms, William, 102
Toothill, 112-114, 301, 304, 306
Tuck, F.A., 140
Tuck, Nan, 140
Tugwell, Nancy, 140
Twyford, 129
Twynham, 34
Tyrrell, Walter, 33

Umbala, 130

umbrellas, 102-103

Underwood, Peter, 222, 321

Valiente, Doreen, 5, 113, 116, 126, 190, 198, 207, 209, 214-215, 227, 237-241, 243, 262-263, 276, 301
Vanda, 26
veganism, 251
vegetarianism, 251
Venus, 43, 45, 175
Victoria and Albert Museum, 302
Victoria Station, London, 27
volunteers, 233, 263-264

Wakefield, Bill, 102, 105-108
Wakefield, Colin, 102, 107
Walhampton, 159
Walkford, 35, 125, 133-136, 212, 266-267
Ward, Amy, (see Woodforde-Finden)
Ward, J.S.M., 27, 274
Watford, 128-130
Watkins, Alfred, 121
weather, 25, 59, 82, 149, 218, 220-221, 224, 236, 254, 257-259, 275
Webb, David, 158
Wells, Christine, 147, 150, 159, 163
Welwyn, 129
West Moors, 28, 298
Westcott, William Wynn, 53-54
Westlake, Aubrey, 295
Westlake, Ernest, 295
Whitcher, Ruth, 140
Whitchurch, 133
Whitcombe, Lottie, 140
Whitehorn, A.C., 77
wica, 177-178, 184-185, 281
Wight, Isle of, 15, 30, 32, 35, 102, 152, 219
Wilkinson, Louis, 209-210, 227, 235, 250, 292

William Rufus, 33, 112, 149, 174, 231-232, 306
Williams, Aronica ('Annie'), 149
Williams, Henry, 129
Williamson, Cecil, 42, 116, 196, 217, 253, 262, 274, 302
Williamson, Hugh Ross, 33
Wiltshire, 27, 165-166, 236
Wimbledon, 94
Winchester, 33, 102, 129, 152, 306
Window of Hudson's Pagoda, The, 62
witch blood, 3
Wittenham, Long, 132
Wodehouse, P.G., 198
Woodford-Grimes, Edith Rose, 43, 110, 116-117, 120-122, 126, 178, 190, 205-206, 262-267, 269, 292, 302, 304
Woodford-Grimes, Rosanne, 121, 124, 263-266, 307
Woodforde-Finden, Amy, 120-121
Woods, McAlpine, 21
Workers' Educational Association, 123
Wray, Caroline, 118
Wray, Edith (see Woodford-Grimes)
Wray, William Henry, 118
Wyatt, Eveline, 77

York, 119
Yorkshire, 117-118, 129, 169

Zen, 269

FREE DETAILED CATALOGUE

Capall Bann is owned and run by people actively involved in many of the areas in which we publish. A detailed illustrated catalogue is available on request, SAE or International Postal Coupon appreciated. **Titles can be ordered direct from Capall Bann, post free in the UK** (cheque or PO with order) or from good bookshops and specialist outlets.

Do contact us for details on the latest releases at: **Capall Bann Publishing, Freshfields, Chieveley, Berks, RG20 8TF.** Titles include:

A Breath Behind Time, Terri Hector
Angels and Goddesses - Celtic Christianity & Paganism, M. Howard
Arthur - The Legend Unveiled, C Johnson & E Lung
Astrology The Inner Eye - A Guide in Everyday Language, E Smith
Auguries and Omens - The Magical Lore of Birds, Yvonne Aburrow
Asyniur - Womens Mysteries in the Northern Tradition, S McGrath
Beginnings - Geomancy, Builder's Rites & Electional Astrology in the
    European Tradition, Nigel Pennick
Between Earth and Sky, Julia Day
Book of the Veil, Peter Paddon
Caer Sidhe - Celtic Astrology and Astronomy, Vol 1, Michael Bayley
Caer Sidhe - Celtic Astrology and Astronomy, Vol 2 M Bayley
Call of the Horned Piper, Nigel Jackson
Cat's Company, Ann Walker
Celtic Faery Shamanism, Catrin James
Celtic Faery Shamanism - The Wisdom of the Otherworld, Catrin James
Celtic Lore & Druidic Ritual, Rhiannon Ryall
Celtic Sacrifice - Pre Christian Ritual & Religion, Marion Pearce
Celtic Saints and the Glastonbury Zodiac, Mary Caine
Circle and the Square, Jack Gale
Compleat Vampyre - The Vampyre Shaman, Nigel Jackson
Creating Form From the Mist - The Wisdom of Women in Celtic Myth and
    Culture, Lynne Sinclair-Wood
Crystal Clear - A Guide to Quartz Crystal, Jennifer Dent
Crystal Doorways, Simon & Sue Lilly
Crossing the Borderlines - Guising, Masking & Ritual Animal Disguise in the
    European Tradition, Nigel Pennick
Dragons of the West, Nigel Pennick
Earth Dance - A Year of Pagan Rituals, Jan Brodie
Earth Harmony - Places of Power, Holiness & Healing, Nigel Pennick
Earth Magic, Margaret McArthur
Eildon Tree (The) Romany Language & Lore, Michael Hoadley

Enchanted Forest - The Magical Lore of Trees, Yvonne Aburrow
Eternal Priestess, Sage Weston
Eternally Yours Faithfully, Roy Radford & Evelyn Gregory
Everything You Always Wanted To Know About Your Body, But So Far
    Nobody's Been Able To Tell You, Chris Thomas & D Baker
Face of the Deep - Healing Body & Soul, Penny Allen
Fairies in the Irish Tradition, Molly Gowen
Familiars - Animal Powers of Britain, Anna Franklin
Fool's First Steps, (The) Chris Thomas
Forest Paths - Tree Divination, Brian Harrison, Ill. S. Rouse
From Past to Future Life, Dr Roger Webber
Gardening For Wildlife Ron Wilson
God Year, The, Nigel Pennick & Helen Field
Goddess on the Cross, Dr George Young
Goddess Year, The, Nigel Pennick & Helen Field
Goddesses, Guardians & Groves, Jack Gale
Handbook For Pagan Healers, Liz Joan
Handbook of Fairies, Ronan Coghlan
Healing Book, The, Chris Thomas and Diane Baker
Healing Homes, Jennifer Dent
Healing Journeys, Paul Williamson
Healing Stones, Sue Philips
Herb Craft - Shamanic & Ritual Use of Herbs, Lavender & Franklin
Hidden Heritage - Exploring Ancient Essex, Terry Johnson
Hub of the Wheel, Skytoucher
In Search of Herne the Hunter, Eric Fitch
Inner Celtia, Alan Richardson & David Annwn
Inner Mysteries of the Goths, Nigel Pennick
Inner Space Workbook - Develop Thru Tarot, C Summers & J Vayne
Intuitive Journey, Ann Walker Isis - African Queen, Akkadia Ford
Journey Home, The, Chris Thomas
Kecks, Keddles & Kesh - Celtic Lang & The Cog Almanac, Bayley
Language of the Psycards, Berenice
Legend of Robin Hood, The, Richard Rutherford-Moore
Lid Off the Cauldron, Patricia Crowther
Light From the Shadows - Modern Traditional Witchcraft, Gwyn
Living Tarot, Ann Walker
Lore of the Sacred Horse, Marion Davies
Lost Lands & Sunken Cities (2nd ed.), Nigel Pennick
Magic of Herbs - A Complete Home Herbal, Rhiannon Ryall
Magical Guardians - Exploring the Spirit and Nature of Trees, Philip Heselton
Magical History of the Horse, Janet Farrar & Virginia Russell
Magical Lore of Animals, Yvonne Aburrow
Magical Lore of Cats, Marion Davies
Magical Lore of Herbs, Marion Davies
Magick Without Peers, Ariadne Rainbird & David Rankine
Masks of Misrule - Horned God & His Cult in Europe, Nigel Jackson

Medicine For The Coming Age, Lisa Sand MD
Medium Rare - Reminiscences of a Clairvoyant, Muriel Renard
Menopausal Woman on the Run, Jaki da Costa
Mind Massage - 60 Creative Visualisations, Marlene Maundrill
Mirrors of Magic - Evoking the Spirit of the Dewponds, P Heselton
Moon Mysteries, Jan Brodie
Mysteries of the Runes, Michael Howard
Mystic Life of Animals, Ann Walker
New Celtic Oracle The, Nigel Pennick & Nigel Jackson
Oracle of Geomancy, Nigel Pennick
Pagan Feasts - Seasonal Food for the 8 Festivals, Franklin & Phillips
Patchwork of Magic - Living in a Pagan World, Julia Day
Pathworking - A Practical Book of Guided Meditations, Pete Jennings
Personal Power, Anna Franklin
Pickingill Papers - The Origins of Gardnerian Wicca, Bill Liddell
Pillars of Tubal Cain, Nigel Jackson
Places of Pilgrimage and Healing, Adrian Cooper
Practical Divining, Richard Foord
Practical Meditation, Steve Hounsome
Practical Spirituality, Steve Hounsome
Psychic Self Defence - Real Solutions, Jan Brodie
Real Fairies, David Tame
Reality - How It Works & Why It Mostly Doesn't, Rik Dent
Romany Tapestry, Michael Houghton
Runic Astrology, Nigel Pennick
Sacred Animals, Gordon MacLellan
Sacred Celtic Animals, Marion Davies, Ill. Simon Rouse
Sacred Dorset - On the Path of the Dragon, Peter Knight
Sacred Grove - The Mysteries of the Forest, Yvonne Aburrow
Sacred Geometry, Nigel Pennick
Sacred Nature, Ancient Wisdom & Modern Meanings, A Cooper
Sacred Ring - Pagan Origins of British Folk Festivals, M. Howard
Season of Sorcery - On Becoming a Wisewoman, Poppy Palin
Seasonal Magic - Diary of a Village Witch, Paddy Slade
Secret Places of the Goddess, Philip Heselton
Secret Signs & Sigils, Nigel Pennick
Self Enlightenment, Mayan O'Brien
Spirits of the Air, Jaq D Hawkins
Spirits of the Earth, Jaq D Hawkins
Spirits of the Earth, Jaq D Hawkins
Stony Gaze, Investigating Celtic Heads John Billingsley
Stumbling Through the Undergrowth , Mark Kirwan-Heyhoe
Subterranean Kingdom, The, revised 2nd ed, Nigel Pennick
Symbols of Ancient Gods, Rhiannon Ryall
Talking to the Earth, Gordon MacLellan
Taming the Wolf - Full Moon Meditations, Steve Hounsome
Teachings of the Wisewomen, Rhiannon Ryall

The Other Kingdoms Speak, Helena Hawley
Tree: Essence of Healing, Simon & Sue Lilly
Tree: Essence, Spirit & Teacher, Simon & Sue Lilly
Through the Veil, Peter Paddon
Torch and the Spear, Patrick Regan
Understanding Chaos Magic, Jaq D Hawkins
Vortex - The End of History, Mary Russell
Warp and Weft - In Search of the I-Ching, William de Fancourt
Warriors at the Edge of Time, Jan Fry
Water Witches, Tony Steele
Way of the Magus, Michael Howard
Weaving a Web of Magic, Rhiannon Ryall
West Country Wicca, Rhiannon Ryall
Wildwitch - The Craft of the Natural Psychic, Poppy Palin
Wildwood King, Philip Kane
Witches of Oz, Matthew & Julia Philips
Wondrous Land - The Faery Faith of Ireland by Dr Kay Mullin
Working With the Merlin, Geoff Hughes
Your Talking Pet, Ann Walker

FREE detailed catalogue and FREE 'Inspiration' magazine
Contact: Capall Bann Publishing, Freshfields, Chieveley, Berks, RG20 8TF